RURAL SOCIETY
IN
COLONIAL MORELOS

RURAL SOCIETY
IN
COLONIAL MORELOS

Cheryl English Martin

University of New Mexico Press
Albuquerque

For my parents

Library of Congress Cataloging in Publication Data

Martin, Cheryl English, 1945–
    Rural society in colonial Morelos.

    Bibliography: p.
    Includes index.
    1. Morelos (Mexico)—Rural conditions. 2. Sugar
growing—Mexico—Morelos—History. 3. Mexico—History—
Spanish colony, 1540–1810. I. Title.
HN120.M58M37   1985   307.7′2′097249   84–29784
ISBN 0–8263–0797–3

First edition

HN
120
.M 58
M 37
1985

Contents

Maps

Appendixes

Tables

Acknowledgments

Recognizing the help of mentors, guides, and friends who contributed to the completion of a project is one of the more pleasant steps in the preparation of a manuscript.

I would like to begin by acknowledging the training and encouragement I received from two outstanding authorities in the field of colonial Mexico. Richard E. Greenleaf, director of my doctoral dissertation, subjected my early work to incisive but always constructive criticism and shared with me his extensive knowledge of Mexican archives. The late France V. Scholes communicated to me, as to so many of his students in paleography, the joy that comes from deciphering colonial documents.

This project first took form during my participation in a seminar for college teachers conducted by Richard Herr at the University of California at Berkeley in the summer of 1979. Professor Herr gave generously of his time and expertise then and at succeeding points in the preparation of the manuscript. William B. Taylor also offered valuable insights and help during the early phases of my research. I am especially grateful to David Holtby of the University of New Mexico Press, who has given enthusiastic encouragement and superb editorial guidance along the way.

I also thank my colleagues and friends in the Department of History at the University of Texas at El Paso for providing steady encouragement and a congenial *ambiente* in which to work. In particular, David Hackett advised me in the use of computers, helping immeasurably in the manipulation of demographic data and displaying the kind of collegiality that can characterize academic life at its best. Rebecca Craver read the entire manuscript at a particularly crucial point in its development. Her alert eye caught many awkward constructions. Sandra Harding also made valuable comments on several of the early chapters. Finally, Kenneth Shover and Carl Jackson were supportive department chairmen during the years that this manuscript was in the making.

Other persons who assisted with the completion of this work include Stanley Hordes and Victoria Cummins, who helped me in obtaining microfilm. Ingeniero Juan Dubernard of Cuernavaca, Morelos graciously allowed me to consult materials in his personal collection. I thank also Robert Haskett, Stephanie Wood, and Eric Van Young, each of whom shared archival citations and lively discussions during coffee breaks in the now renovated patios of Lecumberri. Still others lent help in ways too varied to enumerate; I will simply offer my sincere thanks to Sue Cook, Flo Dick, David Marley, Ann Schultis, Jonathan Amith, Lee Byrd, Bob Byrd, Carl Erickson, Rebeca Ramos, Teresa Rojas, Robert Schmidt, Emilio Bejarano, and Michael E. Smith.

The completion of this book also owes much to the generous support of the National Endowment for the Humanities. A grant from that agency funded Professor Herr's seminar at Berkeley. Later, an NEH Fellowship for College Teachers freed me from teaching during the 1982–83 academic year, enabling me to finish the project.

I turn now to acknowledgments of a more personal nature. My parents, Hal and Helen English, stimulated my long interest in Latin America by sending me to Ecuador as a exchange student in 1962, and in so many other ways created for me the opportunities to do the things that I wanted to do.

Finally, it is customary, and perhaps trite, to state that without the assistance and support of one's spouse a work would never have reached completion. In this case it is also true. To Charles H. Martin—husband, fellow historian, toughest critic, and best friend—and to our son Jeff, my heartfelt gratitude for allowing the campesinos of colonial Morelos to encamp in our household for so many years.

Introduction

Two sharply contrasting images—of recreation and revolution—come to mind when the Mexican state of Morelos is mentioned. For centuries its lush, semitropical valleys have provided residents of Tenochtitlán-Mexico City a welcome relief from the capital's chilly climate and hectic urban pace. The Emperor Moctezuma I relaxed in his fabled gardens at Oaxtepec; half a millenium later, weekend vacationers flock to the same spot to enjoy the bathing resort maintained by the Instituto Mexicano de Seguro Social. Cuernavaca, playground of the international jet set in the twentieth century, has long been a favored retreat for foreigners in Mexico, from Fernando Cortés to Maximilian von Hapsburg and the Shah of Iran.

During the second decade of the twentieth century, however, the state of Morelos was hardly a haven for relaxation and repose. Instead, it spawned the most forthrightly agrarian component of the Revolution of 1910 and witnessed some of that tragic era's most bitter fighting. The sturdy campesinos and townsmen who rallied to Emiliano Zapata's revolt did so in angry response to profound political, social, and economic changes that had come to their state and their nation since Porfirio Díaz's accession to the presidency thirty-four years earlier. Large landowners (*hacendados*) in Porfirian Mexico encountered few seri-

1

ous obstacles in their efforts to expand their holdings at the expense of small farmers (*rancheros*) or Indian villages. In Morelos, hacendados sought to increase their output of sugarcane with the help of recently introduced rail transportation and steam-powered mills, symbols themselves of the dazzling, if short-sighted "progress" that Díaz and his supporters tried to bring to Mexico. Year after year, the country people of Morelos saw the hacendados take from them the lands they had claimed and successfully defended for centuries. They endured too the humiliation of the hacendados' flippant dismissal of their concerns. A hacienda owner's suggestion that the land-hungry villagers of Anenecuilco "farm in a flower pot" typifies the disdainful attitude of the landowners.[1]

In the spring of 1910, political ferment generated by Díaz's bid for yet another term as president gave Emiliano Zapata, newly elected president of Anenecuilco's village council, the opportunity he needed to articulate his own and his neighbors' rage at the repeated abuses they had suffered. At the same time, the great landowners' long domination of local and national politics gave frustrated townsmen ample reason to support Zapata's attack on the Díaz regime. For the next ten years, the *zapatistas* hounded a sequence of national governments, "revolutionary" and otherwise, for their failure to implement an equitable distribution of farmland. Their solemn adherence to this goal finally forced most of those scrambling to seize leadership of the Revolution to acknowledge, with varying degrees of enthusiasm and sincerity, the importance of agrarian concerns in the developing agenda for national change. In the meantime, however, successive waves of military reprisals attempted to silence forever the *morelenses*' objections to the "progress" pursued by President Díaz and by several of his so-called revolutionary successors.[2]

The deep historical roots of Zapata's rebellion, and the local perspective which was at once its greatest weakness and its greatest strength, have commanded the attention of scholars who have studied the movement. John Womack has simply but eloquently described the zapatistas of Morelos as "country people who did not want to move . . . [who] insisted on staying in the villages and little towns where they had grown up, and where before them their ancestors for hundreds of years had lived and died."[3] That Anenecuilco supplied both the roots of, and the reason for, Zapata's actions is suggested by the evocative title of

Jesús Sotelo Inclán's work, *Raiz y razón de Zapata*.[4] To cite just one other example, Arturo Warman has incorporated into the title of his recent book on the peasants of Morelos the age-old formula invoked by Indian villagers to register formally their protests against encroachments on their lands, "Venimos a contradecir," or, in English, "We come to object."[5] What these authors, together, indicate is that the campesinos of Morelos, whatever the deficiencies in their formal education, possessed a profound sense of their state's history. By the opening decade of the twentieth century, the villagers found that historical relics affirmed the permanence of their communities more soundly than the miserable condition to which they had been reduced in the present. Crumbling churches stood as testimony to the past importance of the villages as civic and ceremonial centers. Those villages fortunate enough to have retained precious colonial maps and titles documenting their land claims treated those papers with more reverence than any historian has ever shown for primary sources.[6]

The sugar haciendas of Morelos, most of which could trace their origins to the sixteenth or seventeenth centuries, provided the foil against which the villagers fashioned their deep-seated historical consciousness. The present study traces the development and mutual interaction of the haciendas, villages, and small farms of Morelos from the late sixteenth century to the end of the colonial period. Those who built, owned, and managed the haciendas necessarily figure heavily in the unfolding drama. Fluctuations in hacienda fortunes left their impact on many aspects of life in colonial Morelos, and hacienda records are indispensable in reconstructing the region's social history. But this study is not, strictly speaking, a history of the haciendas. Ward Barrett has written a splendid account of the operations of one representative hacienda, a book that is richly detailed in its attention to the technical and managerial aspects of colonial sugar production.[7] His findings are substantially applicable to other haciendas. A purely economic analysis of the haciendas' profitability, based on exhaustive scrutiny of the scattered financial accounts that are extant, might be possible, but also lies outside the scope and purpose of the present study. For the time being, the broad rhythms of change in the sugar industry can be traced with sufficient precision to permit the kind of social analysis attempted here, wherein the fundamental concern remains the relationships between the haciendas and other components of rural society, and the extent to which the presence of sugar haciendas shaped the social history of Morelos.

This analytical focus, stressing the interaction of sugar estates and other elements of rural society, helps define the chronological and geographical limits of this study. The year 1580 is a logical starting point. Although Fernando Cortés and two other enterprising Spaniards established the state's first sugar haciendas in the 1520s and 1530s, a major expansion of the industry, as well as important changes in the structure of land tenure at the Cortés mill, began during the last two decades of the sixteenth century.

Reasons admittedly more pragmatic than analytical have influenced the choice of 1810 as the end date for this study. The political turmoil of the nineteenth century and the resultant disruption in record keeping pose serious, though perhaps not insurmountable, obstacles to the study of the early national period. The present work therefore ventures only a brief concluding sketch of the region's development after 1810. Perhaps, in time, some courageous scholar will undertake the mighty task of piecing together the social history of Morelos from 1810 to 1880. In the meantime, the colonial forebears of Zapata, who built the historical legacy on which he drew so heavily and so effectively, warrant our attention.

The importance of sugar cultivation also defines the geographical limits of this study. The area under consideration includes much, but not all, of the territory comprising the present-day state of Morelos. Of direct concern are those parts of the state, located at the foot of the escarpment of the volcanic plateau, where sugarcane can be grown. The contour line of 1,500 meters above sea level roughly delimits these areas. This altitude, at least 700 meters below that of Mexico City, gives the region temperatures several degrees higher than those of the capital. Under normal conditions this climate is sufficiently warm to permit the cultivation of sugarcane, although the possibility of frost posed a serious threat to the canefields on several occasions during the colonial period, especially in the late seventeenth and early eighteenth centuries. Other geographic features combined with Morelos's milder climate to encourage the cultivation of sugarcane. Its location at the base of the plateau accounts for its particularly rich soil, nourished by volcanic deposits, and for the relative abundance of water draining into the basin from the escarpment.[8]

Technically, the area belongs to what geographers call *tierra templada*, which extends from about 700 to about 2,000 meters above sea level.[9] However, the term *tierra caliente* is often used to designate much or even all of the sugar-growing region of Morelos. Arturo Warman, for example, specifies the 1,500-meter marker as the dividing line between tierra caliente and tierra templada; areas above 1,750 meters he describes as *tierra fría*.[10] G. Michael Riley, however, places the Yautepec Valley and the upper reaches of the Cuautla and Cuernavaca Valleys in the tierra templada and the lower extensions of the latter two valleys, as well as the Valley of Jojutla, in the tierra caliente.[11]

Documents from the colonial period, such as one penned by the famous eighteenth-century scientist José Antonio Alzate y Ramírez, referred indiscriminately to the entire basin as tierra caliente.[12] This terminology endured into the nineteenth century. When asked to describe the climate of their parishes in 1848, the curates of Tlaltizapán and Oaxtepec both responded, without hesitation, "tierra caliente."[13] Their contemporary, Fanny Calderón de la Barca, used the same words when recounting her travels in the area.[14] To avoid confusion, the present study will refer to "tierra caliente" only in those contexts where its use helps convey the way in which colonial thinkers regarded the region—a warm, fertile area whose climate and agricultural production suitably complemented those of the higher and cooler Valley of Mexico. The reader is urged to consult Appendix 1, which lists elevations and mean annual temperatures of many places mentioned in this work, and which will offer some sense of the differences among specific localities.

Places at higher elevations but adjacent to the 1,500-meter marker, in areas called tierra templada in Warman's work, became heavily involved in the provision, voluntary or otherwise, of labor and other resources for the sugar industry, and they too enter the analysis presented here. Portions of what are now the neighboring states of Mexico and Puebla shared the ecological features of the area under study, but in order to keep the project within manageable proportions, they have been excluded.

The designation "Morelos" is, of course, an anachronism. The insurgent hero, José María Morelos y Pavón, for whom the state is named, was not born until 1765, and the area only became the state of Morelos in 1869. During the colonial period, it fell under two distinct political

jurisdictions. One was the so-called Marquesado del Valle, the personal fiefdom claimed by the the conqueror Fernando Cortés, first
Marqués del Valle de Oaxaca. Except for intervals when the crown
temporarily suspended the Cortés family's prerogatives, the conqueror
and his descendants retained the right to collect tributes and appoint
civil officials who governed Marquesado territories in Morelos and elsewhere in Mexico. For most of the colonial period Cortés's heirs lived
in Europe, and general supervision of the family's affairs in Mexico
fell to the appointed governor of the Marquesado del Valle, who resided
in the viceregal capital. The Morelos portion of the Marquesado was
subject to the administrative control of the *alcalde mayor*, or local magistrate, of Cuernavaca, who in turn appointed *tenientes* (lieutenants) to
represent him in principal towns throughout his district, or *alcaldía
mayor*. Another part of the region lay under crown jurisdiction, pre-
sided over by a royally appointed alcalde mayor in Cuautla Amilpas.
Following the reorganization of local government in 1786, both the Cuernavaca and Cuautla districts were considered part of the intendancy of
Mexico. They formed part of the state of Mexico from 1821 until the
creation of the separate states of Morelos and Guerrero in 1869.[15]

Institutions and developments outside the state of Morelos receive
attention to the extent, often considerable, that they influenced the
social history of the area. In particular, the role of Mexico City was
paramount. Eric Van Young has pointed out, both in a theoretical
discussion of regional history and in the very design of his work on
Guadalajara, the importance of cities in understanding the social and
economic development of the hinterlands over which major urban centers "sat like spiders at the center of administrative, political, and
commercial networks with identifiable regional boundaries."[16] Relationships with Tenochtitlán-Mexico City have shaped the history of
Morelos for at least half a millennium. The region gave the Aztec
emperors easy access to a range of agricultural products not produced
in the Valley of Mexico. The demand for fruits, vegetables, maize,
and other crops to feed the ever-growing population of Mexico City
has influenced the structure of agricultural production in Morelos from
colonial times to the present. Especially in the eighteenth century, provision of such staples for the metropolitan market had important social
and economic consequences in the region.

Most important of all, however, was Mexico City's preponderant influence on the sugar industry of Morelos. Merchants in the viceregal capital marketed most of the region's sugar, with the exception of small amounts sold locally or sent to Puebla de los Angeles and to the mines of Taxco. Moreover, ecclesiastical institutions and other lenders in Mexico City provided most of the capital on which the industry's initial development and continued operations so vitally depended. Fluctuations in Mexico City's demand for sugar and in its available pool of capital thus had profound effects on the sugar industry and on rural society in Morelos.

Without doubt changes in production patterns elsewhere in the Western Hemisphere exerted some influence—the precise extent of which remains to be determined—on prices and therefore on the financial history of sugar haciendas in colonial Mexico. In part, the Mexican industry's development in the sixteenth century came in response to the phenomenal growth in international demand for sugar. However, the contemporaneous expansion of sugar cultivation in Brazil and the spectacular rise of the West Indian industry after 1650 effectively ended Mexican participation in the world market.[17] After the early seventeenth century Mexican sugar entered international trade in appreciable amounts only for a brief period following the destruction of plantations in Saint-Domingue in the 1790s and again during the age of Porfirio Díaz. For most of the colonial period Mexican production was oriented toward domestic consumption, with sugar-producing enclaves, each tied to a specific city or mining region, scattered throughout New Spain and New Galicia.[18] Therefore, domestic rather than international factors offer the most satisfactory explanations for the pronounced fluctuations in the fortunes of Mexican sugar estates. For haciendas in Morelos, the role of sugar and credit markets in Mexico City was decisive.

Successive changes in the sugar industry brought continued alterations in patterns of land tenure and utilization, which in turn shaped the social history of Morelos. After a half-century of expansion lasting roughly from 1580 to 1630 the industry entered a phase of stagnation and eventual decline. By the opening of the eighteenth century, many long-established haciendas had plunged into bankruptcy, from which most of them did not fully recover until after 1760. The depression of the sugar industry engendered considerable variety in land usage and associated forms of settlement. Indian villagers and modest non-Indian farmers alike enjoyed increased access to land and water as the sugar estates' demands for these resources diminished. After 1760, however, the revival of the haciendas brought a sharp rise in land and water values, and in the level of social conflict.

The shifting fortunes of the sugar haciendas were accompanied by major changes in the composition of their work forces and in the rhythms of life and labor on the haciendas. The presence of the sugar industry also affected the internal development of Indian villages in Morelos. In periods of expansion the haciendas attracted to the region large numbers of non-Indians, many of whom in time became permanent residents of major villages. By the end of the colonial period most of these communities had become, in effect, Spanish-mestizo farming communities and provincial trading centers, in which Indian governors and leading villagers (*gobernadores* and *principales*) nevertheless continued to exercise political power.

A major repository of documents from which this study is drawn is the Ramo de Tierras of the Archivo General de la Nación (AGN) in Mexico City. Although the contents of this ramo are derived in large part from the land and water disputes that recurred throughout the colonial history of central Mexico, the bulky *expedientes* often include hacienda inventories, ledgers, correspondence, and personal testimony that provide valuable clues for the social historian. The archive of the Hospital de Jesús, also in the AGN, contains papers generated by administrators of the Cortés estate and local officials in Marquesado domains. These documents also contain information on land and water disputes, as well as records of tribute receipts, internal affairs of the Indian communities, and the personal grievances of slaves, Indians, and others who appealed to Marquesado authorities for help. Several other ramos of the AGN provided less extensive but still useful information.

These documentary staples of the colonial historian have been supplemented with demographic information derived from parish registers, obtained on microfilm from the magnificent collections of the Genealogical Society of Utah. Selected for most detailed scrutiny were records of the parish of Nuestra Señora de la Asunción in Yautepec, an Indian *cabecera*, or head town, which attracted many non-Indian settlers throughout the colonial period. The parish included two outlying Indian *sujetos*, or subject settlements, as well as several Spanish haciendas and ranchos. Data derived from other parishes are also included, but Yautepec's central location in the sugar region, together with the generally superior quality and quantity of its surviving registers, warrant the special attention that it has received in this study. Moreover, the parish's relatively compact territorial extent probably minimized the underreporting that often occurred in larger parishes, where priests or the faithful had to travel great distances for the sacraments. A summary of general tendencies revealed in the Yautepec registers can be found in the tables and graph of the Appendixes. More specific findings appear at pertinent points throughout the text.

Insights derived from this demographic analysis have been invaluable in charting fluctuations in the relative size and ethnic composition of populations resident on haciendas and in "Indian" communities, especially for the years prior to the late eighteenth century, for which little census material exists. Baptismal registers, which reflect demographic reality more faithfully than records of burials and marriages,[19] figure most prominently in this particular line of inquiry. Thus the fact that in the seventeenth century the curates of Yautepec baptized increasing numbers of Indian and Afro-Indian children whose parents are listed as residents of this or that hacienda suggests significant changes in the size and racial makeup of hacienda populations. Baptismal records also reveal ties of ritual kinship (*compadrazgo*) formed by residents of haciendas and villages.

Because parishioners were more likely to forego church burial than any other rite, burial registers are the least reliable of parish records. These documents nonetheless permit the historian to identify periods of demographic calamity, and, through a cautious comparison of figures from different parishes all affected by a particular crisis, to assess variations in the magnitude of epidemics and crop failures from one place to another. Burial figures for Yautepec have revealed an ecological and epidemiological history that differed in important respects from that of other parts of central Mexico. Marriage records, while by definition excluding all but church-sanctioned unions, nevertheless have offered additional information employed in this study. Most important, they show a surprisingly high degree of racial endogamy among Indians, a tendency not easily discernible in other types of sources. Moreover, the registers often listed the place of origin of both brides and grooms, confirming the importance of migration in shaping the social history of colonial Morelos.

The chapters that follow survey Morelos's changing patterns of land tenure and usage and the resulting alterations in social relations from the sixteenth to the early nineteenth centuries. Chapter 1 provides an overview, drawn in large part from secondary sources, of the region's social and economic history from the arrival of the Spanish conquerors to the beginning of the sugar industry's expansion after 1580. Chapter 2 traces the development of the sugar haciendas, while the following two chapters examine demographic trends and shifts in the structure of agricultural production during the seventeenth and early eighteenth centuries. Hacienda growth and the acceleration of social conflict in the late colonial era form the subject of Chapter 5. Chapters 6 and 7 explore the internal social development of the haciendas and the Indian villages, respectively, while Chapter 8 offers a case study of local politics in one community, Yautepec, on the eve of Mexican independence. Finally, the Conclusion ventures a few observations, again based largely on secondary sources, on the nature of society in Morelos following independence.

1
The Aftermath of Conquest, 1521–1580

When Spanish conquerors first arrived in the valleys of Morelos in the spring of 1521, they found a densely populated, agriculturally diverse region that had provided a variety of foodstuffs, textiles, and other commodities in tribute to the Aztec rulers since its definitive subjugation by Emperor Moctezuma I in the mid-fifteenth century. As many as 725,000 persons lived within the bounds of the present-day state of Morelos, an area comprising both the highland region, occupied by the Xochimilcas Indians, as well as the lowlands, home to the Tlahuicas.

Fernando Cortés quickly appropriated for himself *encomienda* rights over the five cabeceras of Cuernavaca, Yautepec, Oaxtepec, Yecapixtla, and Tepoztlán. As holder of an encomienda, Cortés received the tributes that the towns' Indians would have paid to the Spanish crown had they not been granted in encomienda. In theory at least, Cortés and other *encomenderos* incurred obligations to promote the physical well-being of the Indians they held and to see that they received adequate instruction in the Christian faith. Like other early encomenderos, Cortés used the Aztec tribute system as a basis for the demands he made on his Indians. By mid-1522, less than a year after the fall of the Aztec capital of Tenochtitlán, Indians from the five Morelos cabeceras and their sujetos were delivering cotton textiles, gold, and food valued at six thousand gold pesos per year to the conqueror's agents. The Indians also provided labor to service Cortés's ambitious enterprises in Morelos and elsewhere in New Spain.[1]

Other conquerors' bitter opposition to Cortés resulted in the temporary loss of his encomienda holdings to rival Spanish claimants between 1524 and 1529. During that interval, he journeyed to Spain to press before King Charles I and the Council of the Indies his claim to extensive encomiendas throughout New Spain and the other prerogatives that he felt were his by right. Royal decrees of July 1529 did not grant the conqueror all that he asked, but restored his encomiendas in Morelos. In addition, Cortés and his descendants received permission to consolidate their holdings into a *mayorazgo*, or entailed estate, and to exercise civil and criminal jurisdiction in territories comprising those holdings, thereafter known as the Marquesado del Valle de Oaxaca. The conqueror returned to Mexico in 1530, and in November of the following year took up residence in Cuernavaca, which quickly became the headquarters of his multifaceted undertakings in the rapidly developing colony of New Spain.[2]

Once established in Cuernavaca, Cortés altered his tribute demands, expanding the range of products to be furnished by the Indians of the five Morelos towns. The items included in this new list reflect the diversity of Cortés's enterprises in Morelos. In addition to the food staples, gold, textiles, and labor services previously rendered, the Indians now began supplying kindling, charcoal, ropes, cooking utensils, rabbits, doves, eggs, frogs, and fish. They also prepared for him *tortillas de pan*, or tortillas made from wheat flour—an indication of the rapid cultural fusion taking place.[3]

By this time the warm, fertile valleys of the Morelos lowlands had also witnessed the introduction of sugarcane, the Old World crop that was to have such an impact on the region's subsequent history. Sometime before 1529, Antonio Serrano de Cardona, encomendero of Cuernavaca during the period when Cortés was deprived of his holdings, had planted cane on land rented and later purchased from the Indians of Cuernavaca. Within two years he constructed a water-powered mill at a site called Atlacomulco. Following his return to the area, Cortés tried repeatedly but without success to impede the development of Serrano's hacienda. Although a compromise eventually gave the conqueror a one-seventh share in his rival's mill, litigation continued for several decades, long after the deaths of both men.[4]

Meanwhile, Cortés himself began sugar production in Cuernavaca. His prior residence in Cuba brought him into contact with the early development of the industry there. In New Spain Cortés established a sugar mill at Tuxtla, in the present-day state of Veracruz, as early as 1522 or 1523. In 1532 he constructed a modest animal-powered mill, or *trapiche*, near Serrano's mill in Cuernavaca. A few years later the conqueror transferred his milling operations to a larger, water-powered *ingenio*, located at Tlaltenango, a sujeto of Cuernavaca. By the end of the 1530s this mill's annual production reached 125,000 pounds of sugar, sold both in Mexico and in Spain. The development of the conqueror's sugar hacienda explains Cortés's interest in obtaining sizable amounts of kindling wood from his tributaries. Indians from his Morelos encomiendas also performed much of the labor involved in transporting raw sugarcane from the fields to Tlaltenango.[5] Meanwhile, Cortés helped his friend Bernardino del Castillo develop a small sugar hacienda in Cuernavaca's *barrio* (neighborhood subdivision) of Amanalco. The conqueror gave del Castillo a tract of land measuring 300 by 200 *varas*, or about 10.4 acres, in a grant (*merced*) dated 26 November 1531. Five years later Cortés granted him an adjoining piece of property of identical size.[6]

Impressive though his efforts at sugar cultivation were, Cortés engaged in many other enterprises in Morelos, which again reflected the region's diverse potential for agricultural production. Crops cultivated on his scattered holdings included grapevines, a wide variety of European fruits, wheat, and mulberry trees for silkworms. He also built a wine press at Yautepec and a fulling mill at Cuernavaca, and introduced European livestock on several *estancias*, or ranches, in the region. During the quarter-century between the initial establishment of Cortés's encomienda and his death in 1547, the Indians of Morelos thus acquired substantial exposure to a wide variety of Old World agricultural products and practices.

The conqueror also laid the basis for the long process of racial and cultural blending of Indian and African that was to characterize the later social history of the region. Although Indians, including slaves, encomienda workers, and some salaried employees, supplied the bulk of labor needed for the operation of his mill at Tlaltenango, Cortés also imported African slaves to form a more permanent labor force for his many undertakings. In 1549, some eighty Africans worked at Tlaltenango, and two others at his outlying cattle ranches, while twenty-one black slaves served his household in Cuernavaca. Antonio Serrano also began using African slaves, who numbered twenty-three in 1549.[7]

The generation of Indians who witnessed and participated in the establishment of Cortés's varied enterprises also experienced the manifold political, cultural, and biological changes that accompanied the arrival of Europeans in the New World. Probably no generation in history has faced so much change compressed within a few decades as did the Indians of Mexico and Peru following the Spanish conquest. Smallpox, measles, and other diseases, to which New World natives lacked previous exposure, produced demographic crises in proportions probably never before or since equalled in human history. The studies of Sherburne F. Cook and Woodrow Borah have shown that the indigenous population of central Mexico dropped from perhaps as many as 25 million to about 7 million between 1519 and 1548, a decline of about 75 percent.[8] While some experts consider the Borah-Cook preconquest estimates excessive, there is no doubt that a substantial decline occurred.[9]

Evidence from Morelos indicates that the region shared fully in the demographic disaster. Using data published by Borah and Cook, G. Michael Riley has estimated that the preconquest population of the state of Morelos was approximately 725,000.[10] Peter Gerhard in turn has calculated a figure of 600,000 for 1524.[11] By the mid-sixteenth century, following a devastating series of epidemics in the 1540s, a substantial reduction had taken place. In 1551, a census of the Marquesado portions of Morelos, probably excluding *caciques* (local rulers) and others exempt from tribute, revealed a total population of 81,852.[12] For the entire state Peter Gerhard has suggested a midcentury population of about 158,000.[13] Although the divergence between these two figures is perhaps wider than the difference in the areas covered might warrant, both calculations nonetheless indicate heavy mortality, perhaps at rates exceeding those observed elsewhere in central Mexico.

While coping with the drastic effects of epidemic disease, Indians in postconquest Morelos also witnessed dramatic political, religious, and cultural change. Native rulers, though continuing to exercise jurisdiction within their communities, experienced a marked deterioration in their positions. The caciques of Cuernavaca, for example, lost portions of their personal landholdings to the ambitious Marqués del Valle. To maintain their position, native rulers found it expedient to adapt quickly—if superficially—to the new culture and religion imposed by the conquerors. The apparent hispanization of native rulers is evidenced by their rapid assumption of Spanish names and the extent to which they claimed to have supported the introduction and spread of Catholicism in the region. This "spiritual conquest" of Morelos began officially in 1525, when Franciscan friars founded their convent in Cuernavaca. From there they proceeded to other towns of the region. By the end of the 1520s the Franciscans were joined by Dominicans, who built their first Indian mission in Oaxtepec and then undertook the conversion of such surrounding communities as Yautepec and Tepoztlán. Beginning in 1533, the Augustinians also entered the missionary field in Morelos, concentrating their efforts in the region now comprising the eastern portion of the state.[14]

By 1550 the Indians of Morelos had felt pervasive change as a result of the Spanish conquest. A bewildering array of new diseases, plants, and animals altered forever the region's ecology, while political, economic, and religious innovation also swept the area. The towering figure of the conqueror Fernando Cortés, with his ambitious economic enterprises and ubiquitous tribute-collectors and other agents, symbolized the extent of change experienced in Morelos. Yet by midcentury a relatively small amount of land had passed from Indian owners to Spaniards. Cortés, by far the largest landholder in Morelos, owned outright a total of 1,402 acres at the time of his death. More than half of these lands, or 786 acres, were in the vicinity of his sugar mill at Tlaltenango. He owned another 111 acres in Yautepec and its sujetos, and 269 more in Oaxtepec and its sujeto Texcalpa. His remaining holdings consisted of scattered small parcels, most comprising far less than one hundred acres, and located primarily within the various barrios of Cuernavaca. Cortés acquired these properties either through simple appropriation of personal property belonging to Moctezuma or local caciques, or through purchase of land from Indian leaders.[15]

In addition to the lands he owned outright, the Marqués del Valle rented others from Indians in and around Cuernavaca. Following the conqueror's death, the Indians continued to make occasional land cessions to his son and heir, Don Martín Cortés, second Marqués del Valle. In 1559, for example, several principales of Ahuehuepa sold the Marqués a small piece of property for four hundred pesos, which they evidently divided among themselves.[16]

G. Michael Riley has identified only two other Spanish landholders in the Marquesado territories as of 1549. One was Isabel de Ojeda, widow of Antonio Serrano de Cardona. The bulk of her lands, some 672 acres, were located in the Cuernavaca barrios of Tetela and Iztayuca. She held another three acres in Cuernavaca itself, together with 1.8 acres at Atlacomulco, site of her sugar mill. Finally, Bernaldino del Castillo owned a small amount of land at Amanalco.[17] Although Riley states that del Castillo's total holdings amounted to only 6.5 acres in 1549, the donations made by Fernando Cortés to del Castillo comprised over 20 acres. In addition, del Castillo purchased an undetermined amount of land directly from the Indians of Cuernavaca in 1550.[18] Nevertheless, his holdings hardly amounted to a vast latifundium. Like the Marqués, del Castillo grew sugarcane on additional lands rented from Indian leaders.[19]

This relatively modest scale of Spanish land acquisition was due to a combination of factors, some general to New Spain, others unique to Morelos. Lesser conquerors, in sharp contrast to the entrepreneurial Cortés, showed relatively little interest in commercial agriculture during the first few decades after the conquest. Moreover, the still sizable Indian population occupied much of the best agricultural land. Therefore, Spanish land acquisition proceeded rather slowly until at least 1550. Those Spanish estates that began to emerge after midcentury were concentrated around the fringes of the Valley of Mexico, and along major thoroughfares connecting the viceregal capital with the port of Veracruz and with the northern mining centers that began their impressive development following the discovery of the Zacatecas mines in 1546. The very success of Zacatecas and other mining centers, however, lured many enterprising Spaniards into mining ventures and exploration further northward rather than into commercial agriculture in central and southern Mexico.[20]

Other circumstances also contributed to the slow pace of Spanish land acquisition in Morelos. Cortés, after 1530 the region's only encomendero, understandably discouraged the development of agricultural enterprises that might have competed with his own.[21] Moreover, at least until the second Marqués's alleged complicity in the treasonous conspiracy of 1566, which brought the temporary sequestration of all rights and perquisites pertaining to the Marquesado, the viceroys of New Spain evidently respected the Cortés family's claimed control over land allocation in the Marquesado. Finally, because no "Spanish" municipalities were ever founded in Morelos, there was no local authority to allocate to Spanish settlers, as did the *cabildos* (town councils) of Mexico City and Puebla de los Angeles. For all of these reasons, major land alienations did not begin in Morelos until after 1580.[22]

Nevertheless, the number of non-Indian residents evidently began to grow during the third quarter of the sixteenth century. By 1570, according to Peter Gerhard, about nine hundred Negroes and mulattoes and some one hundred Spaniards, about half of them members of the clergy, lived in the region.[23] Oaxtepec was one location favored by Spanish newcomers. In 1571 at least five Spaniards, in addition to the Dominican friars attached to the local monastery, were well-established *vecinos*, or householders, in the town. One of these residents reported that he had lived in the town for eight or nine years, another for two. A third, a scribe who had served various officials assigned to the district, said he had visited Oaxtepec on numerous occasions for the previous eleven years but now considered himself a permanent resident.[24] Such individuals probably bought small tracts of land from Indians who claimed them as private property. In 1582, for example, Pedro de Morales purchased a piece of property from Isabel Cortés, an Indian *cacica* who later sold large portions of land to other Spaniards.[25] The Indians of Oaxtepec noted in 1580 the fairly recent introduction of wheat farming in their area—a sure sign of the presence of Spaniards, since Indians in sixteenth-century Mexico cultivated this grain only with great reluctance.[26]

Another indication of the growing Spanish presence in the region was the establishment of a hospital for the incurably ill at Oaxtepec. In 1566 a Spaniard named Bernardino Alvarez founded the Hospital de San Hipólito in Mexico City as an asylum for the insane and for convalescents dismissed from other hospitals of the viceregal capital.[27] Shortly after San Hipólito began operations, Alvarez turned his energies to the founding of a clinic for incurables at Oaxtepec, famous since Aztec times for its salubrious climate and healing mineral springs. In 1569 Alvarez dispatched an associate, Domingo de Ibarra, to Oaxtepec to ask the town's Indian leaders for a plot on which to build a hospital. Even before Ibarra's arrival in Oaxtepec, Archbishop Alonso de Montúfar had granted a license for the hospital's creation, and Viceroy Martín Enríquez had ordered local Indians to assist in building the projected facility. In a deed dated 20 July 1569, the Indians of Oaxtepec formally gave Ibarra a plot measuring 30 by 60 *brazas*, or about 70 by 140 yards, near the town's monastery and central plaza. It is likely that not all of the proper formalities were observed in drawing up the deed, or perhaps some of the town's Indians contested the grant. Nonetheless, local officials revalidated the donation in 1571, following a hearing at which three Spanish residents testified that the grant would do no harm to the Indians.

The names of the Indian leaders who made the formal donation to the newly founded Hospital de Santa Cruz give something of a clue to the extent of acculturation among Oaxtepec's Indian leaders after a half-century of Spanish rule. While all of the officials listed in the grant had Spanish given names, the Indian governor (*gobernador*) and the members of his council (two *alcaldes* and several *regidores*) also had Spanish surnames. However, other local leaders, described only as *mandones*, or rulers, still used Indian surnames.[28]

The establishment of the Hospital de Santa Cruz accelerated the influx of Spaniards into Oaxtepec. The hospital quickly acquired deserved renown throughout New Spain, attracting patients from throughout the realm and winning particular acclaim for its treatment of incurables and syphilitics of all races and social classes. Meanwhile, Bernardino Alvarez organized his followers into a religious corporation, known officially as the Order of Charity and informally as the Brothers of San Hipólito, who continued the operation of the Oaxtepec clinic and its sister institutions throughout New Spain for the remainder of the colonial period. In addition to the brothers who managed its daily operations, the Oaxtepec hospital also provided a home for Gregorio López, the famous late sixteenth-century hermit and mystic whose proposed canonization was a favorite cause for many later generations in Mexico.[29]

Meanwhile, the Indians of Oaxtepec and surrounding areas supplied laborers to help with the construction of additional hospital facilities and to assist in its daily operations. In the 1580s, for example, the town of Yecapixtla sent twenty-five workers to the hospital each week. For some, assignment to the Oaxtepec hospital brought welcome relief from more arduous work at the mines of Huautla, located in the southernmost portion of the modern state of Morelos. In 1587 Viceroy Villamanrique ordered that instead of sending a weekly contingent to the mines, the town of Tetelcingo should send four men to the Oaxtepec hospital.[30]

The Brothers of San Hipólito obtained space for the construction of their hospital in Oaxtepec by winning the good will of the town's Indian leadership. During the second half of the sixteenth century other ecclesiastical institutions evidently received comparable donations from Indians throughout the region. Donations made to local convents in such towns as Oaxtepec, Yautepec, Cuautla, Jonacatepec, and others, as well as lands received by the Brothers of San Hipólito in addition to their hospital site, soon became the nuclei for sugar haciendas that developed in the period after 1580.[31]

In 1580 the Indian leaders of Oaxtepec prepared a report, one of the famous *Relaciones Geográficas*, providing a detailed description of their community and the manifold changes they had witnessed during the preceding sixty years. They gave considerable attention to the "botanical conquest" of New Spain, noting the Indians' marked enthusiasm for many Castilian fruits, including melons, figs, oranges, limes, and quinces, all of which thrived in the warm climate and fertile soil of their region. As early as the mid-sixteenth century, the Indians of Oaxtepec and Cuernavaca had sold sizable quantities of both Old World and indigenous fruits to Indian buyers from the markets of Mexico City.[32] A variety of European vegetables, such as cabbage, lettuce, radishes, garlic, and onions, while also well suited to the climate and soil of Morelos, had proven less popular with the Indians; their cultivation was restricted to the well-tended gardens of the monasteries. Mulberry trees dating from Cortés's abortive effort to promote silk raising could still be found in Oaxtepec and its environs. The coming of the Spaniards had also brought the addition of beef and poultry to the Indians' diets. Finally, the caciques commented on the social and economic changes introduced after 1521, especially the marked commercialization of their society. Before the Spanish conquest, everyone had worked hard; by 1580 people spent far less time at work and much more in trade. While in former times most had been content to wear a single, simple *manta*, or cloak, now they had added other, frivolous items to their wardrobes.

The Relación de Oaxtepec also details the profound impact of Old

World diseases on the Indians' lives. In the old days, according to the caciques, their forebears had risen two hours before dawn and bathed thrice daily. Despite the rigors of their daily regimen, Indians in prehispanic times "did not know what sickness was," save for attacks of fever and *bubas* (probably syphilis), from which, their descendants said, they quickly recovered. Many therefore survived to enjoy the special deference reserved for the elderly. Now, by contrast, they suffered from illnesses previously unknown, which, the Indians averred, the Spaniards had brought to their land. New cures introduced by the Europeans, including bleeding and purging, brought scant relief from these afflictions. Even the Indians' customary baths now gave them headaches.[33]

It is likely that the caciques of 1580 idealized the pre-Cortesian past, now nearly sixty years removed and beyond the personal memory of most of the population. In describing the gruesome effects of Old World diseases, however, they drew on very recent experience. The years since 1576 had brought a devastating epidemic to the indigenous peoples of Mexico and Central America. Called *matlazáhuatl* in Mexico, the illness may have been typhus, or perhaps bubonic plague.[34] Whatever its identity, it produced another sharp decline in the already depleted indigenous population. Estimated at 2.6 million in 1568, the Indians of central Mexico had been reduced to approximately 1.9 million by 1580.[35]

The plague of 1576 opened the way for the expansion of Spanish agriculture throughout New Spain. Lands vacated by deceased Indians now became available for incorporation into emerging haciendas. Moreover, the growing urban, hispanized population could no longer depend confidently on the Indians to provide them with a steady food supply. The plague probably did much to demoralize the Indians, who found reason to placate their new gods by ceding additional lands to churches and monasteries in their villages. Then too, the commercialization of Indian society, so lamented by the caciques of Oaxtepec, gave added inducement to alienate other surplus lands to Spaniards and mestizos willing to pay cash for them. Finally, it is likely that the epidemic brought a heavy turnover in the Indian leadership, further confusing the question of land tenure. Contemporary documents certainly suggest such a development in Oaxtepec. For example, none of the Indian leaders who assisted in the preparation of the Relación of

1580 appear in the list of caciques who had witnessed the town's donation of land to the Brothers of San Hipólito just nine years earlier.[36]

All of these factors coincided with a period of growth in certain sectors of the economy of New Spain, which made additional capital available to those wishing to invest in commercial agriculture. These circumstances, taken together, account for the rapid expansion of the sugar industry in Morelos during the years after 1580. Chapter 2 surveys this development in detail.

2

The Development of the
Sugar Industry, 1580–1650

The expansion of sugar plantations in Morelos after 1580 occurred during a period of far-reaching readjustment in patterns of land tenure and utilization throughout central Mexico. The matlazáhuatl epidemic of 1576 took a heavy toll in Indian lives and prompted widespread concern for the future feeding of the colony's growing urban, "Spanish" population, heretofore largely dependent on Indian produce supplied in payment of tribute or sold in the open market. Indigenous population decline left vast tracts of land available for appropriation by non-Indians, who understood that shortages of Indian produce had enhanced their own possibilities for profit in commercial agriculture. Moreover, the concurrent expansion in mining and trade continued through the first few decades of the seventeenth century, despite epidemic-induced labor shortages. Such economic growth furnished both demand and investment capital for the Spanish-owned estates that were developing in many parts of central Mexico.[1] Powerful economic forces, as well as official solicitude for the provision of foodstuffs for the colony's burgeoning cities and mining centers, clearly encouraged Spanish commercial production of such staples as maize and wheat during the late sixteenth and early seventeenth centuries.

Economic trends also made sugar production an attractive investment in the years after 1580. World demand for sugar rose impressively during the sixteenth century, and Mexican shipments to Spain expanded accordingly. Free from the price controls and official requisitions imposed on grain producers, sugar growers sold their crop on a profitable open market.[2] In the 1580s and 1590s, sugar prices in Mexico reached levels rarely again attained for the remainder of the colonial period.[3]

Despite these auspicious circumstances, emerging sugar planters faced opposition from viceroys and other officials, who feared that any expansion of sugar cultivation might divert land and other resources away from commodities considered more essential to the colony's welfare.[4] Moreover, policymakers wished to conserve New Spain's rapidly dwindling indigenous population for labor in mining and other pursuits more essential to the goals of Spanish imperial policy. Finally, the Spanish monarchs preferred to curtail sugar production in Mexico while stimulating the growth of plantations in the Canary Islands and in the strategically located Caribbean colonies, which offered few other lucrative enterprises for potential settlers.[5]

Such concerns lay behind a flurry of viceregal decrees issued in 1599. On 2 April Viceroy Gaspar de Zúñiga y Acevedo, Conde de Monterrey, prohibited the use of *repartimiento* (forced labor draft) Indians in sugar mills, while still permitting the employment of natives who volunteered for such work. Three weeks later he also forbade the erection of any new water-powered mills, or ingenios; even those already under construction could not be finished. In August of the same year he attempted to limit the cultivation of sugarcane itself by requiring that producers secure a license to plant cane. Penalties for growing cane without permission included confiscation of the crop, loss of one's land, and a hefty five-hundred peso fine. Finally, in early October of 1599, the viceroy forbade even the establishment of animal-powered trapiches.[6]

These measures did little, however, to impede the already evident formation of sugar estates in Morelos. The very nature of sugar production attracted investors who were well prepared to challenge official efforts to thwart the industry's development. The relatively high initial capital outlays for labor and equipment meant that only reasonably wealthy individuals could establish major sugar haciendas. Although the social ranking of many of the early planters remains obscure, a significant number of them evidently enjoyed official or unofficial

ties to the bureaucracy. For example, the founder of Hacienda Guajoyuca near Yautepec was Juan Fernández de la Concha, a native of
Asturias who served as secretary to the Viceroy Marqués de Guadalca-
zar.[7] Pedro Cano, developer of the mill that became known as Temilpa,
was a *relator*, or court reporter, of the Audiencia of Mexico.[8] Another
early hacendado, Francisco López Bueno, was alcalde mayor of Cuernavaca during the second decade of the seventeenth century.[9] Menén
Pérez de Solís, founder of a trapiche in Cuautla, had served as a scribe
in that town.[10] Finally, the Brothers of San Hipólito, who developed
three sugar mills in the region, enjoyed high official favor during these
years, in contrast to their great loss of prestige later in the seventeenth
century.[11] As a group, in December 1600 the influential planters in
the alcaldía mayor of Cuernavaca had little trouble in persuading local
authorities to cancel a planned inspection for compliance with the controls on the sugar industry.[12] Although on other occasions local officials evidently enforced the restrictions on the use of Indian labor, a
fortuitous development in international politics softened the impact of
these regulations. The union of the Spanish and Portuguese crowns
from 1580 to 1640 opened the markets of Spanish America to Portuguese traders who dominated the west coast of Africa, and the slave
trade, in the sixteenth and early seventeenth centuries.[13]

Meanwhile, aspiring hacendados were busy acquiring choice lands
for the production of sugarcane. Accumulation of sufficient land, prop-
erly situated and well watered, depended on a skillful combination of
capital, influence, opportunism, and luck. Most would-be sugar planters shrewdly rested their land claims on a variety of overlapping and
even conflicting bases. The hacienda Temisco, for example, included
among its lands seven separate emphiteutic grants (*censos perpetuos*) conferred by the Marqués del Valle, two viceregal grants (mercedes), and
as many as seventeen different parcels bought from Indians of Temisco
and other pueblos.[14] Such multiple bases of landownership in themselves favored those able to finance and manipulate judicial proceedings in defense of their claims.

Some of the earliest land acquisitions came in the form of three viceregal mercedes awarded to the Hospital Order of San Hipólito in the
early 1580s.[15] Although a few others also received mercedes at about
the same time, most emerging landowners had to await the resettlement (*congregación*) of the native population, undertaken between 1603

and 1605, to acquire such governmental grants. More common during the 1580s and 1590s were purchases of small amounts of land, directly or indirectly, from their Indian owners. Indian population decline, which continued at a rapid rate even after the epidemics of the 1570s had abated, left survivors with large amounts of surplus lands. Witnesses who testified in a governmental investigation of land tenure in Yautepec, Oaxtepec, and Cuautla in 1611 uniformly documented the noticeable decline in the population since 1580.[16] Land sales enabled Indian leaders to accumulate cash for the payment of excessive tribute assessments, often based on earlier, higher population counts. In other cases, Indians gave lands to churches or to individuals who had done them favors.

The remarkable will of Isabel Cortés, written in Oaxtepec in 1599, shows the extent of holdings to which some individual Indians laid claim, and the manner in which they disposed of their lands. Doña Isabel asserted that she was a principal of Oaxtepec, and that her first husband, Don Alexo Cortés, had been a gobernador of the town. On his death, Doña Isabel had inherited lands he had received from his father, referred to as Don Alexo el Viejo. It is possible that Doña Isabel, or those to whom she bequeathed her lands, misrepresented her late husband's status; no Alexo Cortés appears among the caciques of Oaxtepec listed in the hospital donation of 1571 or in the Relación of 1580.[17] Nevertheless, Doña Isabel enumerated seventeen specific tracts of land which she had either previously given away or sold, or which she bequeathed in her will. The Convent of Santo Domingo in Oaxtepec received four separate pedazos de tierra (pieces of land), and the cantores, or singers of the church, were given a plot in recompense for singing at their benefactor's funeral and praying for the repose of her soul. A Spaniard named Sebastián Ruíz received three separate pieces of land in exchange for many favors he had done for Doña Isabel. Other individuals, most of them probably Spaniards, had bought or received as gifts other tracts explicitly identified in her will.

In addition to the lands specifically mentioned, Doña Isabel claimed many more plots, which she said could be identified in pictures and documents she had left with español (Spaniard) Juan Rodríguez Boga, whose daughter had received one of her many bequests. Nine such tracts went on sale in a public auction held in Oaxtepec in June 1599, shortly after her death. Moreover, Doña Isabel stated in her will that she had already sold or given away still other pieces of land. Since the plots mentioned in Isabel Cortés's will are usually referred to simply as "pedazos de tierra," it is impossible to determine the size of her holdings. Most of the lands were in or near Oaxtepec, but at least two parcels were as far away as the pueblo of San Lucas, a sujeto of Ahuehuepa, which in turn became a sujeto of Cuautla in the congregación of 1603.[18]

Many of the lands sold or given away between 1580 and 1603 by Doña Isabel and other Indians passed directly or indirectly to individuals then in the process of establishing sugar haciendas. The well-documented acquisitions of Lucio Lopio Lampertengo, described in contemporary documents as a vecino of Mexico City, amply demonstrate the typical modes of land transfer during this period. Between April and September 1598, Lampertengo purchased five separate tracts, three directly from their Indian owners and two through Spanish intermediaries, in and around Oaxtepec. Three of these plots came from the extensive holdings of Isabel Cortés; in the following year he acquired two more parcels from her estate. One of the latter was called Pantitlán, the name by which his rapidly developing hacienda came to be known. In 1600 he bought yet another two tracts from Isabel's estate, paying a total of sixty pesos. On at least one occasion, Lampertengo traded some of his lands for other parcels with the Indian officials of Oaxtepec.[19] The Hacienda Santa Inés, near Cuautla, owed its origins at least in part to similar purchases of small amounts of land from Indians during the 1580s and 1590s.[20]

The transfer of Indian land to emerging Spanish estates accelerated after government officials carried out a major resettlement of the Indian population between 1603 and 1605. Modeled after similar church-sponsored reorganizations of the mid-sixteenth century and the sweeping reforms implemented in Peru by Viceroy Francisco de Toledo in the 1570s, this policy was designed to serve important fiscal and religious objectives. By gathering residents of widely scattered villages into major towns more easily accessible to priests and civil officials, architects of the program hoped to facilitate tribute collection and religious indoctrination of the natives. Communities ordered to move became barrios of the cabeceras to which they were relocated. The disappearance of such communities as separate pueblos left lands available for would-be hacendados.[21]

Although Howard Cline has estimated that only a minority of New Spain's Indians were affected by the congregaciones,[22] several parts of Morelos were major targets of the resettlement. About thirty of Cuernavaca's more than seventy outlying estancias (subject communities) disappeared, while only four of Yautepec's thirteen estancias survived the congregaciones. Cuautla Amilpas underwent a comparable reorganization; only four of its twelve subject communities remained in place after 1603. Yecapixtla lost nearly all of its outlying estancias, while at least three settlements disappeared in the area known in the sixteenth century as "Las Tlalnaguas," in what is now eastern Morelos. By contrast, the highland community of Tepoztlán seems to have been unaffected by the resettlement.[23]

During the years immediately following the congregaciones, aspiring hacendados eagerly sought viceregal mercedes to lands recently evacuated by resettled Indians. Table 2.1 documents the round of mercedes that followed the congregaciones in Morelos. Grantees often ignored stipulations forbidding transfer of their lands to others within a specified period of time, perhaps because they were merely acting as stand-ins for the individuals to whom they sold their property, or because rapidly rising land values tempted them to sell quickly. As a result, Marcio Lopio Lampertengo was able to acquire three separate land grants, which became part of the hacienda Pantitlán after he purchased the property from his brother Lucio in 1605. In 1610 Marcio bought 1.5 caballerías (about 155 acres; a caballería was equivalent to about 105.8 acres) which had been granted to the seller less than a month before. Three years later he purchased rights to another recently conferred merced and then received an additional grant in his own name. Like most emerging haciendas, Pantitlán thus evolved through a combination of small purchases and more sizable viceregal mercedes.[24]

In some cases mercedes simply confirmed recipients' titles to land for which they had already established some other form of claim. One merced given to the Brothers of San Hipólito, for example, ratified their ownership of land previously purchased, perhaps before the congregación, from various Indian principales of the pueblo of Suchimilcatzingo, and from several Spaniards.[25] It is likely that some of Pantitlán's mercedes similarly included lands already transferred to the hacienda by Indian sales or bequests.

Not only did the viceregal mercedes assist emerging hacendados in

Table 2.1

Viceregal Mercedes to Sugar Planters, 1581–1621

Date	Amount of land	Location	Recipient	Resultant Hacienda	Source
1581	2C	Ahuehuepa	Hospital de Oaxtepec	Hospital	AGNM, vol. 11, fol. 31v.
1581	2C	Ahuehuepa	Gordián Casasano	Casasano	AGNM, vol. 11, fol. 60v.
1582	4C; 1 SGME	Olintepec	Hospital de Oaxtepec	Hospital	AGNM, vol. 11, fol. 106v.
1582	2C; 2 SGME	Ahuehuepa	Hospital de Oaxtepec	Hospital	AGNM, vol. 11, fol. 203.
1584	1½C	Suchimilcat-zingo	Juan Gutiérrez	Probably Casasano or Calderón	AGNM, vol. 12, fol. 68.
1605	6C	Cuautlixco, Cuautla, and Ahuehuepa	Diego Caballero	Santa Inés	AGNT, vol. 1825, exp. 1; AGNHJ, leg. 128, exp. 5.
1605	2C	Cuautlixco	Jácome Hernández	?	AGNHJ, leg. 128, exp. 5.
1606	3C	Yautepec	Pedro Díaz de Villegas	?	AGNM, vol. 25, fol. 106; AGNHJ, leg. 128, exp. 5.
1606	3C	San Pedro Ayahualco	Blas de Pedroza	?	AGNHJ, leg. 128, exp. 5.
1606	½C	San Pedro Ayahualco	Cristobal de Oñate	Probably Calderón	AGNJH, leg. 128, exp. 5.
1607	6C: 1 SGMA	Amilcingo and Cuautlixco	Pedro Díaz de Villegas	?	AGNHJ, leg. 128, exp. 5.
1607	1 SGMA	Anenecuilco	Hospital de San Hipólito	Hospital	AGNHJ, leg. 128, exp. 5.
1607	1 SGMA	?	Francisco Barbero	Temisco	AGNT, vol. 3428, exp. 1.
1608	8C	Amacuzac, Guaxintlan and Coatlán	Francisco Barbero	Temisco	AGNT, vol. 3428, exp. 1.
1608	3C	Cuautlixco	Diego Caballero	Santa Inés	AGNHJ, leg. 128, exp. 5.
1608	2 SGME	Yautepec and Tlayacapan	Hospital de San Hipólito	Guausopán and/or Suchi-quesalco, eventually Hospital	AGNHJ, leg. 316, exp. 6.

Table 2.1 (continued)

Date	Amount of land	Location	Recipient	Resultant Hacienda	Source
1608	1 SGME	Anenecuilco and Olintepec	Hospital de San Hipólito	Hospital	AGNHJ, leg. 128, exp. 5.
1608	3C	Cuautla and Olintepec	Hospital de San Hipólito	Hospital	AGNM, vol. 26, fol. 81.
1609	2C; 1 SGME	Yautepec and Itzamatitlán	Hospital de San Hipólito	Guausopán and/or Suchi-quesalco, eventually Hospital	AGNM, vol. 26, fol. 159.
1609	4C	Oaxtepec	Alonso Pérez Carreño	?	AGHNJ, leg. 128, exp. 5.
1610	1½C	Oaxtepec	Pedro de Mendoza	Pantitlán	AGNHJ, leg. 128, exp. 5.
1610	4C; 1 SGME	Yautepec	Juan de Torres Montenegro	Guajoyuca	AGHNJ, leg. 128, exp. 5.
1610	1 SGME	Suchimilcat-zingo	Fernando Calderón	Calderón	AGNM, vol. 39, fol. 233.
1611	2 SGME	Guajoyuca and Yautepec	Hospital de San Hipólito	Guajoyuca (traded)	AGNT, vol. 2157, exp. 1, fol. 58v.
1613	3C	Ticumán	Juan Fernández de la Concha (for Alonzo Martínez López)	Xochimancas	AGNHJ, leg. 96, exp. 4, fol. 418.
1613	2C	Oaxtepec	Sebastián Ruíz de Castro	Pantitlán	AGNM, vol. 27, fol. 208v; AGNT, vol. 1545, exp. 1.
1613	4C	Yautepec	Francisco Parraza y Rojas	Possibly Apan-quesalco	AGNM, vol. 27, fol. 273.
1613	1C	Yautepec	Juan Donato	Probably Pantitlán	AGNM, vol. 29, fols. 24v, 25v.
1613	1C; 1 SGME	Yautepec	Marcio Lopio Lampertengo	Pantitlán	AGNM, vol. 28, fol. 98; AGNT, vol. 1545, exp. 1.
1613	2C	Yautepec	Pedro Rocha	?	AGNM, vol. 28, fol. 230.

Table 2.1 (continued)

Date	Amount of land	Location	Recipient	Resultant Hacienda	Source
1613	4C; 1 SGME	Suchimilcat-zingo	Gonzalo and Alonso Casasano	Casasano	AGNT, vol. 1731, exp. 2, fol. 7.
1614	4C	Xiutepec	Iñigo López de Salcedo (for Inés de Soto)	San Gaspar	AGNHJ, leg. 304, exp. 1.
1615	3C	Yautepec	Juan Uribe	?	AGNM, vol. 30, fol. 51.
1621	4C; 1 SGME	Cuernavaca	María de Guevara (for Gaspar de Contreras)	San Nicolás Obispo	AGNHJ, leg. 96, exp. 2, fol. 176.

Abbreviations:
C: caballería
SGME: sitio de ganado menor
SGMA: sitio de ganado mayor

establishing or confirming their claims to landownership; the prospect of receiving such grants served to clarify questions of land tenure by inducing landholders to settle differences among themselves. In 1610, for example, Alonso and Gonzalo Casasano reached an accord with neighboring landowner Fernando Calderón, resolving five separate disputes over their respective claims in Cuautla, Ahuehuepa, and the deserted pueblo of Suchimilcatzingo. Since both parties had requested additional mercedes, they agreed that neither would henceforth contradict the other's petitions. Their quarrels settled, the Casasano brothers and Calderón were free to develop their newly consolidated and augmented properties. Haciendas Calderón and Casasano soon became two of the region's major sugar estates.[26]

As the viceroys made lavish land grants in the postcongregación period, the heirs of Fernando Cortés also fostered the expansion of Spanish estates. By the early seventeenth century the Cortés family estate faced mounting financial troubles, which tempted the conqueror's descendants to raise funds by transferring land to Spanish agriculturalists. Don Pedro Cortés, the fourth Marqués del Valle, who held his title from 1602 to 1629, made the greatest number of alienations.[27] Between 1608 and 1610 the Marqués issued at least eighteen short-term leases on lands in the alcaldía mayor of Cuernavaca, especially near Yautepec and Oaxtepec.[28] The terms of these agreements restricted the tenants' use of their rented lands in various ways. For example, in 1610 Baltasar Hernández obtained a five-year lease on slightly more than one caballería of land in the abandoned pueblo of Guajoyuca. His lease stipulated that he could not cut more wood than what he needed for the operation of his household nor maintain more livestock than the animals necessary for plowing his fields.[29]

About 1613, the Marqués del Valle began granting firmer titles to land within his claimed jurisdiction. Known as censos perpetuos, such grants conferred perpetual and, in effect, unrestricted rights to the allocated lands, as long as recipients and their descendants continued to pay an annual fee to the Marquesado. From 1613 to 1623 Pedro Cortés bestowed more than two hundred censos perpetuos for lands in Cuernavaca, Oaxaca, and other Marquesado territories.[30] Like viceregal mercedes, censos perpetuos assumed great importance in the formation of sugar estates. Table 2.2 lists those in the Cuernavaca jurisdiction that became the nuclei of major haciendas.

These land allocations made by the Marqués del Valle were challenged repeatedly by royal officials, who argued that only the king and his representatives had authority to dispose of lands left vacant by the deaths of His Majesty's Indian vassals. This assumption underlay the many viceregal mercedes conferred in lands claimed by the Marqués. In 1628, the Council of the Indies decided this issue in the king's favor and ordered that the Marqués surrender to the royal treasury all profits from his land alienations.[31] A quarter-century later a royal decree reversed this ruling, but the status of these censos perpetuos remained a subject of intermittent debate into the eighteenth century. For most of the colonial period, however, the estate of the Marqués del Valle collected annual payments from successors of the original grantees.[32] Some early hacendados sought to protect themselves by securing viceregal mercedes and censos perpetuos to the same lands.[33]

The church also served as a major conduit in the transfer of lands to emerging hacendados during the period of estate formation. Both before and after the congregaciones, individual Indians as well as Indian communities donated land to ecclesiastical corporations, especially to local monasteries whose friars had established close bonds with the people they served. Such donations enabled the Brothers of San Hipólito and

Table 2.2
Censos Perpetuos Granted to Sugar Planters, 1613–1630

Date	Amount of land	Location	Recipient	Resultant Hacienda	Source
1613	½C	Adjoining lands of Oaxtepec hospital	Francisco Bernal and Isabel Ruíz	Cocoyoc	AGNHJ, leg. 96, exp. 3, fol. 537.
1613	8C	Yautepec and Ticumán	Juan Fernández de la Concha	Guajoyuca (ultimately Atlihuayán)	AGNT, vol. 1955, fol. 213.
1613	3C	Ticumán	Alonso Martínez López	Xochimancas	AGNHJ, leg. 96, exp. 4, fol. 418.
1614	5C + 1 SGME	?	Juan Martín Basave	Guadalupe	AGNHJ, leg. 447, exp. 3.
1614	5C + 1 sitio	Yautepec	Sebastián Díaz (for Juan Fernández de la Concha)	Guajoyuca (ultimately Atlihuayán)	AGNT, vol. 239, fol. 40.
1616	2C + 1 SGMA	?	Andrés Gómez Ortiz (for Juan Díaz Guerrero)	Temisco	AGNT, vol. 3428, exp. 1.
1617	2C	Acatlipa	Pedro González de Prado	Temisco	AGNT, vol. 3428, exp. 1.
1618	4C	In or near pueblo San Vicente	Diego Alarcón	San Vicente	AGNHJ, leg. 304, exp. 1.
1619	2C	Yautepec	Juan Fernández de la Concha	Guajoyuca (ultimately Atlihuayan)	AGNT, vol. 239, fol. 40.
1619	6C	Tepoztlán	Marcos de Opangueren (for Marcio Lopio Lampertengo)	Amanalco	AGNT, vol. 1545, exp. 1.
1620	4C	Between pueblos of Tesoyuca and Tetecala	Fernando Cortés de Monroy	Sayula	AGNHJ, leg. 90, exp. 4.
1620	4 sitios de estancia	Cuernavaca	Juan Díaz Guerrero	Temisco	AGNT, vol. 3428, exp. 1.
1621	3 SGMA	Cuernavaca	Juan Díaz Guerrero	Temisco	AGNT, vol. 3428, exp. 1.
1621	1 SGME	?	?	Temisco	AGNT, vol. 3428, exp. 1.

Table 2.2 (continued)

Date	Amount of land	Location	Recipient	Resultant Hacienda	Source
1621	3C + 1 SGMA	?	Juan Martín Basave	Guadalupe	AGNHJ, leg. 447, exp. 3.
1621	4C	Yautepec	Alonzo Martínez López	Xochimancas	AGNHJ, leg. 96, exp. 4, fol. 418v.
1621	2C + 2 SGME	Miacatlán	Francisco de la Fuente	Miacatlán	Sandoval, *La industria,* p. 97.
1621	1 SGME	?	Francisco de la Fuente	Miacatlán	Sandoval, *La industria,* p. 97.
1621	1 SGME + 2C	near Acatlipa	Juana de Villalobos	Temisco	AGNT, vol. 3428, exp. 1.
1623	1½C	?	Andrés Arias Tenorio	Amanalco	AGNT, vol. 1545, exp. 1.
1627	1C	near Yautepec River	Pedro Arias de Ulloa	Barreto	AGNHJ, leg. 96, exp. 1, fol. 235.
1627	1C	Yautepec	Juan de Falcés	Xochimancas	AGNHJ, leg. 96, exp. 4, fol. 419.
1628	2C	near Miacatlán	Francisco de la Vera Zapata	Miacatlan	CJD
1630	1 SGMA	Cuernavaca	Francisco de la Fuente	Temisco	AGNT, vol. 3428, exp. 1.

Abbreviations:
C: caballería
SGME: sitio de ganado menor
SGMA: sitio de ganado mayor

the convent of Santo Domingo in Mexico City to develop thriving sugar haciendas in Morelos. The Dominicans' estate, Cuahuixtla, was based on several gifts made by Indians and *gente de razón* (non-Indians) to the convent in Cuautla, whose superiors then transferred their titles to the order's mother house in Mexico City.[34]

In other cases, gifts to ecclesiastical corporations were absorbed, sooner or later, into haciendas developed and owned by laymen, so that by the eighteenth century virtually every hacienda in the region counted at least some erstwhile ecclesiastical property among its lands.[35] Sometimes, however, convents retained liens or outright ownership of lands but in practice made them available to haciendas. For example, in 1614 a principal of Yautepec presented a one-caballería tract to the town's Dominican convent. Five years later the friars ceded this land to Gerónimo and Diego Sequeira, developers of the hacienda Apanquesalco, but retained a lien of eighteen hundred pesos in principal on the property.[36] Similarly, the hacienda Temilpa incorporated into its lands property that belonged to the Dominican convent of Tlaltizapán, for which the hacienda's owners paid the friars an annual stipend of a hundred pesos.[37]

Direct alienation of land from Indians to sugar planters also continued during the period of the viceregal mercedes and Marquesado censos perpetuos. Sometimes Indians granted lands for which rival claimants had already received titles from the viceroy or the Marqués del Valle. In 1617, a frustrated censo holder complained to Marquesado authorities that the Indians of Jonacatepec had impeded his access to the land he had been granted. He claimed that the Indians had been prompted in their actions by others who wanted to buy or rent from them the land he had received in censo perpetuo.[38] Often, too, individual Indians sold lands to which their claims were tenuous at best. One common pattern involved the transfer of land that Indian women, married to Spaniards or mestizos, had inherited from their parents, in-laws, or previous husbands.[39]

The continuing importance of Indian land alienations in the process of hacienda formation is reflected also in major changes that took place in the prevalent mode of land tenure at the Cortés family estate during the first three decades of the seventeenth century. Since the mill's founding in the 1530s, its managers had relied primarily on land rented from Indians in neighboring communities. In 1549, for example, the hacienda had approximately 531 acres planted in sugarcane, of which about 425 acres, as well as the very ground on which the mill stood, were rented. The estate leased twenty-two separate pieces of land in 1581, most of them at Tlacomulco, or Atlacomulco, to which the mill was eventually transferred in 1642. Early in the seventeenth century, the Cortés estate secured firmer claims to the fields that supplied the mill, in much the same manner as other haciendas. The Indians of Cuernavaca granted the Marqués del Valle a censo perpetuo for four caballerías at Atlacomulco and then apparently sold the land to him outright in 1620. Although the estate continued to rent some Indian land for the remainder of the colonial period, after about 1624 the rental parcels

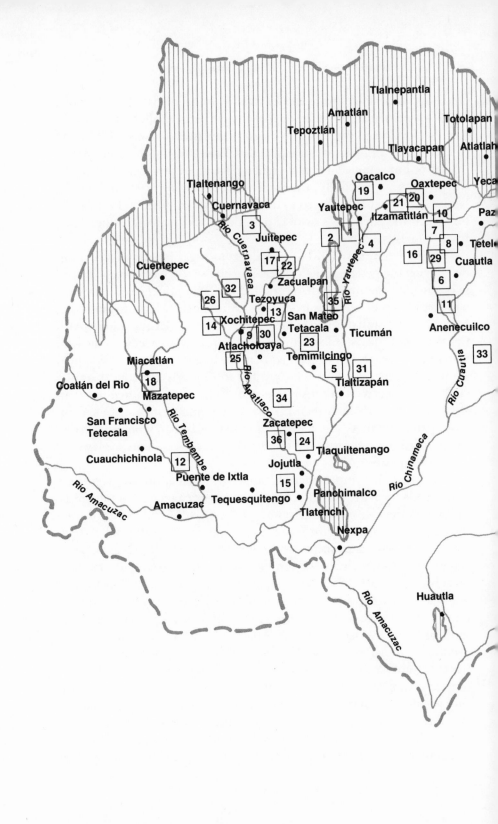

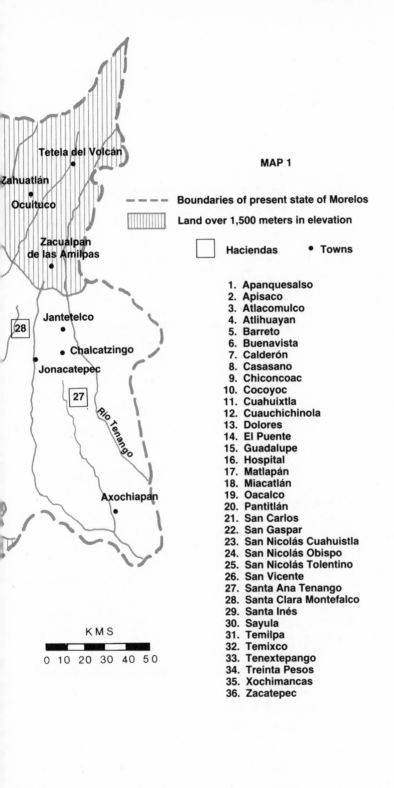

MAP 1

‒ ‒ ‒ ‒   Boundaries of present state of Morelos

▥ Land over 1,500 meters in elevation

☐ Haciendas   • Towns

1. Apanquesalso
2. Apisaco
3. Atlacomulco
4. Atlihuayan
5. Barreto
6. Buenavista
7. Calderón
8. Casasano
9. Chiconcoac
10. Cocoyoc
11. Cuahuixtla
12. Cuauchichinola
13. Dolores
14. El Puente
15. Guadalupe
16. Hospital
17. Matlapán
18. Miacatlán
19. Oacalco
20. Pantitlán
21. San Carlos
22. San Gaspar
23. San Nicolás Cuahuistla
24. San Nicolás Obispo
25. San Nicolás Tolentino
26. San Vicente
27. Santa Ana Tenango
28. Santa Clara Montefalco
29. Santa Inés
30. Sayula
31. Temilpa
32. Temixco
33. Tenextepango
34. Treinta Pesos
35. Xochimancas
36. Zacatepec

Tetela del Volcán
•

Zahuatlán
•

Ocuituco
•

Zacualpan
de las Amilpas
•

Jantetelco
•

Chalcatzingo
•

Jonacatepec

28

27

Río Tenango

Axochiapan
•

K M S

0 10 20 30 40 5 0

were larger in size and leased from the Indian gobernadores of neighboring towns rather than from individual Indian commoners. The hacienda thus changed from an agglomeration of "scattered fields or groups of fields separated by Indian land" to "a single compact unit with a single cluster of irrigated land and an adjacent pasture."[40]

Changes in the Cortés hacienda mirrored the process of land acquisition and consolidation undertaken by other ambitious agriculturalists in the region in the late sixteenth and early seventeenth centuries. Although most haciendas began with the planting of a few fields in sugarcane and the construction of a simple animal-powered trapiche, landowners with access to sufficient water and capital soon installed larger, water-powered ingenios. The Lampertengos, for example, had a trapiche at Pantitlán as early as 1599, but sometime after 1613 established a water-driven mill.[41] The Hospital de Santa Cruz de Oaxtepec, under the auspices of the Brothers of San Hipólito, also had a trapiche in 1599; by 1625 this mill had also become an ingenio.[42] Many other hacendados obtained viceregal licenses to build water-powered mills between 1613 and 1631.[43] Once they had installed these costly mills and the aqueducts necessary to convey water to the ingenios and to their canefields, hacendados had a powerful economic incentive to accumulate as much land as possible and to consolidate holdings into contiguous units, in order to maximize returns on their investments.

Most early hacendados spent additional funds to procure African slaves to work in their fields and mills. Pantitlán already had an unspecified number of slaves when Marcio Lopio Lampertengo bought the hacienda from his brother in 1605.[44] The slave force at Guajoyuca grew rapidly after Juan Fernández de la Concha purchased the estate in 1616. The hacienda had no slaves when he bought it, an unspecified number three years later, and eighty slaves by 1630.[45] In 1632, less than five years after its founding, the nearby hacienda Atlihuayan also had about eighty slaves.[46]

The substantial investments necessary to develop a sugar estate led many ambitious hacendados to borrow heavily from ecclesiastical institutions, which throughout the colonial period diverted to commercial agriculture the wealth derived from mining and commerce. Although some hacendados secured loans from small convents in nearby towns, the powerful nunneries and monasteries of Mexico City quickly assumed a preponderant role in financing the nascent sugar industry of Morelos.

Landowners agreed to pay annual interest equal to 5 percent of the loan's principal, divided in three installments to be paid at four-month intervals, until the borrower repaid in full. In actual practice, the loans were seldom repaid. As a result, leading ecclesiastical institutions of Mexico City acquired sizable perpetual liens on most of the region's haciendas. Whenever a landowner fell behind in the payment of interest, these creditors could, and often did, secure an embargo on his hacienda and its produce.[47] Many hacienda owners further burdened their estates in order to support *capellanías* (endowed chantries) or *obras pías* ("pious works," or religious or charitable foundations) that they had founded.[48] However, the largest encumbrances imposed during the first half of the seventeenth century involved actual transfers of funds used in developing the haciendas.

A few examples will illustrate the chronology, extent, and sources of hacienda indebtedness in the early seventeenth century. Typical was the borrowing pattern of Secretary Juan Fernández de la Concha, developer of the hacienda Guajoyuca. When he bought the estate in 1616, he gave its former owner an unspecified amount in cash and a lien worth two thousand pesos on the property. Two years later, de la Concha borrowed nine thousand pesos from the Convent of Jesús María in Mexico City; the following year he secured another loan, for six thousand pesos, from a capellanía. A nun in Mexico City subsequently loaned his heirs another two thousand pesos. The contracting of these loans coincided with the installation of Guajoyuca's equipment and the expansion of its slave labor force.[49]

Andrés Mendes, who established the ingenio Atlihuayan in 1627, also borrowed heavily in order to develop his estate. In 1632 he obtained two thousand pesos from the convent of San Agustín in Tlayacapan. Three years later he found himself in need of still more funds to meet daily operating expenses for his hacienda. This time he secured a short-term loan of over three thousand pesos from an individual financier in Mexico City, rather than from an ecclesiastical corporation. Although he had promised to repay this loan within one year, he died before doing so. His heirs then turned to the more familiar pattern of ecclesiastical borrowing in order to repay his debts and to maintain the hacienda in operation. In 1637 they received two thousand pesos from the nunnery of San José de Carmelitas Descalzas in Mexico City. Fifteen years later Mendes's daughter and son-in-law further encumbered the hacienda when they obtained loans totaling 21,000 pesos from two other nunneries in the viceregal capital.[50]

The financial records of the Brothers of San Hipólito show that ecclesiastical landowners also borrowed lavishly in order to build up their haciendas during the first half of the seventeenth century. In the 1610s and 1620s the brothers usually rented out their two small trapiches and forfeited a portion of the rental income in return for the tenants' services in developing the land. Like Andrés Mendes, they also turned to individual moneylenders, who supplied over 20,000 pesos to finance the expansion and continued operation of their estates. Such lenders received no liens on the brothers' property but also charged higher interest rates than ecclesiastical institutions. Finally in 1636, the Brothers of San Hipólito began borrowing funds from wealthy nunneries and other ecclesiastical corporations in Mexico City. During the next sixteen years they obtained a total of 59,000 pesos from such sources.[51]

Most haciendas of Morelos thus acquired heavy burdens of debt which their subsequent owners were never able to escape. The infusion of capital borrowed from ecclesiastical institutions made possible the haciendas' early expansion, but also placed their future prosperity in jeopardy. Service on those debts remained a constant obligation of hacienda owners, long after the equipment purchased with the borrowed money had deteriorated and the first generation of slaves had died. The haciendas' creditors, most of whom were located in Mexico City, had easy access to shrewd lawyers and to the tribunals in which they pressed their claims for recovery of back interest. Satisfaction of their demands severely diminished the potential profitability of the sugar industry.

Thus most haciendas already carried substantial encumbrances when the crown imposed a new financial burden on them in the 1640s. During that decade landowners throughout New Spain were required to pay fees for the *composición*, or confirmation, of their land titles. In return, royal officials guaranteed the validity of a person's claims, regardless of any irregularities or outright illegalities in their acquisition. With considerable justification, François Chevalier has emphasized both the importance of the composición in the consolidation of rural estates and the economic burdens which the levy brought.[52] For landowners in Morelos, the amount charged, as well as the relative burden imposed, varied considerably from one hacienda to another. The Brothers of San Hipólito were reportedly assessed the staggering sum of 6,500 pesos,[53] while the owner of the hacienda San Nicolás Cuatecaco paid 4,650 pesos.[54] Although Chevalier assumed that such figures were typical throughout the Cuautla-Cuernavaca region, there is substantial evidence that quotas set for many other landowners were far more moderate. Several sugar hacendados paid amounts ranging from 1,000 to 1,200 pesos.[55] Guajoyuca's levy of 1,200 pesos represented, for example, about 2.3 per cent of the hacienda's stated value of 53,000 pesos.[56] Owners of smaller trapiches and ranchos also paid composición fees, usually 200 pesos or less.[57]

Whatever the amount, the composiciones exacerbated but hardly created the difficulties revealed in the financial records of most haciendas by the mid-seventeenth century. As early as 1637, the owners of Atlihuayan bewailed the adverse circumstances (*"tiempos tan apretados"*) afflicting the industry.[58] Even before he was assessed for the composición fee, the owner of Guajoyuca owed nearly eighteen hundred pesos in unpaid interest on the censos perpetuos granted by the Marqués del Valle. Other hacendados were similarly insolvent. With good reason the official entrusted with collecting the composición fees expressed his frustrations in trying to persuade landowners to make their settlements. Rents of Cocoyoc and one of the trapiches belonging to the Brothers of San Hipólito were embargoed in order to secure at least partial payment of the amounts their owners owed for composiciones and unpaid interest on their censos perpetuos.[59]

The causes for these financial troubles were several. After about 1600 the expansion of the industry in Morelos and elsewhere in Mexico combined with the drop in exports to bring a gradual decline in sugar prices.[60] Meanwhile, planters in Morelos faced mounting costs of production by the second third of the seventeenth century. Prices of livestock, tools, copper kettles and other equipment rose steadily.[61] After 1640 labor costs also rose, as the independence of Portugal and the rise of slave economies in the West Indies disrupted shipments of slaves to Spanish American markets.[62] Moreover, trends in the larger economy of New Spain made it increasingly difficult for hacendados to borrow fresh capital to finance current operations or to make improvements on their estates. Although historians still debate whether the Mexican economy entered a stage of "crisis," "recession," or "depression" by the second third of the seventeenth century, several signs suggest stagnation in trade and in commercial agriculture, and a decline in production in at least some of the colony's major mining centers.[63] At the same time, the hefty liens imposed during the heyday of hacienda expansion proved increasingly burdensome as the century advanced. Finally, even the weather contributed to the haciendas' deterioration; in 1636 and 1637 severe frosts damaged sugarcane on many estates in Morelos.[64]

These financial troubles of the sugar haciendas proved beneficial to other, more modest agriculturalists, to whom impoverished hacendados sometimes rented portions of their lands. For example, in the early 1640s Carlos de Zúñiga y Arellano, the impecunious owner of Hacienda San Carlos Borromeo, subdivided part of his lands and rented them to three separate individuals, in parcels of one, two, and eight caballerías. Rents paid by these persons were embargoed by composición collectors following Zúñiga's failure to pay the stipulated fee.[65]

These tenants of San Carlos Borromeo belonged to an important but usually overlooked segment of rural society in colonial Morelos. Like the sugar planters, these humbler agriculturalists expanded their operations in the region during the years after 1580. Known locally as rancheros or labradores (farmers), such persons lacked the resources to establish a major hacienda but nonetheless succeeded in acquiring temporary or permanent use of lands at about the same time that sugar hacendados were consolidating their holdings. Especially in the western portion of what is now Morelos, where only a few sugar haciendas took root during the early seventeenth century, a thriving ranchero economy developed. Several such farmers rented small parcels of land from the Indians of Jiutepec and other communities.[66] Even in the Yautepec Valley, where the sugar industry assumed greater proportions, some rancheros established for themselves an important niche in the social and economic structure of the region. A survey taken in Yautepec in 1627 revealed the presence of at least fourteen labradores or rancheros, in addition to the owners of sugar mills in the town's jurisdiction.[67] These farmers produced maize, fruits, vegetables, and some sugar, relying on the hacendados' mills for processing their cane.

Sugar haciendas in the process of consolidation often absorbed lands claimed and developed by these less prosperous landholders. For example, many of those who became fixed-term tenants—as opposed to holders of censos perpetuos—of the Marqués del Valle were unable to compete successfully with others who coveted the region's valuable land. The tenant Baltasar Hernández was unable even to occupy either of the two properties he rented. Before he could begin planting, rival claimants, well connected to the Mexico City bureaucracy, seized the land by virtue of viceregal mercedes they had obtained. Juan Fernández de la Concha, secretary to the viceroy, easily incorporated one of the plots into his emerging hacienda, named Guajoyuca for the abandoned pueblo on whose site it stood.[68] By 1625 Hernández had become an employee of Diego de Ovalle, who inherited Guajoyuca from Fernández de la Concha.[69] Two years later, however, he was referred to as the owner of a *hacienda de labor*, or small farm, in Yautepec.[70] Other Marquesado tenants encountered similar frustrations.[71]

The early development of both Casasano and Calderón also owed much to their owners' ability to absorb the holdings of humbler labradores. Martín López de Chartudi was a small farmer whose property passed first to Calderón and later to Casasano. Before his death in 1609, López de Chartudi had acquired 2.5 caballerías of land in the abandoned pueblo of Suchimilcatzingo, near Cuautla, for which he paid annual interest to the Dominican convent of Mexico City. His marriage to Mariana María, an Indian woman who claimed to be a principal of the abandoned village, probably facilitated his acquisition of property there. López de Chartudi ran up debts totaling more than 2,500 pesos to a Mexico City vecino who had served as his *fiador*, or bondsman. As a result, his property went on sale and Casasano eventually acquired title to it.[72]

The history of a rancho in Yautepec further illustrates the changing patterns of land tenure and the fortunes of small farmers during the period of hacienda formation. In 1625 Francisco de Coria Telles paid 910 pesos for a house and a caballería of land at a public auction held to raise funds to cover debts of the rancho's previous owner, who had received the land seven years earlier in a censo perpetuo grant. Within less than ten years Coria Telles sold the rancho to a government official who resided in Mexico City. The rancho's new owner then rented it to a succession of local labradores. In 1636, it rented for 350 pesos per year; its tenant cultivated sugarcane, maize, and other crops. In 1640, however, Andrés Arias Tenorio, owner of the haciendas Pantitlán and Amanalco, absorbed the property into his holdings.[73]

Not all small farmers disappeared, however. Many survived and suc-

ceeded in increasing their access to land and water when the sugar industry began to falter. Juan Pancho Toscano was one such relatively
successful farmer in seventeenth-century Yautepec. Toscano was
described as a labrador in 1627; at that time at least twenty-nine Indians from outside the jurisdiction of Yautepec had settled on his property.[74] Sometime between 1635 and 1644, Toscano bought one caballería
from Mariana Mendes, daughter of the founder of Hacienda Atlihuayan.
At the time of his purchase, the property carried a redeemable lien of
six hundred pesos. Toscano promptly repaid that loan and then paid
crown officials three hundred pesos to confirm his title. He still owned
the property in 1657.[75] Toscano's rancho continued to attract permanent residents in the 1650s and 1660s. During that period, Yautepec's
parish registers show the baptisms of twenty-one children, most of them
Indians, who were listed as residents of "el rancho de Toscano."[76]

The assets of Alonso Moreno, owner of a small rancho near the temporarily abandoned pueblo of Oacalco, offer a good illustration of the
nature and scale of such farmers' endeavors. He built his home and
rancho on a quarter-caballería of land held by virtue of a censo perpetuo
given him by the Marqués del Valle. There he cultivated small amounts
of sugarcane, chilis, and tomatoes. He also possessed a sitio de ganado
menor (grant for grazing sheep, about three square miles) near the upland
pueblo of Amatlán, again given in censo perpetuo by the Marqués.
There he kept a herd of more than six hundred goats leased from the
Convent of Tepoztlán. At the time of his death, his estate included
some twenty mules, two dozen oxen, a few chickens, pigs, and cows,
and a hundred fanegas of maize. His personal effects reveal this modest farmer's pretensions to erudition and culture. He owned a few books,
including a volume of comedies and an account of the conquest of the
Indies, and several paintings.[77] The development of properties such
as those of Juan Pancho Toscano and Alonso Moreno constituted a
significant if unspectacular chapter in the agricultural and social history of Morelos during the early seventeenth century.

Between 1580 and 1630, then, a revolution in land tenure and utilization swept the lowlands of Morelos. Ambitious agriculturalists
employed a variety of strategies to secure titles to lands suitable for the
production of sugarcane. The establishment and consolidation of their
estates, together with the installation of the sugar mills and irrigation
works, altered forever the landscape of the region. The rapid emer-

gence of the sugar haciendas did not, however, eliminate either the more humble haciendas de labor or the Indian villages from the social and agricultural makeup of Morelos. Nevertheless, fluctuations in the fortunes of the sugar haciendas were directly or indirectly responsible for many of the modifications in demography, in patterns of settlement, and in the structure of agricultural production witnessed in the region from the early seventeenth century forward. Chapters 3 and 4 survey these processes from the period of the sugar industry's development through the mid-eighteenth century.

3

Settlement Patterns and Population Change, 1603–1750

The years from 1570 to the mid-seventeenth century brought dramatic and permanent change to the physical landscape and ethnic composition of the Morelos lowlands. The continued ravages of epidemic disease caused still further reductions in the region's remaining indigenous population, prompting the extensive resettlement of the survivors carried out by government officials beginning in 1603. The combined effects of the epidemics and the congregación resulted in the disappearance of numerous villages. Meanwhile, the expansion of Spanish commercial agriculture sharply altered existing patterns of land and water usage, while stimulating the influx of African slaves and other non-Indians to the region.

Dramatic as these changes were, the patterns of settlement and social relations associated with them remained subject to further modification during the remainder of the colonial period. The region's Indian communities, while enduring the loss of considerable portions of their ancestral lands and coping with the multiple effects of the political changes being forced upon them, nonetheless showed some ability to mold events to their advantage. They employed both legal and extralegal means to challenge the congregación decrees, and developed a variety of strategies to defend community lands against unwanted intrusions

47

by burgeoning haciendas. Those villages that by virtue of ecological accident or assertive action succeeded in retaining surplus lands attempted to profit from the expansion of commercial agriculture. They continued the well-established practice of renting or selling plots to hacendados or small farmers.

Meanwhile, major demographic changes continued throughout the remainder of the seventeenth century and beyond. Beginning with the establishment of commercial agriculture, jobs on the sugar haciendas and smaller ranchos lured to the region a steady stream of migrants, many of them Indians, whose arrival further altered the subsequent social history of Morelos. After about 1650, this immigration combined with natural increase to produce a perceptible growth in the Indian population, which in turn intensified pressures to modify congregación arrangements or concessions made previously to hacendados. In the 1690s and again in the 1730s, major epidemics temporarily stalled population growth and stimulated yet additional adjustments in settlement patterns.

The Indians' ability to influence the political and social history of their region is amply illustrated by their response to the congregaciones of 1603. Indeed, the very rationale of the resettlement presumed some indigenous participation in shaping emerging patterns of settlement. Because framers of the policy hoped to guarantee that Indians would be able to pay their tributes, they tried to relocate communities on well-chosen lands adequate for subsistence needs and tribute obligations. For this reason, Indian leaders and their priests had opportunities to air their views on proposed resettlement plans prior to their implementation. Moreover, Indians were permitted to seek reversal of congregación decrees that disregarded their wishes. They could request permission to remain at their original locations or to transfer to sites other than those to which they had been assigned.[1]

Villagers in Morelos made ample use of this prerogative. Residents of Ahuehuepa and Anenecuilco resisted incorporation into Cuautla, explaining that they preferred to remain in their original homes.[2] Those of Cocoyoc secured suspension of an order to relocate at Oaxtepec and then defied a subsequent decree commanding them to destroy their church and attend Mass at Oaxtepec.[3] The villagers of Atlacholoaya also successfully challenged the forced relocation of their community.[4] Other communities accepted resettlement for the time being, but were careful to maintain claims to their original lands, which provided their descendants with a pretext for the eventual reversal of the congregación. The community of Zahuatlán, a sujeto of Yecapixtla, provides an example of this strategy. Although incorporated into the cabecera as the barrio of "Zahuatlán el Nuevo" in 1603, the Indians requested and received permission to maintain a corral and shelter at their old location, so that a few persons might continue care for community livestock kept there.[4] Other towns obtained permission to transfer from one relocation site to another. A number of such instances were, in fact, thinly disguised attempts to remain as close as possible to their original locations. The Indians of Gueguesingo, for example, explained why they preferred to congregate in Mazatepec, rather than in Xochitepec, as ordered. They cited their close ties of friendship and kinship to the Indians of Mazatepec, as well as its geographic proximity, which would enable them to continue to cultivate the lands they had always used.[5] By remaining close to their ancestral lands, they were able to resist permanent absorption as barrios of the cabeceras into which they were incorporated.[6]

Still other communities sought and received licenses to switch from one congregación site to another for reasons that seem less clearly dictated by any desire to remain close to their ancestral lands. The Indians of Cicatlacotla explained that they preferred to congregate in Tlaquiltenango, rather than Ista, in order to save the trouble of erecting new homes, because Tlaquiltenango had many empty houses. The Indians of San Antonio Cuahuistla simply disregarded orders to congregate in Jiutepec. They instead went to Xochitepec, built new homes, and eventually won permission to remain there.[7]

In addition to these collective efforts to resist the policy of congregación, other Indians challenged the resettlement on an individual basis. As many as twenty families refused to be relocated in the pueblo of Tlayacaque, preferring to go instead to Ticumán, Tlaltizapán, and other towns. Another half-dozen individuals fled from their congregación site at Pazulco to Yautepec. A house-to-house investigation of Yecapixtla in 1605 revealed missing Indians, numbering one or two families from each of four or five of its thirteen barrios, who had gone to live elsewhere.[8]

The active role played by Indians in shaping the development of congregación policy or in thwarting its implementation suggests that Indians were alert to possibilities for improving or at least maintaining

their access to vital resources during the period of resettlement. Some
Indians, however, may have willingly accepted congregación decrees
that afforded them the opportunity to move to more favorable locations. Sites chosen for the congregaciones were important prehispanic
sites, presumably among the most attractive for settlement and agricultural production. Although the surviving documentation is admittedly
skimpy, there is no indication that residents of Yautepec's nine estancias offered serious objections when they were asked to move to the
cabecera. Perhaps these Indians readily welcomed the chance to relocate at a spot described in the eighteenth century by José Antonio
Villaseñor y Sánchez as the most favored valley in the region.[9]

At the same time the unhappy experiences of some villages that
resisted congregación may have provided inducement for Indians to
accept the changes enacted by the resettlement program. The village
of Ahuehuepa, whose residents stubbornly refused to move to Cuautla
in 1603, offers a good example of the difficulties faced by villages that
tried to remain in their original locations. Many of the town's inhabitants, including virtually all of its leaders, died in an epidemic between
1629 and 1631. An enterprising commoner named Miguel Martín there-
upon assumed leadership in the community. A native of Tecpanzingo,
seven leagues distant, he had established a foothold in Ahuehuepa only
by virtue of his marriage to a local woman. During the 1630s, he ruled
despotically over Ahuehuepa's few remaining residents, many of whom
were also newcomers to the village. Although Miguel Martín pursued
litigation challenging land claims of Hospital and other haciendas, he
contributed in other ways to the continued alienation of community
resources by selling fruit trees, which hacienda workers used for firewood in the sugar mills. Meanwhile, his land suits did little to arrest
the haciendas' appropriation of land once held by the community, and
his mistreatment of villagers prompted many to abandon their homes
in Ahuehuepa in favor of the haciendas or other towns. By 1635, Miguel
Martín's critics asserted that only ten to twelve tributaries actually lived
in Ahuehuepa. Nevertheless, the town still retained more than one
caballería of land, which probably sufficed to support its remaining
residents.[10] In contrast to Ahuehuepa, Cuautla's other outlying sujeto,
Anenecuilco, enjoyed somewhat greater success in protecting community lands, obtaining in 1614 a viceregal merced confirming the town's
claim to two caballerías and a sitio de ganado menor.[11]

Congregación brought both benefits and burdens to communities that served as hosts to relocated people. By incorporating the caciques of relocated villages into local government, consolidated communities may have been able to avoid lapses in leadership such as occurred in Ahuehuepa.[12] Moreover, incoming populations assisted their new towns in maintaining effective occupation of community land, so that consolidated communities were better able to protect their lands and other resources. For example, as the principales of Yautepec viewed the continued seizure of their lands by recipients of mercedes and censos perpetuos, they resolved to prevent further encroachments by obtaining mercedes of their own. In March 1614, they received one such grant, giving them title to three caballerías.[13] Two years later, shortly after taking formal possession of this land, they sought an additional grant for a sitio de ganado menor. In their application the Indians specifically stated that they wanted official title to this land in order to prevent its acquisition by others. The land evidently lay at a site much coveted by aspiring hacendados. Among those notified of the impending grant were owners of several developing haciendas, including Benito Lobo, whose property eventually became the hacienda Apanquesalco, Juan Paniagua, whose property evolved into San Carlos Borromeo, and the mayordomo of the hacienda Guajoyuca—all of whom held land bordering on or close to that sought by the community of Yautepec. Witnesses testifying in the town's behalf frankly admitted that the Indians did not cultivate all of the land they currently held; far less was needed for their plantings of maize, vegetables, sugarcane, and cotton. Yautepec nevertheless received this second merced in 1617.[14] In 1634, when surrounding landowners challenged the Indians' claims to the three caballerías granted in 1614, community leaders obtained a viceregal *amparo*, or guarantee confirming their rights to the land.[15]

The Indians of Jiutepec demonstrated similar assertiveness in defending their extensive landholdings, obtaining amparos in the 1630s and even submitting to the process of composición to confirm their titles a decade later. The town thus retained control of lands sufficient for their own subsistence, as well as numerous tracts rented to non-Indians. They probably derived additional revenue from the sale of produce in Mexico City, as evidenced by the appearance of a witness identified as a fruit vendor in the plaza of the viceregal capital, who testified in support of the village's land claims. Documents dealing with Jiutepec's composicion suggest that other communities also validated their titles in this manner.[16]

Nevertheless, even the most forward of leaders in the most favored of Indian communities proved unable, and sometimes unwilling, to halt a slow but steady accretion in hacienda holdings and prerogatives during the seventeenth century. The principales of Yautepec, for example, failed to block the Brothers of San Hipólito from securing a license to increase their production of sugarcane in Yautepec and Itzamatitlán.[17] In 1635, the Indians of Oaxtepec also tried unsuccessfully to limit the expansion of the hipólitos' operations. When the Indians filed a formal complaint with the teniente of Yautepec, the brothers argued that as an ecclesiastical corporation they were exempt from the jurisdiction of the teniente and other civil magistrates. An ecclesiastical judge in Mexico City understandably upheld the brothers' position and ordered the teniente to forward the Indians' brief to his court for review. Although the alcalde mayor of Cuernavaca intervened on the Indians' behalf, the Audiencia of Mexico upheld the brothers' claim to ecclesiastical immunity. Oaxtepec's complaint thus foundered amidst the tangle of conflicting jurisdictions that marked litigation in seventeenth-century New Spain.[18]

In other ways Indian caciques played an active, though sometimes unwilling, role in the alienation of community resources. Lands abandoned by Indians who had died or moved elsewhere remained at the disposition of community leaders who rented and occasionally sold them to hacendados and rancheros. Such rentals occurred wherever communities had surplus land, but they were especially numerous in areas where viceregal mercedes or Marquesado censos perpetuos had not already alienated much of the land. Village leaders in Tesoyuca and Jiutepec were particularly active in making such grants to non-Indian agriculturalists.[19] The growing command of Indian caciques over surplus land is also evident in changes noticed by Ward Barrett in records of the Cortés hacienda. Before about 1624, administrators of the mill paid small rental fees directly to as many as twenty-seven individual Indians who provided land for the hacienda's use. After that date, however, the Indian gobernadores and principales collected the rents.[20]

Indian leaders also provided house sites, or *solares*, within their towns to gente de razón willing to pay nominal fees. In 1613, Diego López

Macedo received permission from the Marqués del Valle to claim a vacant solar in Yecapixtla. In return, he agreed to pay the town's Indian government an annual pension of two pesos.[21] The leaders of Yautepec granted perpetual rights to house sites without any formal intervention of Marquesado authorities. In 1626, they sold to Lorenzo de Guzmán a solar belonging to the community. Guzmán and his heirs incurred the obligation to pay the Indians eight pesos in annual dues and to maintain the property in good condition. Ten years later Juan de Pedraza purchased in censo perpetuo rights over two more solares in Yautepec, agreeing to pay eight and one-half pesos per year for the two lots.[22]

Rental of unused community lands to non-Indians provided village leaders with funds to meet tribute obligations. Especially before a series of readjustments made between 1627 and 1642, these assessments were particularly onerous, because they were based on outdated, and therefore higher, population counts, as the figures in the first two columns of Table 3.1 demonstrate. By the early seventeenth century, Indian tributaries throughout the alcaldía mayor of Cuernavaca were paying all of their tributes in cash, rather than continuing to pay a portion in maize, as they had apparently done theretofore.[23] Cash receipts from rental payments could easily be surrendered to satisfy tribute obligations. In the 1630s, the community of Jiutepec received more than eight hundred pesos per year from hacendado Melchor Arias Tenorio, and additional sums from tenants of smaller parcels of land. These funds paid for religious festivals and other community needs.[24] Revenues from land rentals were so important to Indian community leaders that many of them protested when the crown imposed a general moratorium on rental payments in the 1630s and 1640s while authorities investigated whether such rentals had left the communities with sufficient lands for their own subsistence.[25]

Sometimes, too, tribute liabilities provided occasions for land alienations against the caciques' wishes. Between 1627 and 1632, for example, Indian leaders of Yautepec were asked to pay tribute for about 646 tributaries, of which approximately 163 were migrants from other jurisdictions who had found jobs on emerging haciendas and ranchos in the town's vicinity.[26] An occasional migrant willingly came forward to pay his tribute. For example, Pedro Bartolomé, an Indian from the pueblo of Tepeojuma, paid tribute in Yautepec even though he worked

Table 3.1
Numbers of Indian Tributaries, Selected Towns, 1625–1686

Town	1625 payments	Early seventeenth-century assessment (date)	1672 payments	% change over previous assessment	1686 assessment	% change over previous assessment
Oaxtepec	220	98 (1627)	98	0	53	– 45.9
Yautepec (cabecera)	—	—	202	—	161	– 20.3
Yautepec (with sujetos)	1,050	479 (1642)	465	– 2.9	361	– 22.4
Tepoztlán	1,116.5	810 (1638)	810	0	763	5.8
Tlaquiltenango (with sujetos)	—	449.5 (1635)	496	+10.3	443.5	– 10.6
Yecapixtla	729	—	183	—	259	+ 41.5
Cuernavaca	4,000	2,050.5 (1635)	2,170	+ 5.8	2,388	+ 10.0
Jonacatepec	178.5	126 (1632)	126	0	91	– 27.8
Jantetelco	115	72 (1630)	19	– 73.6	53.5	+181.6
Chalcatzingo	140.5	69 (1636)	89	+29.0	54	– 39.3
Pazulco	—	—	80	—	142	+ 77.5

Sources: AGNHJ, leg. 251, exp. 15; leg. 312, exp. 13; vol. 49 (leg. 28), exps. 3, 12.

on the hacienda of the Brothers of San Hipólito near Cuautla. Pedro Bartolomé's situation was somewhat exceptional, though. Because his wife was a native of Yautepec, he enjoyed access to a plot of land there.[27]

Migrants lacking such ties to Yautepec had little reason to pay tribute to the town's gobernadores. Landowners who employed these outsiders often prevented the gobernador and his assistants from collecting the necessary money or commodities from the tributaries. In 1629, Viceroy Rodrigo Pacheco y Osorio, Marqués de Cerralvo, finally ordered hacendados to pay the tributes for their workers, and several of Yautepec's landowners complied, while the number of *extravagantes* (outsiders) continued to rise. In 1631, the town was assessed for 1,042.5 tributaries, including natives and newcomers residing at the cabecera, in its sujetos, or at surrounding haciendas and ranchos. By the following year, hacendados had stopped making payments for their workers. Francisco Martínez de Oruña, in charge of tribute collection throughout the alcaldía mayor of Cuernavaca, therefore ordered the imprisonment of Yautepec's gobernador and principales until they paid outstanding tribute liabilities. The leaders proclaimed their willingness to pay the amount owed for natives of Yautepec, but protested that they had no funds with which to meet quotas for the extravagantes. Martínez de Oruña then confiscated one caballería of community land, as well as a solar already rented to a Spanish resident of the town, and placed the land on public auction so that the proceeds could be used to pay the tributes. Although details of the sale are not recorded in surviving documents, the lands without doubt found an eager buyer among the ambitious agriculturalists of Yautepec.[28] Despite this setback, the town's Indian leaders finally secured a more equitable assessment in 1642, when a new count held them liable for the quotas of 479 tributaries within their jurisdiction. A portion of the reduction was probably due to the effects of epidemics which evidently swept the area during the 1630s.[29]

Beginning at some time in the middle third of the seventeenth century, the Indian population of central Mexico began to grow again, after having experienced a steady decline ever since the introduction of European diseases in 1519. The rate and timing of this population increase varied from place to place. According to José Miranda's calculations, the total number of Indian tributaries in the dioceses of Mexico,

Puebla, and Michoacán rose from 132,721 at midcentury to 170,476 by 1692, an increase of more than 28 percent. In the diocese of Mexico the rate of growth approached 33 percent; from 57,751 tributaries in 1644, the diocese's indigenous population increased to 76,626 by 1692.[30]

Without doubt, the most important factor accounting for this change was a small but significant strengthening of the Indians' resistance to Old World diseases. As William H. McNeill has noted, the vulnerability of human populations to new infections begins to subside after 120 to 150 years of exposure.[31] By about 1640 a greater percentage of Indians survived bouts of smallpox and measles in childhood and were therefore immune when new epidemics struck. While these diseases continued to take heavy tolls among the young, their reduced severity among those of reproductive age lessened their long-term demographic impact. Socioeconomic factors may have also contributed to the population recovery. In some locations, Indians may have taken advantage of the congregación program to move to more desirable locations. Then too, José Carlos Chiaramonte has ventured the hypothesis that the development of haciendas fostered growth among the Indian and mestizo sectors of the population. Because hacendados had to devise means of attracting workers and of using their labor efficiently, the haciendas may have offered living conditions preferable to those prevailing in the peasant villages.[32]

The timing and rate of population change after 1650 is difficult to ascertain with great precision for the lowlands of Morelos. Figures drawn from Yautepec's baptismal registers show that the parish's indigenous population was definitely growing by midcentury. During the quinquennium 1635–39, the earliest for which Indian baptismal records are available, an average of thirty-one Indian children were baptized each year. Twenty years later, the annual average had risen to fifty-one.[33] Undoubtedly, this growth owed much to immigration as well as to the Indians' heightened resistance to European diseases. As early as 1627, at least 304 Indians from other parts of the lowlands, and from adjacent highland areas such as Tepoztlán and Tlayacapan, had become residents of Yautepec and its surrounding haciendas.[34]

Although the Yautepec parish registers indicate that the Indians were growing in number by midcentury, tributary counts suggest a declining population for many locations in Morelos. According to José Miranda's figures, the total number of tributaries in the Cuernavaca jurisdiction dropped from 5313 in 1644 to 5,079 in 1692, a fall of 4.4 percent.[35] Peter Gerhard cites slightly different figures (8,084 in 1620, 5,258 in 1643, and 4,326 in 1680), but also documents a downward trend lasting at least until the final two decades of the seventeenth century.[36] The discrepancy between Gerhard's figure for 1680 and Miranda's count for 1692 may indicate that the number of tributaries was rising after 1680. Addition of all the totals given in a new assessment of 1686 yields a total of 4,926.5 tributaries.[37] Table 3.1 (above) shows the number of Indian tributaries in selected towns in the Cuernavaca jurisdiction at various points during the seventeenth century. The first set of figures shows the counts in effect as of 1625; the second set is based on assessments made between 1627 and 1642; the third set shows the number of persons for whom tribute was actually paid in 1672; the fourth set shows the results of a new assessment made throughout the jurisdiction in 1686.[38] The figures show declining numbers of tributaries for most towns, although the rate of change varied considerably from one community to another.

The best explanation for these otherwise puzzling declines in the number of tributaries is that Indians were abandoning the villages in favor of residence on the haciendas, where they were less likely to be counted for tribute purposes.[39] Figures derived from the parish registers of Yautepec, discussed in considerable detail below in Chapter 6, suggest that hacienda populations, including Indians, were expanding during the second half of the seventeenth century. Towns showing falling tributary populations were located in or near the sugar-growing region. Thus Oaxtepec and Yautepec experienced marked declines.

Population growth, immigration, and movement to the haciendas were accompanied by important sociopolitical changes within the Indian communities. Again, the parish registers of Yautepec provide useful information. According to Peter Gerhard's account of the congregación of 1603, the surviving populations of nine outlying estancias of Yautepec moved to the cabecera to become barrios.[40] Baptismal records reveal that these new barrios, or perhaps others already existing in Yautepec before 1603, retained their separate identities until well into the second half of the seventeenth century. Names of barrios appearing as residences of children baptized in Yautepec, together with the numbers of baptisms recorded for them, appear in Table 3.2.

The figures in the table document Yautepec's internal evolution from

Table 3.2
Baptisms of Barrio Residents, Yautepec, 1632–1709

Barrio	1632–1639	1640–1649	1650–1659	1660–1669	1670–1679	1680–1689	1690–1692	1703–1704	1705–1709
Pochtla	34	40	51	58	39	19	4	0	0
Tepetenchi	17	16	21	8	7	6	0	0	0
Panchimalco	8	26	19	26	15	6	2	0	0
Molotla	6	5	9	3	1	1	0	0	0
Tecpan	15	27	26	25	21	8	1	0	0
Tecpilpan	10	10	6	8	1	0	0	0	0
Tlacpac	2	8	1	1	0	0	0	0	0
Chiautla	2	3	12	6	1	0	0	0	0
Atlán	0	4	9	1	1	0	0	0	0
Chiautla Atitlan	9	0	0	0	0	0	0	0	0
Chiautla Tlacpac	7	0	0	0	0	0	0	0	0
Mitla	2	2	0	2	0	0	0	0	0
Popotzingo	0	0	5	4	7	2	4	1	0
San Juan	2	13	17	28	23	109	64	43	102
Santiago	7	24	34	55	71	58	37	27	53

Source: Yautepec Baptismal Registers, GSU, microfilm, rolls 655–833 and 655–834.

as many as thirteen separate barrios to the two that survived in the eighteenth century, San Juan and Santiago. The baptismal registers permit at least tentative assignments of the seventeenth-century subdivisions to the eighteenth-century barrios. Baptismal records, particularly after 1650, often located particular barrios in the pueblos (as they were usually called) of San Juan or of Santiago. Thus there are frequent references to *"el barrio de Pochtla, en San Juan"* or *"el barrio de Tlacpac, del pueblo de Santiago."* Such references are sufficiently numerous and consistent to permit the tentative conclusion that Pochtla, Tepetenchi, Panchimalco, Molotla, and possibly Tecpan and Tecpilpan all evolved into the eighteenth-century barrio known as San Juan, while Tlacpac, Chiautla and Atlán became part of Santiago. The eventual identities of Mitla and Popotzingo remain uncertain. According to Pedro Carrasco, Tepetenchi, Panchimalco, and Molotla were probably the names of preconquest *calpulli* (barrios) in Yautepec.[41]

The early appearance of such designations as Chiautla Atitlan and Chiautla Tlacpac hints that these may have been subdivisions of an estancia congregated into Yautepec. Both of these compound barrio names appeared only in the 1630s; the single designation "Tlacpac" appeared twice in the 1630s, eight times in the 1640s, once during each of the following two decades, and then vanished forever. The single designation "Chiautla," however, reached its peak in the 1650s and did not drop from view until the 1680s. The disappearance of barrios as separate entities testifies to the enormity of population loss suffered by these communities since the sixteenth century. The barrio of Molotla, last mentioned in the baptismal registers of the 1680s, was once itself subdivided into nine calpulli and may have had more than a thousand inhabitants as late as two decades after the Spanish conquest.[42]

The baptismal registers also indicate that one of Yautepec's sujetos, Itzamatitlán, may have had as many as five separate barrios in the early seventeenth century.[43] By the end of that century, and for the remainder of the colonial period, no barrios are mentioned, either in the parish registers or in any other type of documentation. Seventeenth-century parish registers from Oaxtepec, despite many gaps and the poor organization of the surviving records, nonetheless indicate that even the tiny pueblo of Cocoyoc had at least one barrio, called Techichihualpa, as late as 1668.[44]

The disappearance of barrio identities represented, in a sense, the political and cultural ratification of the settlement patterns imposed by the congregations of 1603. A number of factors contributed to this process. The simple passage of time, aided by the continuation of major epidemics for a generation following the resettlement, gradually took the lives of all those old enough to remember their former locations. Meanwhile, migrants arrived, forming a segment of the population with no ties to the extinct communities. Then too, the growth of haciendas with claims to lands once occupied by abandoned pueblos sometimes—but not always—prevented barrio residents from returning to their old sites. More subtly, loss of lands designated for the support of a barrio's religious festivities might have brought the suspension of celebrations vital to the maintenance of a community's separate identity.

Other barrios in Morelos reversed the policy of congregación as the seventeenth century advanced. The community of Oacalco, whose relocation to Yautepec was probably included in the congregación decree, was abandoned after 1603. In 1619 Alonso Moreno received a grant of land in censo perpetuo at the *pueblo despoblado* (abandoned village) of Oacalco. During the subsequent decade he developed a modest rancho on the property, even occupying a portion of the town's abandoned church as his dwelling.[45] Within a few years, however, Indians began moving back to Oacalco. Indian children listed as residents of the pueblo of Oacalco appeared in the baptismal registers in steadily increasing numbers as the seventeenth century advanced, as the figures in Table 3.3 demonstrate. The greatest proportional increases in the pueblo's population occurred between 1650 and 1670.

Complaints aired by Oacalco's leaders during the final quarter of the century reflect this dramatic growth. In 1688 they claimed that the number of tributaries had risen from four (probably an underestimate, given the baptismal figures in Table 3.3) to twenty-six since 1665.[46] In the late seventeenth century, residents of Oacalco requested title to the six hundred varas of land in all directions guaranteed by colonial law to all indigenous pueblos. The attorney for the Marquesado approved the Indians' petition, even though the land in question had been allocated to the Brothers of San Hipólito in viceregal mercedes granted shortly after the congregación.[47]

Communities in other parts of Morelos duplicated the process observed in Oacalco. Barrios began, or stubbornly sustained, a reversal of the congregación policy by returning to live permanently at their

Table 3.3
Baptisms of Residents of the Pueblo or Barrio of Oacalco,
1635–1729

Period	Number	Avg. per year	% change over previous period
1632–34	3	1	—
1635–39	8	1.6	+ 60
1640–49	13	1.3	− 18.8
1650–59	28	2.8	+ 115.4
1660–69	69	6.9	+ 146.4
1670–79	86	8.6	+ 24.6
1680–89	93	9.3	+ 8.1
1690–92	33	11	+ 18.3
1705–9	55	11	0
1710–19	145	14.5	+ 31.8
1720–29	180	18.0	+ 24.1

Source: Yautepec Parish Registers, GSU, microfilm, rolls 655–833, 655–834, 655–835.

original locations. Sometime after 1650, residents of Yecapixtla's barrio, Zahuatlán el Nuevo, intensified their use of lands located at the site of their old pueblo. Although they had won permission to keep livestock there in 1603, they now planted maize and other crops within sight of the ruins of the church and homes abandoned by their ancestors. Finally in the first half of the eighteenth century, some barrio residents left the cabecera to live permanently at Zahuatlán el Viejo. Although the hacienda Cuahuixtla had a long-established claim to the community's lands, its owners were unable to challenge the Indians' presence until after 1750.[48]

In southwestern Morelos, Indians of a barrio called Nexpa in the town of Tlaquiltenango similarly persisted in cultivating their old lands despite relocation. The expansion of commercial agriculture near Tlaquiltenango during the late seventeenth and early eighteenth centuries solidified the Indians' determination to maintain their claim to "Nexpa el Viejo" and led them into conflict with an ambitious hacendado in 1705.[49] Meanwhile, further to the north the Indians of Cuentepec had substantially altered the original edicts of congregación. Although the town's removal to Mazatepec had been mandated in 1603, the inhabi-

tants evidently remained in their original site. Moreover, the Indians
of two other towns, San Mateo Tlamaxaque and San Miguel Tlacotla,
settled in Cuentepec, even though at least the latter had originally
been ordered to move to Mazatepec also. By the second half of the
seventeenth century, the descendants of Indians from the two towns
congregated at Cuentepec continued cultivating a portion of their
ancestral lands, and rented out other tracts of these once-abandoned
lands to Spanish rancheros. Like their counterparts at Nexpa, the
Indians of Cuentepec met opposition to their claims from surrounding hacendados. Finally, in 1718 a group of Indians attempted to establish permanent residences at the abandoned pueblo of San Mateo
Tlamaxaque.[50] In other locations the settlements refounded at once-
abandoned locations were well established by the second third of the
eighteenth century, although surviving documents do not indicate when
this dispersal began. To the east, the pueblo of Amayuca, once a barrio of Jantetelco, had returned to its old location by 1727, much to the
annoyance of landowners in the region.[51] South of Cuernavaca, a
refounded pueblo named Zacualpan received cabecera status and its
fundo legal (land allotment) in 1757.[52]

The Another case from the southwestern portion of present-day Morelos
shows elements of the reversal of congregación as well as the oblitera-
tion of old community identities. At some time during the first half of
the seventeenth century, perhaps in the late 1630s, the Indians of the
pueblo San Gerónimo Metla had moved to Tlatenchi after an epidemic
left only four surviving families. Although residents of the cabecera
continued to observe the traditional festivities honoring the image of
San Gerónimo brought there by the survivors of Metla, apparently
the former pueblo failed to survive as a clearly defined barrio in Tlatenchi. Nevertheless, the Indians of Tlatenchi, as well as those of the
neighboring town of Panchimalco, maintained their claims to the lands
once occupied by the extinct pueblo. During the second half of the
seventeenth century they planted maize and cotton at the site, although
they too encountered strong opposition from the expanding agricultural enterprises of the non-Indian sector.[53]

The rapid population growth that prompted these shifting patterns
of settlement halted temporarily during the 1690s, a period of devastating crop failure and disease in many parts of the world.[54] In Mexico,
bad weather, floods, and insects severely damaged crops over a wide

area during 1691 and 1692. By June of the latter year, food shortages in Mexico City sparked the best-known example of mass violence in seventeenth-century Mexico. An angry, hungry mob stormed the vice-regal palace, setting it afire. A few months later a measles epidemic further devastated an already weakened population. Disease, in particular a matlazáhuatl epidemic at mid-decade, as well as bad weather and food shortages, continued with little respite for the next several years, interfering with tribute payments and other activities in many places.[55]

The decade's events also disrupted life in Morelos, although perhaps less severely than elsewhere in central Mexico. The fact that Indians throughout the alcaldía mayor of Cuernavaca paid their tributes with reasonable punctuality, at least through 1696, suggests that peasant agriculture retained a certain vitality.[56] Although there are unfortunate lapses in the parish registers of Yautepec and Oaxtepec for a portion of the decade—lacunae which may in themselves point to a major crisis during these years—the records for Yautepec nonetheless suggest that the region escaped the devastating hunger of 1692. The parish's burial registers for that year show that crop failure was directly responsible for few, if any, deaths in Yautepec. Although burials for 1692 were twice as high as during the three preceding years (see Appendix 2), Elsa Malvido found that in Cholula deaths in 1692 were three times as heavy as in previous years.[57] Moreover, deaths in Yautepec were concentrated in the months of October through December, coinciding exactly with the measles epidemic raging throughout central Mexico. During the first nine months of 1692, when food shortages reached such critical proportions elsewhere, death rates in Yautepec differed little from rates prevailing during the previous three years.

Surviving parish registers permit less precise analysis of events in Yautepec after 1692. No burial registers are available from 1693 until after 1700, and baptismal registers survive only for non-Indians during that period. Marriage records are apparently more complete, but show a lapse during the middle of the 1690s, and therefore should be used with some caution. Nevertheless, it is possible to conclude that the decade witnessed sufficient mortality to blunt the forward thrust of population growth suggested by the growing numbers of baptisms recorded in the 1670s and 1680s. Available figures for non-Indians show a sharp drop for 1693, followed by a steady recovery that brought the figures close to pre-1692 levels by 1696. Baptisms again dipped in 1697 and then took several years to recover. When complete figures, including Indians, again become available for the period after 1703, the totals do not approach the pre-1692 levels until after 1715. Moreover, the substantial numbers of widows and widowers among Indians who mar-·ried in the late 1690s indicate that the decade's events struck the Indian population with particular severity. Among Indians who married between 1695 and 1699, one-third of the brides and almost as many grooms (31 percent) had been married before. By contrast, of those who married twenty years later, only 13 percent of the grooms and 18 percent of the brides had been widowed.[58]

Information from Yautepec's parish registers also suggests that the decade's events had important social implications. Particularly worthy of note is the high proportion of children identified as *hijos de padres no conocidos* (children of unknown parents), baptized in Yautepec during the 1690s, indicated in Appendix 3. These figures suggest considerable social instability, as poverty, death, or migration evidently interfered with the formation of stable family units. Nevertheless, it should be emphasized that the decade's events did no more than augment already high percentages of hijos de padres no conocidos baptized in Yautepec. During the 1680s, an average of 20 percent of the children baptized were so listed. The figures for the years after 1692 are also somewhat inflated because they give rates only for non-Indians, who traditionally, in Yautepec and elsewhere in colonial Mexico, had higher rates of child abandonment than did Indians.[59]

Nevertheless, whatever the disruptive effects of the decade's events, they did little to reduce a persistent Indian tendency toward marital endogamy. While the high numbers of mixed-bloods among the hijos de padres no conocidos suggest that many Indians formed temporary unions with persons of other races, over 92 percent of the Indian men and nearly 88 percent of the Indian women who married during the 1690s chose Indians for their partners. These rates of Indian endogamy are only slightly lower than they had been previously.[60] The implications of this consistent endogamy among Indians will be considered at greater length in Chapter 7.

If the events of the 1690s produced a slightly higher tendency to form temporary or permanent unions with gente de razón, the longer-term effects of the decade's events may have been just the opposite. There is evidence to suggest that by the first decade of the eighteenth century the sociopolitical boundaries between Indians and non-Indians, and between haciendas and villages, had increased. After 1705, when Indian as well as non-Indian baptismal registers are again available, the proportion of Indians among hacienda residents declined sharply from levels observed earlier.[61] Two separate social processes combined to produce this effect. Some Indian hacienda residents who lost actual or potential Indian mates during the 1690s chose new partners, with or without benefit of a church ceremony, from among black and mulatto hacienda residents. These Indians then became parents of a new generation of mulattoes, who had few ties with the Indian villages. Others returned to the villages, where the epidemics' effects had probably made homes, land allotments, and perhaps marriage partners more readily available than before the 1690s. These people became, once again, "Indians" in the full sociopolitical sense of the term.

Difficulties experienced by the long-established sugar haciendas further reduced their attractiveness to Indians in the 1690s. Declining sugar prices, accumulated debts, and a series of winter frosts brought many of the haciendas of the Cuautla and Yautepec valleys to the verge of bankruptcy by the end of the seventeenth century. As the haciendas curtailed or completely ceased sugar production, they reduced their demands for land and for water, both for irrigation of canefields and the operation of ingenios. Indian villagers and other small producers were therefore able to increase their own production of irrigated fruits and vegetables. These brightened prospects for peasant agriculture quite probably lured Indians away from the haciendas and back to the villages in the years after 1700.

The relative prosperity of small-scale agriculture was both a stimulus and a response to the growth in Indian population during the first third of the eighteenth century. With the important exception of 1727-28, when a measles epidemic took many lives, baptisms in Yautepec routinely outnumbered recorded burials in this period. (See Appendix 2.) It is of course possible that underreporting of burials masked a certain amount of mortality. In general, however, this period seems to have been one in which the Indian population throughout New Spain recovered remarkably from the setbacks of the 1690s, deterred only by sporadic incidences of disease and bad weather, and by the absence of the *generación hueca*—those children who died, or were never born, as a result of the epidemics of the 1690s.[62] As the Indian population grew, migration to the lowlands of Morelos and to the region's haciendas again increased, most notably in the late 1720s.

This period of population growth stopped abruptly in many parts of New Spain during the 1730s. The outbreak of matlazáhuatl, again usually identified as typhus, in the summer of 1736 signaled a new period of demographic crisis. From its original location in the Valley of Mexico the contagion spread rapidly throughout central New Spain, taking an especially heavy toll among the Indian population. In many places this epidemic brought an appreciable and permanent decline in this group's relative importance in the total population.[63]

The epidemic arrived in Yautepec in April 1737, reached its peak in August of that year, and abated substantially by the early months of 1738. As elsewhere, its effects were concentrated disproportionately among the Indians. Some 84 percent of the burials in 1737 were of Indians, while that group's share of total baptisms had fluctuated between 52 and 75 percent during several previous years. (See Appendix 2.) Nevertheless, several signs point to the epidemic's reduced severity in the lowlands of Morelos. A report addressed to the governor of the Marquesado del Valle in 1738 noted that the illness had taken fewer victims in the lowlands than in adjacent highland regions. Moreover, tierra caliente residents who did become infected recovered more often than their neighbors in higher, cooler areas.[64] This report gains plausibility when we remember that typhus flourishes more readily in cooler climates.

Evidence from Yautepec supports the conclusion that the lowlands were less severely affected by the epidemic. Burial figures again offer marked contrast with Elsa Malvido's findings for Cholula. The total number of deaths in Yautepec for 1737 was 273, between four and five times the total for 1736. In Cholula, however, deaths in 1737 were seventeen times as numerous as in the preceding year. Moreover, the epidemic in Yautepec took a greater proportion of its victims from among the young. Malvido estimates that only one-fourth of those who died in Cholula were youngsters, although at the height of the epidemic priests recorded only the burials of adults.[65] In Yautepec, 43 percent of the burials in 1737, and 42 percent of those in the following year, were of *párvulos* (infants or small children) or *niños* (children). Moreover, mortality never became so severe that priests in Yautepec stopped recording the burials of children.[66] Yet another indicator of the relatively mild nature of the epidemic in Yautepec can be found in the marriage records for the years immediately following the epidemic. In general, periods of high adult mortality in colonial Mexico were followed by intervals of increased racial intermarriage, as recent widows and widowers sought new partners.[67] Indians in Yautepec continued to display their customary propensity toward endogamy during the years after the matlazáhuatl epidemic, however. Between 1737 and 1744, over 86 percent of Indian grooms and more than 90 percent of Indian brides selected spouses from their own racial group.[68]

Despite the epidemic's reduced severity, it was not without major social and economic consequences in the region. One of the most important effects was an influx of immigrants from the heavily affected highland regions to the immediate north, a factor noted by the author of the report sent to the Marquesado authorities.[69] Baptismal records from Yautepec for the decade following the epidemic confirm this observation. The most startling demographic feature of this period is the dramatic rise in the total number of baptisms in the early 1740s. In 1741 the figure reached 225—a level *never* again attained for the remainder of the eighteenth century. This remarkable recovery from a major epidemic could only have been possible if substantial numbers of healthy adults migrated into the area. Yautepec stands in sharp contrast with Zacatelco, near Puebla, where baptisms reached their colonial-period high in 1736, immediately *preceding* the epidemic.[70]

The matlazáhuatl epidemic also brought a noticeable and permanent decline in the percentage of Indians among total baptisms in Yautepec. Although Indian baptisms rose during the early 1740s, other racial groups showed greater proportionate increases, as the figures in Table 3.4 demonstrate. Until 1740, Indians often accounted for more than 60 percent of all baptisms, while with few exceptions they failed to do so thereafter. (See Appendix 2.) Given the high rates of Indian endogamy reflected in marriage registers of the post-epidemic period, much of the long-term proportionate decline in Indian baptisms was due to factors other than increased intermarriage. Some of the change can of course be attributed to the formation of common law unions between Indians and gente de razón. It is likely, too, that a greater proportion of non-Indians born during the "baby boom" of the early 1740s survived to maturity. In most years during the 1740s, Indians continued to account for more than 70 percent of the burials in Yautepec, even

Table 3.4
Baptismal Trends, Yautepec Parish, 1730–1747

Year	Total Baptisms[a]		Indians			Mulattoes			Other Mixtures		
	#	% change from 1730–37	#	% of total	% change from 1730–37	#	% of total	% change from 1730–37	#	% of total	% change from 1730–37
Average 1730–37	141	—	89	63.1	—	26	18.4	—	20	14.2	—
1738	145	+ 2.8	88	60.7	– 1.1	31	21.4	+ 19.2	14	9.7	– 30.0
1739	177	+ 25.5	101	57.1	+ 13.5	37	21.0	+ 42.3	26	14.7	+ 30.0
1740	174	+ 23.4	91	52.3	+ 2.2	34	19.5	+ 30.8	17	9.8	– 15.0
1741	225	+ 59.6	132	58.7	+ 48.3	45	20.0	+ 73.1	35	15.6	+ 75.0
1742	206	+ 46.1	121	58.7	+ 36.0	49	23.8	+ 88.5	24	11.7	+ 20.0
1743	195	+ 38.3	111	56.9	+ 24.7	45	23.1	+ 73.1	29	14.9	+ 45.0
1744	186	+ 31.9	109	58.6	+ 22.5	47	25.3	+ 80.8	25	13.4	+ 25.0
1745	176	+ 24.8	96	54.5	+ 7.9	40	22.7	+ 53.8	30	17.0	+ 50.0
1746	181	+ 28.4	94	51.9	+ 5.6	43	23.8	+ 65.4	35	19.3	+ 75.0
1747	162	+ 14.9	90	55.6	+ 1.1	33	20.4	+ 26.9	29	17.9	+ 45.0
Average 1738–47	183	+ 29.8	103	56.3	+ 15.7	40	21.9	+ 53.8	26	14.2	+ 30.0

Source: Yautepec Parish Registers, GSU, microfilm, roll 655–835.
[a]Totals include Spaniards, Negroes, and persons of indeterminate racial classification.

though they now comprised a shrinking share of baptisms. A large number of these deaths were of young children born in the post-epidemic period. Beginning in 1747 and continuing for the remainder of the colonial period, periodic epidemics of smallpox and measles erupted with greater ferocity than they had during the first half of the eighteenth century. While the effects on the Indian population hardly approached the scale of the deadly pandemics of the sixteenth century, they nevertheless took a disproportionate share of their victims from among the Indians.

There is evidence also that the matlazáhuatl epidemic produced important changes in residence patterns. The two Indian barrios of Yautepec, San Juan and Santiago, show absolute and proportional increases in the number of non-Indian baptisms during the early 1740s, as the figures in Table 3.5 demonstrate. Mulattoes and other non-Indians evidently took advantage of the immediate post-epidemic circumstances to become village residents, acquiring homes, lands, and mates left available by the deaths of Indians in 1737. Changing settlement patterns are also reflected in the growth of a community called "*el barrio del Rancho Nuevo*," which still survives on present-day maps of the city of Yautepec, and whose population in the eighteenth century was composed almost entirely of mulattoes. The first residents of El Rancho Nuevo to appear in Yautepec's parish registers were two children baptized between 1725 and 1729. Four more infants from this new "barrio" were baptized between 1730 and 1734, and seven in the following quinquennium. During the first half of the 1740s, however, that figure jumped to twenty-one, and the second half of the decade witnessed the baptisms of twenty-two children from El Rancho Nuevo.[71]

In Cuautla, where large numbers of non-Indians had acquired permanent house sites long before 1737, the epidemic probably brought yet another influx of non-Indian residents. In 1797, a sixty-year-old mulatto explained how so many of the town's solares had been occupied by gente de razón. He said that at some unspecified time in the past, an epidemic of matlazáhuatl had left many homes unoccupied, and non-Indians had faced little opposition when they moved in.[72] Since this witness was probably born about 1737, it is likely that his elders had been referring to the 1737 epidemic when they relayed this information to him. The outbreak of matlazáhuatl thus had significant social repercussions in the Indian villages.

Table 3.5
Non-Indian Baptisms, Yautepec Indian Barrios, 1705–1754

| | Barrio San Juan | | Barrio Santiago | |
Period	#	% of total	#	% of total
1705–9	8	7.8	5	9.4
1710–14	6	6.8	3	6.7
1715–19	10	9.0	4	7.1
1720–24	10	8.5	3	7.5
1725–29	12	11.1	2	3.3
1730–34	14	10.6	1	1.5
1735–39	21	12.7	3	4.1
1740–44	34	17.8	8	10.1
1745–49	28	20.4	5	7.0
1750–54	20	15.6	2	3.9

Source: Yautepec Parish Registers, GSU, microfilm, rolls 655–834, 655–835, 655–836.

From 1603 to 1750, the lowlands of Morelos witnessed a nearly uninterrupted series of changes in demography and in patterns of settlement. The governmentally ordered resettlement of 1603 was subjected to frequent modification, particularly after the Indian population began its recovery after about 1650. Meanwhile, non-Indians became permanent residents of major "Indian" villages, especially when epidemics disrupted growth in the Indian population. At the same time, the haciendas developed as alternative forms of community that attracted sizable numbers of Indian migrants during the seventeenth century and again after 1720. Migration into the lowlands of Morelos reached particularly heavy proportions during the years following the epidemic of matlazáhuatl of 1737. These extensive social and demographic changes were accompanied by marked shifts in patterns of agricultural production and land tenure, which form the subject of Chapter 4.

4

Changing Patterns of
Land Use, 1650–1760

The matlazáhuatl epidemic of 1737 climaxed a shift in the structure of agricultural production evident in many parts of Morelos for several decades. Since the late seventeenth century most of the region's long-established sugar haciendas had been suffering the effects of a prolonged recession. The growing financial troubles of these estates reached crisis proportions in the 1690s, coinciding with the climatic and demographic calamities of the decade. During the first half of the eighteenth century the virtual collapse of the sugar industry in the Yautepec and Cuautla Valleys opened the way for the expansion of an agricultural economy in which small-scale rancheros or labradores assumed important roles in the production of foodstuffs for the growing population of the region and of New Spain as a whole. At the same time, Indian villagers found that their own agricultural prospects had improved with the haciendas' reduced demands for land and water. Meanwhile, hacendados still producing sugar in the 1730s faced severe labor shortages following the matlazáhuatl epidemic, as skilled personnel, even slaves, fled the haciendas in search of better opportunities. In the early 1740s, prices for maize and other staples rose sharply in Mexico City markets, further encouraging the production of crops other than sugar.

In what is now the western third of the state of Morelos, somewhat

71

different patterns developed, initially the reverse but ultimately comparable to those observed in Cuautla and Yautepec. South and west of Cuernavaca, the sugar industry had not taken root in the early seventeenth century as firmly or as extensively as it had further east. Instead, a ranchero and village economy prevailed for much of the seventeenth century. After 1680, thanks in part to the concurrent decline of the industry elsewhere in Morelos, new mills were established and rancheros displaced by aspiring hacendados. However, within a few decades, many of these mills fell victim to the same financial, labor, and market difficulties that retarded the recovery of older mills until after 1760.

Signs of impending crisis for the sugar haciendas of the Cuautla and Yautepec Valleys, evident as early as 1650, gathered momentum during the next three decades. Debts incurred during the industry's years of expansion and consolidation remained unpaid, and interest charges consumed a considerable portion of hacendados' declining profits. From midcentury forward, landowners were increasingly hard-pressed to meet current and past-due payments demanded by their insistent creditors. In 1657, for example, officials of the Marquesado del Valle tried to force landowners to pay overdue interest on their censos perpetuos.[1] Goods belonging to the owner of Barreto, as well as those of other hacendados, were embargoed for failure to pay the sums they owed the Marquesado.[2]

In addition to the fact that increasing amounts of hacienda income were committed for the satisfaction of overdue interest charges, several other factors compounded the hacendados' financial difficulties during the second half of the seventeenth century. Due in part to the expansion of sugar production in western Morelos and elsewhere in Mexico after 1680, sugar prices plummeted from the fairly consistent levels they had held since about the 1620s, further diminishing the profit margins of hacendados in the Cuautla and Yautepec valleys.[3] Moreover, soil exhaustion probably contributed to declining productivity on haciendas that had cultivated sugar for many decades, while deterioration of mill equipment, evident at such haciendas as Atlihuayan by 1674, brought heavy replacement costs.[4] Winter frosts, beginning in the 1680s and recurring with added severity in the following two decades, destroyed canefields and pushed many a struggling hacendado over the brink of bankruptcy.[5]

At the same time, shortages of labor and capital brought constant worry to many hacendados. Slaves were increasingly expensive and difficult to obtain, while the epidemics of the 1690s temporarily halted the growth of a free labor supply. Moreover, the transition to salaried labor compounded many landowners' already formidable cash-flow difficulties. Landowners reported crippling labor shortages even when they offered unskilled workers a daily wage of two and one-half reales, a rate 25 percent above prevailing wages. Meanwhile, few lenders were willing to relieve landowners' chronic shortages of *avío*, or operating capital. In November 1684, one Cuautla hacendado bewailed his predicament in a letter to his agent in Mexico City: "I find myself this week without a single *real*, and there is no one in these parts who will lend money."[6] As a result, numerous hacendados owed their workers considerable sums in unpaid wages.[7]

These multiple disasters struck hacendados with little regard to particular features of ownership or management. Atlihuayan, evidently the Yautepec Valley's most impressive hacienda in the mid-seventeenth century,[8] had fallen on hard times by the 1690s. The hacienda's difficulties may be traced in part to a tenant's ambitious attempt to build an expensive new aqueduct in 1689 and 1690. By 1701, the same tenant lacked sufficient resources to provide food for the estate's slaves; he reported a supply of only thirteen fanegas of maize, from which he had to feed one hundred persons.[9] Seven years later the hacienda's owner, Diego Barrientos, requested and received from the audiencia a moratorium on the payment of more than 13,000 pesos in overdue interest owed to holders of censos on his property. He explained that the most recent freeze had destroyed most of his current sugarcane crop.[10] After 1708 Atlihuayan deteriorated further as negligent administrators allowed cattle from neighboring estates to roam at will over its once-productive fields.[11]

Haciendas owned by ecclesiastical corporations, including even the Society of Jesus, suffered troubles comparable to those afflicting estates owned by laymen. At the time of the Jesuits' purchase, the hacienda Xochimancas already carried liens valued at 28,260 pesos, which represented just over a third of its stated value of 82,000 pesos. By 1683 the Jesuits had increased its burden of debt to 141,081 pesos in principal, with annual interest charges amounting to 7,054 pesos.[12]

The two trapiches and ingenio of the Brothers of San Hipólito also encountered serious financial difficulties during the second half of the seventeenth century. By the 1670s, principals of outstanding mortgages on the brothers' property had reached a total of 87,000 pesos. Holders of these censos included several of the most prominent nunneries in the viceregal capital, as well as the *capellanes de coro*, or holders of a group of endowed chantries at the Mexico City cathedral. Interest charges amounted to 4,350 pesos per year, almost a third of the 13,767 pesos paid by the tenants of the three haciendas. In 1677 the brothers owed more than 7,000 pesos in overdue interest to their censo-holders, as well as an additional 12,000 pesos in short-term credits extended by Mexico City merchants to cover operating costs for the haciendas and for their hospitals in Oaxtepec and Mexico City.

The brothers' mounting debts prompted their creditors to initiate a *concurso de acreedores*, a procedure soon to become a familiar one for most sugar hacendados in Morelos. In a concurso, the audiencia (or, in the case of an ecclesiastical defendant such as the Brothers of San Hipólito, a church court) placed an embargo on a debtor's property and rationed his current income among the creditors, usually giving priority to holders of the longest-standing claims. Concurso proceedings did little to help the fortunes of a financially strapped hacendado. Eric Van Young has colorfully described the embargoes as "judicial free-for-alls in which the assembled creditors tore at the remaining assets of the debtor like piranhas scenting blood, in a frenzy to recover as much of their money as possible."[14] These concursos might result in the sale of the debtor's assets, the proceeds of which the courts then allocated among the creditors.

Ecclesiastical judges presiding over the San Hipólito concursos in the late seventeenth century resisted strong pressure from the brotherhood's creditors to order the sale of their estates. Instead the judges directed the haciendas' tenants to deliver their rents directly to the court. After setting aside allowances to cover needs of the Hospitals of San Hipólito and Oaxtepec, the judges then divided the remaining funds among the creditors. However, deteriorating economic conditions soon interfered with the implementation of the settlement reached in the concurso proceedings of 1677. Within three years a series of unreliable tenants and other misfortunes reduced the haciendas' rental income by several hundred pesos, rendering the judges' allocation inoperable. The haciendas continued to decline for the remainder of the century. By the 1690s, the combined income from all three mills totaled only 9,000 pesos, 31 percent below the amount they had received fourteen years earlier.[15]

Even the Cortés family mill, though spared the heavy encumbrances imposed on other haciendas, experienced financial difficulties during this period. In 1679 the ingenio's tenant, José Ruíz, and his bondsman (fiador) took refuge in the Mexico City cathedral to avoid imprisonment for their many debts. A later tenant, Esteban Suárez Narciso, traced his considerable financial troubles to conditions prevailing at the hacienda. Following a fire that damaged several of the hacienda's buildings, Suárez had invested money of his own as well as other borrowed funds in rebuilding the facilities. Repeated frosts in the early 1690s destroyed so much cane that no one was willing to lend him the additional sums he needed to continue operations. Finally in 1693, some four years after his rental began, Suárez declared bankruptcy and asked to be released from the remaining five years of his lease. Although Marquesado officials granted this request, they nonetheless had him jailed for failure to pay past due rent. He died in prison in 1694.[16]

The sad experiences of the owners and tenants of Atlihuayan, Hospital, and Atlacomulco became common occurrences throughout the region in the four decades after 1680. Concursos de acreedores, embargoes, and forced sales appear in the surviving records of almost every estate. In 1699, the hacienda Temilpa, near Tlaltizapán, owed more than three years' interest on censos whose principals totaled nearly 40,000 pesos. Although the hacienda's owner, Alonso Isidro de Velasco y Hermosilla, secured a temporary moratorium on the payment of these debts, he finally had to sell the estate in 1704 to a new owner who promised to resume interest payments.[17] By 1701 the owner of Pantitlán and Amanalco owed over 9,000 pesos in back interest on more than 36,000 pesos borrowed from the treasury of the Inquisition.[18] The ingenio Zacatepec was subjected to repeated embargoes and forced sales between 1694 and 1715, as successive owners proved unable to liquidate its accumulated debts.[19]

By the opening years of the eighteenth century, owners and creditors of most sugar mills in the Cuautla and Yautepec Valleys lamented that few investors were willing to buy or rent these debt-ridden, decrepit estates. When prospective buyers or tenants did come forward, they offered payments far below what the estates had been worth in former times. The hacienda San Diego Ticumán, also known as Barreto, offers a good example. Pedro López de San Vicente rented the estate in 1689 for 6,000 pesos per year. Because its canefields were heavily damaged by frosts in the 1690s, the hacienda lay idle for a full year following the expiration of his lease in 1698. The following year a new tenant took over, paying only 3,000 pesos per year. In 1702 the hacienda passed to a new owner, who offered a mere 2,200 pesos in cash while agreeing to assume interest payments on mortgages whose principals totaled 11,000 thousand pesos.[20]

Others acquired haciendas without making any cash payments at all. The priest Manuel de Verástegui became the owner of Zacatepec in 1715 simply by acknowledging future liability for interest charges on 21,000 pesos' worth of outstanding mortgages.[21] In 1712 Mexico City merchant Miguel Ortega Ojores had taken over San Carlos Borromeo in a similar manner, despite vigorous protests from the hacienda's creditors, who argued that the buyer should make some cash payment which could be allocated in partial satisfaction of their claims. However, Ortega Ojores was unable to maintain his interest payments, and the hacienda passed to a succession of court-appointed receivers, known as *depositarios*, until it was finally returned to its owner, Josefa de La Higuera.[22]

Few knowledgeable persons held much optimism for the potential profitability of these sadly deteriorated haciendas. Felipe Ramírez de Arellano, who acquired a small trapiche in Cuautla in lieu of repayment for loans he had made to its owner, harbored few illusions about the worth of his new property. Shortly after receiving title to the hacienda, he stated that he intended to sell or lease it as soon as he could get its mill back in operation. He cited lack of operating capital as the principal reason why sugar hacendados in the area faced sure financial ruin.[23]

Signs of the sugar industry's decadence were visible throughout the Cuautla and Yautepec Valleys in the opening decades of the eighteenth century. Milling ceased at Pantitlán in 1704, and the ingenio was declared *despoblado*, or abandoned.[24] Nearby, at San Carlos Borromeo, neither of the hacienda's two trapiches was in operation by 1711. Its irrigation channels were blocked with accumulated soil; little cane grew in its fields. Even the earth itself showed little respect for the hapless hacienda; a recent tremor had severely damaged its chapel. The estate's deterioration had sent many of its resident workers elsewhere in search of better opportunities, even though they had not collected wages owed them.[25]

The combined effects of the depression in the sugar industry and the demographic setback of the 1690s are clearly reflected in population figures for haciendas in the Yautepec Valley. An ecclesiastical census taken in 1715 listed only twenty-nine communicants residing at San Carlos Borromeo. Marginal notes made shortly after the census was completed revealed that of these another three had subsequently fled. Nearby, the trapiches Apisaco and Apanquesalco reported forty-seven and thirty-two communicants respectively. Atlihuayan had a much larger population, one hundred twenty, but almost two-thirds, or seventy-five communicants, were slaves.[26] In succeeding years many slaves took advantage of lapses in hacienda administration to flee; slave flights were more numerous during the first half of the eighteenth century then at any other time during the colonial period.[27]

Workers who remained at the haciendas proved increasingly restive during the early eighteenth century. Many actively protested in an effort to improve their living and working conditions. In 1728 slaves at the bankrupt hacienda Calderón boldly resisted a rumored plan to transfer them either to Casasano or Hospital. Armed with knives and *coas* (hoes), they threatened to burn the mill to the ground if their concerns went ignored. One of their spokesmen stated that they would refuse to acknowledge official transfer (*"darse por recibidos"*) to anyone but a master acceptable to them (*"amo que les conviniese"*).[28]

Meanwhile, free workers also resisted employers' unreasonable demands. Indians from Tepoztlán, for example, evidently refused advances intended to lure them to jobs at Atlacomulco. They explained that the hacienda's administrator assigned them tasks in excess of customary requirements.[29] Probably with considerable justification, hacendados in this period generally regarded their workers as an unruly lot. In 1735, landowners in the Cuernavaca region expressed their opposition to a projected inspection by Marquesado authorities of labor conditions on all haciendas in the jurisdiction. According to the hacendados, such examinations provoked only uproar and scandal, because the work forces on most sugar estates were composed of slaves and other ignorant persons sent to the ingenios against their will. The landowners feared that this undependable horde of workers would see the inspector as a liberator.[30]

The epidemics of the late 1730s evidently exacerbated the shortage of skilled and dependable workers. In 1739, the owner of Chiconcoac expressed his deteriorating confidence in his prospects for recruiting and paying sufficient numbers of workers to keep his mill in operation.[31] Although demographic evidence from Yautepec, as well as other types of sources, indicate that the region received substantial immigration in the years following the matlazáhuatl epidemic of 1737, newcomers probably preferred to take up residence in the villages rather than to seek positions on the haciendas. Moreover, most of them probably lacked the specialized skills needed for sugar production.

Labor difficulties during the first half of the eighteenth century thus precluded an easy recovery for the sugar haciendas. At the same time, conditions prevailing in the Mexican economy further jeopardized a quick return to profitable sugar cultivation on haciendas in the Cuautla and Yautepec Valleys. Instability of ownership and other signs of financial trouble can be detected in the records of haciendas in widely scattered parts of Mexico during the first half of the eighteenth century.[32] For sugar growers, persistently low prices for their product compounded their difficulties. Frustrated hacendados often cited the failure of sugar prices to return to levels prevailing before 1680. As one landowner explained in 1723, prices had been unsatisfactory for producers since long before 1710; any increases were of very short duration.[33] Again in 1732 another hacienda owner decried the "*decadencia y atraso de los azúcares*" ("decadence and setbacks of sugar") in recent years.[34] Given these circumstances, even massive infusions of capital could do little to restore the haciendas' profitability.

The efforts of Pedro Carbajal Machado, owner of Cocoyoc and Pantitlán after 1715, amply illustrate the problems confronting even the most ambitious of hacendados during this period. Carbajal Machado had acquired the haciendas in lieu of repayment for the sizable loans he had made to their former owner, José de Gurbizar, who was also his wife's stepfather.[35] The new owner attempted to expand sugar production at Cocoyoc, sharply curtailed since about 1700, and to rebuild a mill originally founded in the 1680s at the rancho Oacalco, which was incorporated into the lands claimed by Pantitlán. The latter project seriously drained Carbajal Machado's assets. Before the mill even began operations in May 1725, he had invested over 28,000 pesos. During its first two years of milling, Oacalco's production costs exceeded receipts by 50 percent. By the summer of 1728 Carbajal Machado had spent over 115,000 pesos in building and operating the mill, without receiving any net profits from the venture. At that point he expressed his understandable reluctance to invest any more funds in it.[36] The rise and equally rapid decline of Hacienda Oacalco are reflected in the parish registers of Yautepec. Table 4.1 shows the number of children baptized at Yautepec, who were explicitly listed as residents of the hacienda, and not the pueblo or barrio, of Oacalco.

Carbajal Machado's ambitious plans for a new mill at Oacalco contributed to the rapid depletion of his assets, which had exceeded 120,000 pesos at the time of his marriage, before he acquired his sugar haciendas.[37] Following his death in 1730, his heirs faced repeated demands from his many creditors.[38] A decade later Cocoyoc, the only one of Carbajal Machado's sugar estates to show any signs of profitability dur-

Table 4.1
Baptisms, Residents of Hacienda Oacalco, 1726–1740

Year	Number
Before 1726	0
1726	3
1727	14
1728	5
1729	7
1730	4
1731	5
1732	5
1733	4
1734	4
1735	3
1736	1
1737	2
1738	0
1739	1
1740	0
After 1740	0

Source: Yautepec Parish Registers, GSU, microfilm, roll 655–835.

ing the period of his ownership, had so badly deteriorated that sugar milling ceased. In 1740, the hacienda was described as *"perdida, sin caña ni ganados"* ("lost, without cane or livestock"). Nine years later an inventory of the estate vividly documented its decadence. What once had been a *tienda*, or store, now served as the principal residence, while the former headquarters was completely uninhabitable, lacking doors, windows, and a roof. Mill equipment was entirely useless; slaves and other workers had stolen most movable tools. The decrepit hacienda provided scant revenue to sustain the pretentious life-style of Carbajal Machado's heirs. When his daughter María Rosa married Antonio Moro y Manrique in 1741, she had no dowry.[39]

The plans of Pedro Carbajal Machado failed even though he was able to utilize assets from neighboring haciendas, probably at little or no cost to himself. As one of the few financially solvent landowners in the Yautepec Valley during the 1720s, Carbajal Machado served as court-appointed depositario of other bankrupt haciendas. He evidently took advantage of the opportunity to transfer slaves and equipment from these haciendas to his own estates, employing them in the construction and operation of his new mill at Oacalco. An inventory of that mill taken in 1728 revealed the presence of thirteen slaves and 800 pesos' worth of equipment belonging to the haciendas Apisaco and Apanquesalco. Although Carbajal Machado characteristically and with perhaps some justification blamed his financial troubles on the administrator to whom he had entrusted the new mill, the formidable problems confronting the sugar industry throughout the region during the first half of the eighteenth century undoubtedly shared the responsibility.[40]

The crisis of the long-established haciendas of the Cuautla and Yautepec Valleys was accompanied and to some extent exacerbated by a simultaneous expansion of the industry in the region directly south of Cuernavaca, extending along the Cuernavaca and Tetlama Rivers to the latter stream's confluence with the Yautepec River. Although Pedro Cortés, fourth Marqués del Valle, had granted censos perpetuos in this area as liberally as in other parts of Morelos, fewer permanent sugar mills were established there than in the Cuautla or Yautepec Valleys. Instead, for much of the seventeenth century mestizo and Spanish rancheros developed a mixed farming economy, producing maize and other foodstuffs on modest-sized holdings granted in censos perpetuos either by the Marqués or by the Indians in such pueblos as Jiutepec. Beginning shortly after midcentury, and especially after 1680, these labradores, as they were also known, began cultivating sugarcane and constructing simple animal-powered trapiches. A few of these humble estates eventually became important sugar haciendas.

Indian communities with surplus lands facilitated the expansion of some sugar haciendas by renting out additional lands and granting others in new censos perpetuos. For example, on several occasions during the seventeenth century the Indians of Jiutepec had leased to rancheros lands at a site once occupied by a long-abandoned sujeto called Matlapán. Until 1696 tenants produced maize and other crops, but in that year former alcalde mayor Francisco de Morales established a trapiche. Within five years the mill had passed to Francisco del Pozo, who secured a more permanent claim to the property in the form of a censo perpetuo granted by the Indians. He also secured their consent to draw water from the Tetlama River for the irrigation of his fields.[41] Francisco Jiménez Cubero, developer of the trapiche Asesentla, also persuaded the Indians of Jiutepec to grant him a censo perpetuo for lands he had first rented from them.[42] Meanwhile, authorities of the Marquesado del Valle abetted the expansion of commercial agriculture in western Morelos during the first two decades of the eighteenth century by granting several new censos perpetuos to rancheros and hacendados.[43]

Yet these new sugar producers soon faced many of the same difficulties that had brought financial ruin to their counterparts in Cuautla and Yautepec. Labor difficulties plagued landowners throughout Morelos during the first third of the eighteenth century. The need for operating capital, which proved so troublesome to longer-established hacendados farther east, soon forced owners of these newer estates into debt. The Mexico City merchants who supplied capital to the developing haciendas of western Morelos inevitably acquired title to them when the owners were unable to repay their loans. For such investors, these newer estates offered seemingly more attractive prospects for profit than the heavily encumbered and deteriorating haciendas of Cuautla and Yautepec.

The history of the hacienda Nuestra Señora de Guadalupe, located in southwestern Morelos near Jojutla, illustrates the development of the sugar industry out of the ranchero economy of the seventeenth

century. Between 1614 and 1621, Pedro Cortés had allocated the land
which eventually became the nucleus for this hacienda. One of the original recipients, Juan Martínez Basabe, founded a trapiche sometime
before 1626, and the mill was still operating in 1631.[44] By the 1660s,
however, the trapiche had disappeared. The property, known as a
rancho de labor and owned by an español named Alonso de la Cruz,
produced maize, wheat, tomatoes, chilis, and livestock. After de la Cruz
died, about 1670, Esteban Maldonado took over the property and began
growing sugarcane in addition to other crops. Sometime thereafter, he
established a trapiche, which he bequeathed to his son Juan before 1691.
This mill ultimately became known as Nuestra Señora de Guadalupe.[45]
Meanwhile, Esteban and Juan Maldonado also farmed the property
which was later to become the hacienda Nuestra Señora de Dolores.
In the 1640s, Juan Pérez de Figueroa had developed a rancho de labor
on land originally rented and later granted in censo perpetuo by the
Indians of Tesoyuca. In 1657 Esteban Maldonado acquired Pérez's
rancho, where he produced maize, wheat, and other foodstuffs.

The Maldonado family evidently lacked the necessary capital to convert their haciendas to substantial sugar plantations. Sometime before
1701, Juan sold the Guadalupe property to Martín Rodríguez Mariscal,
who then cleared up discrepancies in the estate's titles by agreeing to
pay the Marquesado 150 pesos per year in perpetuity. Rodríguez Mariscal also obtained a license to convert the trapiche to a water-powered
ingenio, but in the meantime was forced to borrow heavily from Mexico City merchant (and tenant of Atlacomulco) Francisco García Cano.
By the fall of 1702 he owed García over 13,000 pesos and had no assets,
other than his hacienda, with which to pay. Title to the hacienda therefore passed to García Cano.

Juan Maldonado also ceded the Dolores property to an aspiring
hacendado who enjoyed access to more substantial amounts of capital.
A secular priest from Mexico City, Antonio Zubia Pacheco, bought
the hacienda in 1696 and the following year secured a license to build
a sugar mill.[46] Meanwhile, the Maldonado family, unable to maintain
a position in the hacendado ranks, continued farming operations on a
more modest scale. José Maldonado, Juan's brother, described himself
as a labrador in 1704, while Juan's son Francisco was a farmer and
livestock producer in Tlaquiltenango.[47] By 1710, Francisco had estab-

lished a modest rancho of about twenty-six acres at the site of an abandoned pueblo.[48]

Other properties followed similar patterns of development from ranchos to sugar mills, which were subsequently taken over by persons possessing greater amounts of capital than the original owners. Bernabé Gómez was another would-be hacendado who met frustrations similar to those of the Maldonados. In 1684, he purchased a rancho called San Antonio Cuahuistla from Miguel de Noguerón, yet another aspiring sugar producer. Gómez quickly built a modest two-room dwelling and a trapiche, which was in operation by 1686. Marquesado authorities temporarily evicted him from his hacienda for failure to obtain the necessary permission for producing sugar.[49] Gómez's ambitions, however, did not stop with the restitution of the mill at San Antonio Cuahuistla. In 1692, he bought another trapiche, San Nicolás Sayula. He had evidently learned from his previous encounter with Marquesado authorities; he promptly secured a license for the establishment of this second trapiche, even though it had already been in operation for a number of years. Soon, however, Gómez found himself unable to meet operating expenses for his undertakings. In 1702 the hacienda was embargoed and eventually auctioned to Manuel del Hierro for 9,320 pesos, approximately 1,800 pesos more than Gómez had paid. In that year accumulated debts allegedly exceeded the value of the hacienda. Gómez's other mill, San Antonio Cuahuistla, may have ceased operations by 1702, for an inventory of his assets referred to this property as a rancho rather than a trapiche.[50]

Miguel de Noguerón, who sold the Cuahuistla property to Bernabé Gómez, met with more success than either Gómez or the Maldonados, but ultimately his property likewise fell to entrepreneurs with access to greater amounts of capital. Sometime before his death in 1686, Noguerón built the trapiche San Nicolás Cuaumecatitián on a rancho rented from the Indians of Tetecala and Temimilcingo. At the time of his death his estate, valued at 16,905 pesos, included eleven slaves who worked on the hacienda. Like other trapiche owners, Miguel's son and heir Francisco began borrowing from Francisco García Cano. In 1707 García Cano added this mill to his holdings at a bargain price of 5,400 pesos.[51]

The development of the trapiche Nuestra Señora de la Concepción Guimac in Cuernavaca also resembled that of other new mills in the area. Originally granted in censo perpetuo in 1643, the property was referred to as a rancho de labor in numerous transfers of ownership during the next forty-five years. Sometime between 1688 and 1693, Cuernavaca resident Diego López de Solís established a trapiche there. In 1693 he sold the property to Vicente Ferrer de Rojas, also a resident of Cuernavaca and holder of the right to collect *alcabalas* (sales taxes). At the time of this sale the trapiche consisted of three small buildings of mud and stone and a small amount of sugarcane. A lone slave, purchased in 1689, also passed to the trapiche's new owner. Like other aspiring hacendados in this period, Ferrer was unable to maintain his property. In 1700, the trapiche passed to Lucas García, a Mexico City merchant, in satisfaction of a debt of 2,738 pesos owed him by Ferrer. This amount represented less than half the sum (6,530 pesos) which Ferrer had paid for the property just seven years previously. García quickly sold the property to Cristóbal Mateos, another resident of Cuernavaca and holder of the local meat supply monopoly. Within five years, Mateos, in turn, sold the property to a priest. At a later unspecified date, sugar production ceased at Nuestra Señora de la Concepción Guimac, and the property again became known as a rancho. Finally in 1791, the administrator of the Marquesado's assets bought the property to provide additional pasture for the livestock of Atlacomulco.[52]

If the rancheros-turned-hacendados were rapidly forced out of sugar production due to insufficient operating capital, the wealthier individuals who replaced them found that even their superior resources and the economies of scale achieved through consolidation could not guarantee sustained profits in sugar production. These new owners soon faced the consequences of bad weather, low sugar prices, shortages of labor and capital, and inefficient management that hampered recovery of the older mills in Cuautla and Yautepec. Conflict among the hacendados over water use also hampered the continued expansion of the industry in the west.[53] Moreover, owners of these recently developed estates confronted mounting hostility from Indian villagers who resisted the new pressures placed on regional land and water resources by the expanding sugar industry.

Again, the history of Nuestra Señora de Guadalupe is instructive. This hacienda's nucleus lay on a site formerly occupied by the abandoned pueblos of San Gerónimo Metla and Zinahuatlán. Exactly when these settlements disappeared is not clear from surviving documentation. In 1604, residents of Tlatenchi, Panchimalco, and Zinahuatlán had been given the choice of congregating either in Tetelpa or in Metla.[54] Testimony presented by these pueblos in 1705 suggests that the Indians of Tlatenchi and Panchimalco ignored the congregación order. Elderly witnesses recalled that about sixty years previously an epidemic had so reduced the population of Metla that the few survivors—totaling four families at most—had heeded their priest's suggestion that they move to Tlatenchi. They had dutifully removed a large painting of San Gerónimo from the church at Metla and transferred it to their new village, where they celebrated San Gerónimo's feast annually.

Just when the Indians of Tlatenchi and Panchimalco began planting maize and cotton at Metla is unclear, but sometime between 1670 and 1690 they challenged Esteban Maldonado's claim to the land. According to testimony given by his son José, Esteban Maldonado had become blind toward the end of his life, and neither he nor his young sons were able to defend their lands. The pueblos succeeded in winning an order from the alcalde mayor upholding their claim to the sites of Zinahuatlán and Metla. While carrying on their struggle with the Maldonados, the Indians of Panchimalco and Tlatenchi also battled with Andrés de Rebollar, owner of Zacatepec, one of the few long-established mills in southwestern Morelos. In 1690, they registered a formal complaint that Rebollar's livestock had been damaging their *milpas*, or cornfields. In response, alcalde mayor Francisco de Morales reminded Rebollar to be more careful with his livestock.

Whatever their temporary success in restraining the Maldonados and Rebollar, the Indians of Panchimalco and Tlatenchi found a tougher adversary in Francisco García Cano. In 1704 García, accompanied by a number of his servants as well as the teniente of Jojutla, forcibly took possession of the land at San Gerónimo Metla. Some witnesses later claimed that one of García's servants struck a former gobernador of Tlatenchi and took another Indian prisoner. Despite the Indians' objections, the teniente proceeded to erect markers delimiting the lands claimed by García, placing one in the middle of a cottonfield belonging to the Indians.[55]

Angry villagers quickly sought revenge. A crowd, allegedly numbering over two hundred, set fire to Guadalupe's canefields and then apprehended and threatened to kill García Cano. Fellow hacendado

Andrés de Rebollar responded readily, undoubtedly because he feared that he might become the Indians' next target. He mustered a force of forty armed men, who put out the fire, secured García Cano's release, and rounded up the leaders of the rebellion. Although García Cano later won formal confirmation of his censo perpetuo to the site of San Gerónimo Metla, the Indians' animosity toward him continued. They repeatedly protested that his livestock damaged their crops, while at the same time they stubbornly refused to fence their fields, arguing that it was García Cano's responsibility to restrain his animals. In 1723 the Indians of Panchimalco again set fire to the hacienda's canefields.[56]

While challenging the claims of Panchimalco and Tlatenchi, García Cano also struggled with the Indians of a settlement called Nexpa. At some time prior to 1705, this pueblo had been moved from its location near the Río Amacuzac to a site adjacent to the town of Tlaquiltenango. The Indians had insisted on planting crops at the site of Nexpa el Viejo, despite the fact that they had been given lands to farm at their new location. Apparently their decision to plant at Nexpa el Viejo was prompted by the spot's attractiveness to local farmers, among them García Cano, who wished to pasture livestock there. García Cano offered to trade the Indians six *fanegas de sembradura* (approximately fifty-three acres) near Tlaquiltenango in exchange for their surrender of Nexpa el Viejo, where he claimed they planted two fanegas de sembradura at most. Although the Indians showed little interest in García Cano's proposal, he nonetheless received title to the property by virtue of a censo perpetuo granted by administrators for the Marqués del Valle. The "rancho de Nexpa" remained incorporated into García Cano's hacienda for the remainder of the eighteenth century. Financial interests of the Marquesado clearly coincided with those of García Cano.[57]

Even though he ultimately won most of his battles with neighboring pueblos, the destruction of García Cano's canefields by angry Indians combined with other circumstances to prevent him from achieving all of his objectives. Guadalupe's previous owner had obtained a license to convert the mill to a water-powered ingenio, but inventories taken after García Cano's death still referred only to a trapiche. In the 1720s and 1730s his widow and heir, Antonia de Aranda Echeverría, experienced the debilitating effects of insufficient capital, while a series of incompetent administrators further contributed to the hacienda's deterioration. In 1732 the administrator was unable or unwilling to allocate to the hacienda's fifty-three slaves their customary, and therefore expected, rations and perquisites. As a result, discipline within the labor force was seriously undermined. A decade later, lack of funds with which to buy firewood and other supplies forced another administrator to destroy a large amount of unmilled cane. Further evidence of the decline in García Cano's estate can be found in the fact that by this time his other trapiche, San Nicolás Cuaumecatitlán, had long been demolished. After his widow's death in the early 1740s, several of the hacienda's slaves were embargoed because taxes and interest on several mortgages remained unpaid.[58]

Other hacendados in western Morelos also encountered serious obstacles in their attempt to sustain the expansive momentum generated in the final two decades of the seventeenth century. As early as 1717, officials of the Marquesado complained of their difficulties in collecting annual premiums for the censos perpetuos held by developers of these new trapiches. By that time, several of the new mills had already been demolished.[59] San Antonio Cuahuistla, the smaller of the two mills founded by ranchero Bernabé Gómez, may have disappeared as early as 1705.[60] The trapiche San Nicolás Tolentino, established in the 1690s by Tomás González de Rebolledo, had ceased operations by the mid-eighteenth century.[61] A similar fate befell the trapiche Nuestra Señora de la Concepción Guimac.

The few landowners able to build relatively prosperous haciendas in the west during the first half of the eighteenth century were persons with access to sufficient capital to buy several estates and consolidate them into single enterprises, thereby achieving some economies of scale. Juan Antonio de Palacios bought both Miacatlán and San Gaspar before his death in 1722. Sometime after 1738, José de Palacio, a *gachupín* (European-born) merchant resident in Mexico City, bought these two haciendas, to which he later added Temisco and El Puente.[62] Another relatively successful hacendado was Manuel García de Aranda, who also consolidated his holdings, though on a less impressive scale than José de Palacio. García de Aranda bought Santa Rosa, also known as Treinta Pesos, as early as 1703. In 1707, he purchased Matlapán from Francisco del Pozo, whose adopted daughter he had married. Finally, in 1716, he added the decrepit hacienda Amanalco to his holdings.[63] At Amanalco he soon established a new mill, christened San Vicente, while continuing to rent out a portion of Amanalco's lands to small farmers. García de Aranda continued as owner of this agricultural enterprise until he died in 1754. Following his death, however, lawsuits brought against his estate revealed the precarious base on which his apparent success rested. An inventory of his estate showed over 51,000 pesos in mortgages imposed on the haciendas Amanalco, San Vicente, and Matlapán, 35,000 pesos of which he had borrowed between 1747 and 1751. The combined value of the three haciendas in 1754 was 73,021 pesos; their debt burden amounted to approximately 70 percent of their total value.[64]

Throughout Morelos, few sugar producers found sustained opportunities for profit during the first half of the eighteenth century. The hacendados' difficulties produced significant alterations in patterns of land tenure and agricultural production, most noticeably in the Cuautla and Yautepec Valleys, where the sugar industry had taken hold most decisively a century earlier. As landowners cut back or eliminated sugar production altogether, they adopted a new strategy that required neither the heavy inputs of capital nor the trained labor force needed for sugar. They subdivided their properties into modest-sized ranchos leased to labradores of various racial classifications, who produced maize and a wide variety of other crops for their own subsistence and for sale locally and in the expanding markets of Mexico City. Hacendados rented other lands in tiny parcels to Indian *terrazgueros*, who were usually residents of villages which lacked sufficient lands to support their growing populations.

José de Gurbizar, owner of Cocoyoc, began experimenting with these land tenure patterns soon after 1700. He rented unused tracts of land from the Indians of Oaxtepec and from the Brothers of San Hipólito, and then sublet these and other parcels to Spanish and mestizo rancheros. Gurbizar made a profit on his transaction with the Indians of Oaxtepec, paying 8.3 pesos in annual rent per caballería and charging his subtenants forty pesos per caballería. One such tenant was an español named Nicolás de Cervantes, who produced a variety of crops on his half-caballería. Cervantes irrigated his crops using water formerly appropriated by Pantitlán, which had recently ceased sugar production as a result of its financial difficulties.[65] The practice of renting land to rancheros continued after Pedro Carbajal Machado acquired Cocoyoc, even though he attempted also to expand its production of sugar.[66]

At Atlihuayan, where some sugar production also continued throughout this period, several individuals rented parcels of land for the production of maize and other crops. In 1731, ten persons, including the hacienda's mayordomo, paid tithes for crops produced on land rented from Atlihuayan. All but one of the tenants, also called *pegujaleros*, used the title "Don." Together the nine tenants produced 3,650 fanegas of maize, 230 fanegas of frijoles, and 120 fanegas of garbanzos. The most substantial pegujalero operation was that of Don Sebastián González, who produced 700 fanegas of maize and 100 of frijoles. Francisco Ramírez diversified his endeavors by producing 620 fanegas of maize, 40 of frijoles, 40 of garbanzos, and a small amount of sugarcane. Don Cristóbal de Mendoza, the ingenio's mayordomo, harvested 190 fanegas of maize on his own account. Records for Atlihuayan also give pegujalero production for 1732. In that year six individuals, in addition to the hacienda's administrator, planted maize and other crops. Evidently there was considerable fluctuation among pegujaleros; only two of the people who rented lands in 1732 had also done so the previous year. The pegujaleros' harvest for 1732 was appreciably lower than that recorded for 1731; they produced only 1,680 fanegas of maize, 120 fanegas of frijoles, and a small amount of sugarcane. The administrator, Don Nicolás Sánchez, reported a harvest of 500 fanegas of maize, however.[67]

Other haciendas abandoned sugar production completely. Following the dismantling of the mill at Santa Inés, for example, lands formerly used to pasture livestock for the ingenio were converted to maize production. The lands were divided into small plots rented by Indians from Pazulco and Tetelcingo, and into larger ranchos leased by non-Indians.[68] At Apanquesalco and Apisaco, where accumulated debts forced the cessation of sugar production by the early 1720s, rancheros and terrazgueros occupied a total of about 500 acres. In 1724 forty persons shared 32.5 fanegas de sembradura at Apanquesalco, while at Apisaco twenty-one persons cultivated a total of 24.5 fanegas de sembradura. Although two tenants rented plots measuring 5 and 3 fanegas de sembradura, the others rented much smaller pieces of land, usually a fanega de sembradura or less. The tenants included Indians from neighboring towns, as well as others who had migrated into the region from the highlands ("tierra fria"). Other tenants were gente de razón who cultivated maize and small amounts of frijoles, paying their rent in kind at harvest time.[69]

The Brothers of San Hipólito also ceased sugar production at their two trapiches, Guausopán and Suchiquesalco. Sebastián de San Martín, tenant of the brothers' haciendas from the 1720s to the 1740s, sublet the lands at Guausopán in small parcels to Indians from Tepoztlán.[70] He also rented the "rancho" Suchiquesalco to Alonso de Guzmán, who tried briefly to resume sugar production in the mid-1720s. Guzmán even experimented with technical innovation by copying a furnace design recently developed in Cuba, but was soon ordered to dismantle the new equipment because he had not paid required royalties to its inventor.[71] Thereafter, he dedicated his efforts to the production of maize, garbanzos, and other crops, remaining at Suchiquesalco until San Martín terminated their unwritten rental agreement in 1743.[72]

Some favored Indian communities also abetted the expansion of the ranchero economy by renting surplus lands to small farmers in much the same fashion as hacienda owners. In the 1730s, the Indians of Oaxtepec reclaimed two separate but adjoining parcels of land, totaling four caballerías, formerly leased to hacendado Pedro Carbajal Machado and his predecessors.[73] They then proceeded to rent the land in small parcels to non-Indian labradores. Three such tenants testified on Oaxtepec's behalf in a land dispute with the highland village of Tlayacapan. One of these pegujaleros was an español, another a mestizo, and the third a castizo.[74]

Production of basic foodstuffs, especially maize, assumed increased importance in the early 1740s, when a succession of poor to mediocre harvests in many parts of central Mexico drove up food prices.[75] Harvests in Morelos suffered some ill effects from unfavorable climatic conditions, but shipments of grain to the markets of Mexico City also played a role in creating the shortages reported during these years, especially in Cuernavaca. In August 1741, the town's tithe collector was accused of hoarding maize for later sale at higher prices. That same month an investigation of maize supplies in Yautepec revealed that seven labradores there had on hand a total of 440 fanegas of maize, worth 1,300 pesos at current Mexico City prices. The maize was probably the fruit of an irrigated crop, planted early in 1741 and harvested in the spring. One of the individuals mentioned was Sebastián González, one of Atlihuayan's ranchero tenants a decade earlier. Another was Pedro Valiente, former teniente of Yautepec.[76] The high birth-rates in Yautepec during the early 1740s suggest that food was available in sufficient quantities for women of child-bearing age.

The increasing importance of maize cultivation in the early 1740s is best documented by the history of Hacienda Pantitlán, whose sugar mill had been idle since the beginning of the century. Pedro Carbajal Machado had used much of the Pantitlán's land for pasture, although apparently he had rented some tracts there to small farmers. In 1738, Felipe de Alzate, father of the famous late colonial scientist José Antonio Alzate y Ramírez, rented Pantitlán and the neighboring hacienda Oacalco from heirs of Carbajal Machado. During the next few years, Alzate converted as much as two-thirds of Pantitlán's lands from pasture to farmland, cultivating some of the land himself and subletting other portions to pegujaleros. Most of the tenants produced nonirrigated maize, but one ranchero, Manuel Ruíz, planted garbanzos, some sugarcane, and other crops requiring irrigation. Two of Alzate's tenants, Agustín and Francisco Ramírez, had been pegujaleros at Atlihuayan in 1731 and 1732.

In 1742 the heirs of Pedro Carbajal Machado had Alzate's lease terminated on the grounds that he had seriously undermined the value of Cocoyoc by depriving the hacienda of its traditional pasture land. In his defense, Alzate pointed to the growing importance of maize cultivation on lands that had once served the sugar industry. Tenants and owners of other haciendas, including Calderón, Apisaco, and Bárcena, as well as the trapiches Guausopán and Suchiquesalco, had expanded their production of maize, said Alzate. Recent high prices had prompted still other hacendados to turn greater attention to grain production. At Cocoyoc, additional land was sublet for that purpose beginning in 1740. An inventory taken a decade later revealed that four rancheros rented lands from Cocoyoc, paying rents ranging from 40 to 160 pesos per year. Meanwhile, at the hacienda Hospital, tenant Sebastián de San Martín had recently opened up some 40 fanegas de sembradura, or 352 acres, to maize cultivation, and tenant farmers at Apanquesalco planted indigo and other crops.

Alzate argued that by clearing land for maize and other crops at Pantitlán he had augmented rather than diminished the value of the estate. In renting Pantitlán, claimed Alzate, he had merely obtained use of the hacienda's badly deteriorated *casco*, or headquarters, and its

lands. Lacking the labor force, livestock, water, and equipment necessary for sugar production, the hacienda was an ingenio only in name.
Moreover, Alzate discounted the argument, advanced by Carbajal
Machado's heirs, that sugar production at Cocoyoc depended on the
use of Pantitlán as pasture for its livestock. By the time that Alzate
rented Pantitlán, Cocoyoc was no longer producing sugar. Although
the Carbajal Machado heirs succeeded in terminating Alzate's lease
before the expiration of his nine-year term, the Audiencia of Mexico
ruled in 1745 that they could not force him to pay for his alleged dam-
ages to the hacienda.[77]

Whatever the merits of Alzate's legal arguments, his management of
Pantitlán made good economic sense. Labor difficulties and shortages
of capital prohibited a return to sugar production; subdivision of their
lands for grain cultivation enabled owners and tenants of haciendas to
reap modest profits with little investment. Alzate's experiment also
made a lasting impression on his famous son and, evidently, on the
subsequent agricultural history of Morelos. Until his father's rental of
Pantitlán, wrote the younger Alzate, agriculturalists in the region had
dedicated their efforts almost exclusively to sugar cultivation, producing only enough maize needed for consumption by their workers and
livestock. After 1740, according to Alzate y Ramírez, farmers in the
"tierra caliente" had seen the wisdom of maize production, and the
growing cities of New Spain increased their reliance on the region for
maize and other foodstuffs, especially in times of agricultural crisis.
Although he understandably exaggerated his father's role in bringing
about this change, there is no doubt that the production of maize for
Mexico City had assumed an important position in the structure of the
area's agricultural production.[78]

In his study of the Bajío, David Brading depicted the period from
1680 to 1740 as a "golden age" for rancheros in León. Small landowners and tenants alike enjoyed access to lands sufficient in quantity and
quality to enable them to capitalize on the growing demand for foodstuffs in the cities and mining centers of New Spain. In contrast to
later periods, wrote Brading, "the structure of agricultural production
still offered ample opportunity for all classes in the countryside to profit
in varying degrees from the general renewal of economic activity."[79]

Conditions in Morelos bore a definite, yet limited, similarity to those
prevailing in the Bajío. Outright ownership of land was almost un-

known among labradores in Morelos. It is true that some farmers, especially in what is now the western part of the state, enjoyed relative security in land tenure by paying nominal annual fees for the censos perpetuos granted them or their predecessors by the Marquesado or by Indian communities. Most rancheros, however, remained dependent on hacendados or Indian villages from whom they rented, usually on a year-to-year basis. Nevertheless, the decline in sugar production gave these rancheros a chance to exploit the climate, soil, and favorable location that made the region so ideal for commercial agriculture. While most such farmers described themselves as españoles, castizos, or mestizos, an occasional *pardo libre* (free mulatto) achieved a modest degree of prosperity on lands rented from haciendas.[80] These labradores' dependence on the hacendados was compensated in part by the fact that it was in the landowners' interest to rent surplus lands to individuals who could at least protect an owner's title against encroachments by squatters. During the first half of the eighteenth century, then, labradores carved out for themselves an important niche in the regional economy, one that they would not willingly yield when rising land and water values threatened their position after 1760.

The retreat of the sugar industry also enhanced the agricultural prospects for villagers living in the Indian communities. Again the case of Pantitlán shows the relationship between fluctuations in the sugar industry and other changes in the structure of agricultural production. Idling of the hacienda's mill early in the eighteenth century enabled the villagers of Oaxtepec and Yautepec to enjoy exclusive use of water previously shared with the hacienda. In Oaxtepec, peasants expanded their own production of sugarcane and bananas on lands where they had never before been able to produce those crops. In the 1720s, Pedro Carbajal Machado, the enterprising owner of Cocoyoc, Oacalco, and Pantitlán, tried unsuccessfully to recover this water for his haciendas. Through persistence and intermittent threats of violence, the villagers of Oaxtepec thwarted his ambition to revive sugar production at Pantitlán. Carbajal Machado obtained a court order affirming his right to irrigate his fields with the water formerly used to operate the ingenio, and proceeded to repair his aqueduct accordingly, but armed villagers boldly altered the conduit and rediverted the water to their own *huertas*, or orchards.[81]

Meanwhile, the villagers of Yautepec also successfully challenged the seizure of a portion of their communal lands by Hacienda San Carlos Borromeo. Between 1720 and 1726, the hacienda's owner had leased the tract, measuring about 123 acres, to the teniente of Yautepec for seventy pesos per year. After 1726, the villagers regained control of the land, where they planted frijoles, other vegetables, and sugarcane.[82] Until 1740 the Indians of Santo Domingo Ticumán also expanded their production of maize and watermelons, using land claimed but not cultivated by the Jesuit haciendas Xochimancas and Barreto.[83]

The account of José Antonio Villaseñor y Sánchez, written in the 1740s, attests to the vitality of peasant agriculture in many parts of the Morelos lowlands. According to Villaseñor, the villagers of Yautepec were the most prosperous of all; their beautiful and pleasant valley afforded them comfortable profits from cash crop production. Villaseñor also reported thriving agricultural production by villagers in most other localities extending in an arc from Yecapixtla and Cuautla westward to Yautepec and then southward to Jojutla, Panchimalco, and Tlatenchi. Outside this arc, those barrios of Cuernavaca with access to sufficient water for irrigation also profited from cash crop production, while villagers of Mazatepec and Tetecala, to the southwest of Cuernavaca, also enjoyed reasonable success in agriculture. Peasants in these favored localities cultivated such staples as maize and frijoles, as well as cotton, sugarcane, and a wide variety of *"frutos regionales y de Castilla"* sold locally and in the markets of Mexico City. Even the highland community of Tepoztlán, while lacking the abundant water and warm climate of the lowlands, nonetheless had over fourteen thousand fruit trees at the time Villaseñor made his report. Not all communities of Morelos were so favored, however. Jonacatepec, Jantetelco, and Pazulco to the east, and Xochitepec and Miacatlán to the west, had neither good soil nor sufficient rainfall for irrigated agriculture. The unfortunate inhabitants of these localities were forced to earn the bulk of their subsistence by working for wages.[84]

The relatively favorable prospects for village and rancho agriculture, themselves due in part to setbacks suffered by the sugar industry, made, in turn, the haciendas' recovery all the more difficult. Because landowners lacked means to provide slaves and free workers with expected wages and other benefits, many potential hacienda workers found more attractive opportunities cultivating their own lands in the villages. Despite the landowners' complaints, however, haciendas retained resident populations descended from slaves and Indians who had settled on the estates in the seventeenth century. For those unable or unwilling to seek other livelihoods off the haciendas, continued residence at the declining sugar estates offered a modest degree of material security. Whatever the financial troubles of the landowners, workers who remained as residents on the haciendas simply reverted to subsistence agriculture to meet their needs.[85] For many, flight to a rancho, a village, or another hacienda would have required them to abandon homes where they and their ancestors had lived for decades, even generations.

The years from 1690 to about 1760 witnessed considerable variety in patterns of land usage and associated forms of settlement. While a few haciendas continued to produce sugar, the virtual collapse of many others left sufficient resources for the Indian villages, for rancheros and sharecroppers, for settlements such as Yautepec's mulatto community, El Rancho Nuevo, and for hacienda residents who simply turned to subsistence agriculture. John Womack's characterization of social relations in Morelos before 1880 is essentially accurate for this period:

> Before [1880], various communities and economic enterprises had existed without question . . . Sugar plantations, traditional villages, small-farm settlements, single independent farms, day laborers' hamlets, country towns, provincial cities—not all of these . . . flourished, but they were all grudgingly able to survive . . . Morelos's sugar plantations still functioned in the main tradition of Mexican haciendas, more as symbols than as businesses. . . . Happily or not, social variety seemed eternal.[86]

During the years from 1690 to 1760, many haciendas, reduced like Pantitlán to land and run-down cascos, indeed functioned less as businesses than as symbols of the ambitions and pretensions of their seventeenth-century founders. When they could, hacendados still encroached on land and water claimed by Indian communities, but the landowners' financial troubles gave many villages the opportunity to rectify such abuses. Meanwhile, enterprising rancheros or or labradores could rent entire estates or smaller parcels of land, depending on their individual assets and ambitions. After about 1760, however, the revival of sugar production and other economic changes disrupted the delicate ecological balance on which this remarkable social variety rested.

5

The Expansion of
Commercial Agriculture,
1760–1810

The final third of the eighteenth century brought profound economic and social changes to New Spain. Economic growth, first evident in the revival of silver mining during the early decades of the century, gathered momentum almost without interruption. Mining, trade, and commercial agriculture all offered attractive opportunities to those with capital to invest; persons who succeeded in such enterprises rewarded themselves by building lavish homes and purchasing impressive-sounding titles of nobility. Major readjustments in colonial policy implemented under the energetic leadership of King Charles III (1759–1788) accompanied and to an extent facilitated these economic changes. Hoping to generate more colonial revenue to support Spain's position in international politics, Charles and his ministers introduced new taxes and government-sponsored monopolies, lifted certain restrictions on trade within the empire, and in general sought to promote all aspects of colonial economic development not perceived as competing with metropolitan interests.[1]

Economic growth brought a marked acceleration of social tensions in the late colonial period. Those who lost resources or markets to more successful entrepreneurs voiced dissatisfaction over their exclusion from the profits of economic expansion. In particular, Indian peasants and rancheros complained repeatedly that ascendant hacendados had despoiled them of agricultural land, now rendered increasingly valuable as a result of significant population growth. Meanwhile, periodic subsistence crises, especially the notorious *año de hambre* ("year of hunger") of 1785–86, laid bare the structural inequalities of the late colonial economy. Peasants usually lacked means to withstand such crises, while the wealthy often succeeded in turning such events to their own profit.[2]

These trends in the economy and society of late colonial New Spain had a significant impact in the sugar-growing region of Morelos. Most noticeable was the sugar industry's remarkable recovery from its depressed condition of the early eighteenth century. Population growth raised demand for sugar, so that prices began to rise somewhat after 1750. Toward the end of the eighteenth century the expansion of trade within the Spanish empire permitted the export of some Mexican sugar, further helping to maintain prices at levels more profitable to producers. Especially in the 1790s, the destruction of plantations in Saint-Domingue gave Mexican sugar a chance to enter world markets in modest proporations.[3]

A number of factors enabled planters in Morelos to take advantage of this improved market situation. Beginning about 1760, an influx of new capital, derived primarily from commerce, permitted the rehabilitation of old mills, the conversion of animal-powered trapiches to larger water-driven ingenios, and the establishment of a few new haciendas. Government policies offered further stimulus to the expansion of sugar production in the form of important tax exemptions for the industry. Moreover, in 1796 the government legalized the manufacture of *aguardiente*, a distilled beverage that was an important by-product of sugar manufacture.[4] Meanwhile, haciendas' available labor supplies grew rapidly, thanks both to general population increase and the willingness of Indians to migrate into the sugar region.

At the same time, sugar hacendados evidently achieved significant increases in productivity of land and labor, not as a result of any major technological breakthrough, but rather through a series of minor modifications in their production schedules and techniques. By the end of the eighteenth century, managers of the Cortés hacienda only milled cane cut from the first growth (*planta*) of the sugar plants, which yielded greater amounts of sugar than the second and third growths (ratoons). Moreover, harvesting at the Cortés estate became concentrated in the dry season, when cane also produced a greater sugar content. Because administrators frequently moved from one hacienda to another and were usually well acquainted with new developments on neighboring estates, there is ample reason to assume that these changes observed at the Cortés estate were adopted throughout the region.[5] As a result, the newly invigorated hacendados of Morelos achieved impressive increases in their output, especially during the final two decades of the eighteenth century. Tithe records indicate that annual production in the Archdiocese of Mexico (virtually all of which came from Morelos) expanded from an average of 4,857 tons during the period 1785–89 to 7,952 tons between 1800 and 1804.[6]

The revival of sugar production placed heavy demands on the region's land and water resources. Meanwhile, growing demand for maize and other foodstuffs for the rapidly increasing population of Mexico City insured the continuing importance of those commodities in the local structure of agricultural production, especially during and after the crisis of 1785–86. Peasants and labradores, as well as hacendados, produced those crops and argued indiscriminately with one another for the necessary land and water.

The hacienda Cocoyoc provides a good example of the recovery of the sugar haciendas during the latter part of the eighteenth century. Unlike many other estates in the region, Cocoyoc had attained an impressive but very brief resurgence during the 1720s, when Pedro Carbajal Machado invested a substantial portion of his personal fortune in its rehabilitation. Following Carbajal's death in 1730, the estate rapidly deteriorated; sugar milling was suspended altogether from 1737 to 1749.[7] During the latter part of the 1740s, Sebastián de San Martín, former tenant of Hacienda Hospital, rented Cocoyoc, but ultimately defaulted on his lease and disappeared.[8] Finally in 1750, Antonio Moro y Manrique, son-in-law of Pedro Carbajal Machado, took the first halting steps toward renovating the hacienda. He leased the property from his wife and her coheirs, paying a modest 450 pesos per year. Before his death in 1752, Moro y Manrique succeeded in resuming sugar manufacture, though only on a very modest scale. These efforts evidently depleted his assets; he died owing tithes and the short-term capital that he had borrowed, leaving his widow pleading dire financial straits.

For the next several years litigation surrounding the disposition of

Moro y Manrique's assets, as well as continued legal battles over the Carbajal Machado estate, interfered with the hacienda's recovery. Between August 1752 and November 1753 receipts from sugar sales and the leasing of ranchos totaled only 3,722 pesos, while operating expenses, excluding the 650 pesos owed annually to holders of mortgages on the hacienda, amounted to 3,508 pesos. Members of the audiencia blamed Agustín de Aresti, appointed depositario of Cocoyoc, for the estate's failure to generate any profits. In November, 1753 they therefore barred him from entering a bid to rent the hacienda, but evidently no one else was willing to invest in this still questionable venture. Five months later the *oidores* (judges) therefore reversed their ruling and permitted Aresti to rent the hacienda for a five-year term, at a price at least 350 pesos higher than the sum paid three years earlier by Moro y Manrique. The hacienda's value had begun to rise.[9]

During the next ten years, Aresti's fortunes improved considerably, enabling him to enter a successful bid for the hacienda's purchase in 1764. Aresti paid 10,000 pesos in cash and assumed liability for interest payments on censos whose principals amounted to 13,000 pesos. Over the next two decades Cocoyoc's worth jumped substantially. By 1786, when Antonio Velasco de la Torre bought the hacienda from Aresti's widow, the value of its land and water alone had risen 33,500 pesos; Velasco paid 78,000 pesos for the property. Thereafter, Velasco continued to invest heavily in the estate. In 1800 he announced plans to build a new aqueduct, at a projected cost of 20,000 pesos.[10] Today that conduit, inscribed with the date of its erection, stands astride the road leading from the hacienda, now a luxurious resort, to Cuautla.

The regeneration of the neighboring hacienda Pantitlán closely paralleled that of Cocoyoc. Although the property had served only for grain production and pasture since 1700, sugar production resumed after midcentury. Following the termination of Felipe de Alzate's lease (see above, Chapter 4), Agustín de Aresti managed the estate briefly until Antonio Moro y Manrique took over the property in 1746. However, Moro y Manrique was no more successful with Pantitlán than he was with Cocoyoc. Following his death, the hacienda passed to Pedro de Valiente, a former teniente of Yautepec and son of a former alcalde mayor of Cuernavaca. The new owner promptly rebuilt the hacienda's mill and began sugar production. Through the remainder of the colonial period, Pantitlán remained an important sugar producer, although not without some financial headaches for subsequent owners. By 1810, Antonio Velasco de la Torre had also added this estate to his agricultural empire.[11]

The hacienda Miacatlán also demonstrates the manner in which landowners increased the worth of their properties during the late eighteenth century. José de Palacio, a priest of the Archdiocese of Mexico, doctor in sacred theology, and son of Alferez José de Palacio, inherited Miacatlán from his father. Before the younger Palacio died in 1776, he built a new trapiche, costing 6,000 pesos, and a new irrigation dam, worth 24,500 pesos. By 1776 the total value of Miacatlán was estimated at between 70,000 and 80,000 pesos, in contrast to its worth in 1738, when the elder Palacio had paid only 55,000 pesos for Miacatlán and San Gaspar together.[12]

Atlihuayan also increased substantially in value during the second half of the eighteenth century. Like Cocoyoc, this hacienda had reached what inventories of the 1740s called total deterioration. As of 1741, all of its slaves had been embargoed due to unpaid debts, and the hacienda's administrators lacked funds to pay free workers. Atlihuayan changed owners several times during the next two decades without any improvement in its financial status. After 1768, however, the hacienda's value rose considerably. In 1781 Rodrigo del Valle sold the property to José Vicente de Urueta, who paid 72,000 pesos—an increase in value of approximately 132 percent in less than thirteen years.[13]

Part of this increase was probably due to del Valle's augmentation of the hacienda's slave force. From 1740 to 1764, the number of slave children born at Atlihuayan had remained almost constant, fluctuating between thirteen and fifteen in each of the five quinquennia (see Table 5.1). For the period 1765 to 1769, however, the total number of slave baptisms abruptly jumped to thirty. It is quite unlikely that this increment sprang from any sudden increase in slave fertility at Atlihuayan. A more plausible explanation is that del Valle acquired, through purchase or subterfuge, slaves belonging to the Society of Jesus, expelled from New Spain by a surprise government decree promulgated in June 1767. Del Valle incurred a fine of 2,000 pesos for having concealed titles to a Jesuit-owned rancho in Zitacuaro.[14] It is possible that departing Jesuits also transferred some of their slaves, perhaps from the sugar haciendas Barreto and Xochimancas, to del Valle. It is worth noting that the number of slaves marrying in Yautepec, most of whom probably belonged to Atlihuayan, also rose during the 1760s.[15] The hacienda's free resident population also grew during del Valle's period of ownership. Although Atlihuayan's total of free births had averaged over fifty per quinquennium during the 1740s, that total dipped below forty during the 1750s and to twenty-four for the period 1760–64. Free births amounted to forty-six between 1765 and 1769, sixty-eight for 1770–74, and sixty-one for 1775–79.

Population figures for Yautepec's mulatto "barrio," El Rancho Nuevo, reflect the effects of Atlihuayan's changing fortunes. The sector of Yautepec called El Rancho Nuevo on present-day maps lies near the site of Atlihuayan. Entries in the baptismal registers for the 1730s referred to the barrio as being adjacent to Atlihuayan, or near the road leading from Yautepec to the hacienda.[16] The settlement first appeared in baptismal listings in the 1720s, and evidently grew dramatically during the decade following the matlazáhuatl epidemic of 1737. (See above, Chapter 3.) As the figures in Table 5.2 suggest, the settlement's population expanded until the end of the 1760s, then contracted abruptly

Table 5.1
Baptisms of Residents of Atlihuayan and San Carlos Borromeo,
1720–1785

Period	Atlihuayan		San Carlos	
	Free	Slaves	Free	Slaves
1720–24	31	8	3	0
1725–29	30	12	13	0
1730–34	53	20	27	3
1735–39	36	10	41	3
1740–44	50	14	97	2
1745–49	54	15	52	1
1750–54	37	13	39	0
1755–59	34	15	22	2
1760–64	24	14	42	0
1765–69	46	30	76	0
1770–74	68	19	96	0
1775–79	61	12	75	0
1780–84	31	4	68	3

Source: Yautepec Parish Registers, GSU, microfilm, rolls 655–834, 655–835, 655–836, 655–837.

Table 5.2
Baptisms, Residents of El Rancho Nuevo,
1725–1784

Period	Number of Baptisms
1725–29	2
1730–34	4
1735–39	7
1740–44	21
1745–49	22
1750–54	16
1755–59	33
1760–64	28
1765–69	37
1770–74	20
1775–79	5
1780–84	4

Source: Yautepec Parish Registers, GSU, microfilm, rolls 655–835, 655–836, 655–837.

after 1770, and especially after 1775—precisely the period during which Atlihuayan increased in value under Rodrigo del Valle's ownership.

Baptismal figures for the hacienda San Carlos Borromeo, also given in Table 5.1, reflect its dramatic recovery in the period after 1750. Evidently this hacienda never had a large slave force, even in the seventeenth century. The low numbers of births between 1720 and 1734 correspond to a period of extreme deterioration of the estate, which was often referred to as a "rancho" rather than a hacienda. (Baptisms of children listed as residents of the "Rancho de San Carlos" are included in the figures.) Baptisms at San Carlos rose after 1730, and most dramatically during the first half of the 1740s, probably because this hacienda received a heavy influx of the migrants who entered the Yautepec region following the matlazáhuatl epidemic of 1737. However, the real recovery of San Carlos as a sugar hacienda began only after 1760, a development faithfully mirrored in the rising numbers of baptisms. Like other haciendas, San Carlos Borromeo changed hands several times before finally prospering during the final three decades of the eighteenth century.

The late colonial period also witnessed the foundation of several new sugar mills, the most famous of which was Buenavista, established near Cuautla in the early 1760s. This mill's history demonstrates changing patterns of land use during the second half of the eighteenth century. Manuel Moro, founder of Buenavista, produced some of his sugarcane on a rancho known as Xicamán, leased from the brothers of San Hipólito, who formerly had rented these lands to small producers of maize and vegetables. By the mid-1780s Buenavista had passed to the García Villalobos family, who also purchased the hacienda Santa Inés in 1784. At Santa Inés they converted additional lands, once rented to small producers, to the production of cane to be processed at Buenavista.[17] By the first decade of the nineteenth century, the Buenavista-Santa Inés complex had become the property of a powerful Mexico City merchant, Martín Angel Michaus. Other individuals also tried to form new trapiches in the late colonial period, but evidently enjoyed less success than the developers of Buenavista.[18]

Other features in addition to the revival of the sugar industry also characterized the agricultural history of late colonial Morelos. Many landowners continued the practice of grain production, both on their own desmesnes and on parcels of varying size leased to smaller producers. Such thriving hacendados as Antonio Velasco de la Torre, owner of Cocoyoc after 1786, Nicolás de Icazbalceta of Santa Clara and Tenango; and José Martín de Chávez of Tenextepango rented lands to small producers of maize, garbanzos, frijoles, and other crops.[19] Other hacendados, especially those lacking sufficient capital or water to compete successfully with the great sugar magnates, introduced indigo cultivation. For example, in 1763 Francisco de Urueta acquired Apanquesalco and Apisaco, located downstream from resurgent haciendas such as Cocoyoc and Pantitlán. While continuing to sublet a portion of his lands to maize-producing terrazgueros, Urueta also rebuilt the sugar mill at Apanquesalco and expanded indigo output.[20] The tenant of Oacalco produced the same set of crops in 1791; a mill for the processing of indigo was listed in an inventory taken at the hacienda in 1796.[21] Andrés Payes de San Julián, who rented the badly deteriorated hacienda Temilpa from 1765 to 1775, made no attempt to resume sugar production there, preferring to concentrate his energies on the cultivation of maize and indigo.[22] In addition, owners or tenants of Pantitlán, Miacatlán, Guadalupe, Xochimancas, Barreto, and Guausopán, as well as numerous rancheros, all produced indigo during the late eighteenth century.[23]

Hacienda production of maize and indigo reflected both the growing demands for these commodities and the ecological and economic limits to the expansion of sugar production. Neither indigo nor maize required as substantial an investment in equipment, or as abundant a water supply as sugar. Moreover, labor required for indigo and maize was not as extensive or as highly skilled as that needed for sugar manufacture.[24] For hacendados located downstream from major sugar producers, these alternative crops offered other means of profit. Thus, we can easily explain the emphasis placed on indigo production by owners or tenants of Temilpa, Xochimancas, and Barreto, all located in the lower Yautepec Valley. These haciendas' access to water diminished in direct proportion to the revival of sugar production upstream, especially after Antonio Velasco de la Torre acquired Cocoyoc.

Crop diversification, especially maize cultivation, assumed heightened importance in Morelos during the subsistence crisis of 1785–86. Reduced rainfall, followed by a premature frost on the night of 27 August 1785, destroyed a substantial portion of that year's maize crop throughout a wide area of central Mexico. An estimated 300,000 persons—perhaps 5 percent of the total population—died as a result of food shortages or related epidemics.[25] Specific effects of the crisis varied from place to place. For example, approximately three-fourths of the crop in Toluca and Apam was destroyed, while farmers in Chalco lost only a fourth of their maize. Parts of Morelos referred to in contemporary accounts as "tierra caliente" evidently escaped the killer frost entirely, although scarcity of rainfall somewhat reduced the maize harvest. Reports addressed to Viceroy Bernardo de Gálvez shortly after the frost referred specifically to the jurisdiction of *"Cuautla de las Amilpas, en donde por ser tierra caliente, no llegaron las heladas, y aunque padecieron las milpas la falta de aguas en el mes de agosto se espera razonable cosecha."* ("Cuautla de las Amilpas, where, because it is tierra caliente, the frosts did not come, and although the maize fields suffered from the scarcity of rainfall in August, a reasonable harvest is expected.")[26]

Demographic data from Yautepec confirm the absence of a crisis of the magnitude of that afflicting other regions of New Spain. As the figures in Appendix 2 demonstrate, burials in Yautepec were actually lower in 1786 than they had been the previous year. In Cholula and

León, by contrast, burials in 1786 exceeded those of 1785 by 40 and 300 percent, respectively.[27] Baptisms in Yautepec also failed to show a major disruption, declining only slightly from levels observed before the agricultural crisis. Still another indicator of Yautepec's relative good fortune is the continued tendency toward endogamy among its Indian population during the years after 1785. (See below, Chapter 7.) In León, however, the already permeable racial barriers tumbled after 1786.[28] Finally, the proportion of children listed as "hijos de padres no conocidos" among those baptized at Yautepec did not show a sharp rise until about four years after the crop failure. This belated increase in that important indicator of social disorder was in itself a by-product of the area's relative good fortune during 1785–1786, which reinforced its long-established tendency to attract immigrants in times of general ecological crisis. (See Appendix 3.)

Other communities in the region show somewhat greater effects of the año de hambre. Tables 5.3 and 5.4 give baptism and burial statistics for Tetelcingo, a predominantly Indian village near Cuautla, and Oaxtepec, where gente de razón comprised over half the population. In Tetelcingo, mortality in 1786 increased sharply over the 1785 figure but still fell far short of the 302 burials recorded in the smallpox epidemic of January and February 1780. Births dipped in 1786 but recovered substantially in succeeding years. For the quinquennium 1786–90, the total number of baptisms in Tetelcingo was 10.3 percent lower than in the previous five-year period. In León, by contrast, the figure fell by 31.5 percent.[29] In Oaxtepec, burials also rose in 1786, but baptisms returned to pre-1786 levels almost as quickly as in Tetelcingo. In both parishes, of course, rates of mortality and fertility may have been skewed by the influx of migrants into the region during and after the año de hambre.

Whatever the precise demographic effects of the agricultural crisis, the civic leaders who met in the fall of 1785 to discuss means of alleviating the current emergency focused their attention on the favored tierras calientes of Morelos and Michoacán. José Antonio Alzate y Ramírez, foremost scientist of the realm, proposed that landowners in these warmer areas be urged immediately to plant winter (irrigated) maize, to be harvested in the spring of 1786. Alzate drew on his own close knowledge of the tierra caliente, citing his father's expansion of maize production at Pantitlán in the early 1740s. The committee endorsed

Table 5.3
Baptisms and Burials, Tetelcingo, 1779–1790

Year	Baptisms	Burials
1779	107	52
1780	98	302
1781	102	49
1782	98	54
1783	89	58
1784	88	119
1785	89	55
1786	77	85
1787	90	78
1788	81	52
1789	85	47
1790	85	86

Sources: GSU, microfilm, rolls 706–027, 706–030.

Alzate's plan and also recommended that hacendados in the tierras calientes be encouraged to increase their own and their tenants' output of *maíz de temporal* (nonirrigated maize) during the summer of 1786.[30] In particular, they singled out two of Morelos's most substantial hacendados, José Salvide Goytia and Juan Antonio de Yermo.[31]

Prompted by substantial bounties, the hacendados of Morelos responded eagerly to the committee's requests, and winter maize from this tierra caliente appeared in Mexico City during the difficult summer of 1786.[32] Landowners reportedly garnered handsome profits, selling grain at prices that may have reached six pesos per fanega at some points.[33] Moreover, they received heartfelt acclaim from the highest political officials, as well as a new rationale to use in advancing their own interests. For example, in April 1786, José Vicente de Urueta of Atlihuayan rebuffed a request of downstream landowners for a general inspection and adjustment of aqueducts by all who drew water from the Yautepec River. Urueta persuaded Viceroy Gálvez that the overhaul must await the harvest of his and others' crops of irrigated maize.[34] In 1790, José Nicolás Abad similarly touted his patriotic response to the famine when explaining why the Brothers of San Hipólito should compensate him for improvements made on lands he leased

Table 5.4
Baptisms and Burials, Oaxtepec, 1781–1791

Year	Baptisms	Burials
1781	—	79
1782	—	60
1783	—	78
1784	71	114
1785	69	75
1786	57	119
1787	57	103
1788	56	—
1789	79	—
1790	78	—
1791	91	—

Sources: GSU, microfilm, rolls 606–326; 606–346.

from them. As a conscientious citizen, Abad said that he had spent a considerable sum in clearing portions of the land for cultivation by pegujaleros during the año de hambre.[35]

The more fortunate among the peasants and other small producers also stood some chance of reaping modest windfalls by selling small quantities of surplus grain at famine-inflated prices. For example, the Indians of Oaxtepec obtained a temporary increase in their allotment of water from the Yautepec River in order to produce irrigated maize during the winter of 1785–1786.[36] The Indians of Atlcahualoya, a sujeto of Jonacatepec, received 3,000 pesos from their *cura* (priest) to facilitate the planting of their crops for 1786. Other evidence shows that even in relatively poor communities Indians had maize stockpiled during the early months of 1786. Residents of the upland village of Santa Catarina Zacatepec complained in February that Nicolás Pérez of Tepoztlán was attempting to seize the maize they had stored in their homes because they owed him over 160 pesos for use of his lands. In late March the teniente of Tetecala, a lowland village, seized sixteen *cargas*, or thirty-two fanegas, of maize from three Indians, alleging that they owed him money for bulls he had sold them. Also early in the año de hambre, the Indians of the pueblo of San Felipe, a sujeto of Cuernavaca, complained that the local tithe collector was pressing them to pay what they owed in maize—as much as eighty cargas—instead of in cash, as was their custom.[37] These incidents show that local power holders quickly attempted to seize the Indians' valuable grain, but they also indicate that the villagers had weathered a major agricultural crisis with some staples to spare.

The expansion of sugar and indigo production and the region's role as a supplier of foodstuffs for Mexico City led to an acceleration of social conflict in late colonial Morelos. Hacendados encroached on lands claimed by villagers and rediverted water to the canefields and ingenios. At the same time the villagers needed increased amounts of land and water to feed their growing populations. Therefore, in Morelos as in much of central Mexico, land and water disputes multiplied during the latter half of the eighteenth century. Although each such conflict had its own particular history, some common features characterized many of these late colonial disputes. Leaders of the villages initiated their protests by citing colonial legislation guaranteeing Indian communities the land and other resources necessary for subsistence and the payment of tribute and other financial obligations. Hacienda owners could hardly deny the existence of such legislation, but they could belittle a village's pretensions to the privileges stipulated in the laws. Whenever possible, hacendados alleged that a protesting community was not a cabecera but simply a barrio that had defied the settlement orders set forth in the congregaciones of 1603, or that a village's seeming shortage of land was due to Indian leaders' selfish and short-sighted willingness to rent substantial portions of community holdings to gente de razón.

Often such charges had considerable validity. For a century a number of barrios had been attempting to resettle at their original sites and regain their status as pueblos, and non-Indians outnumbered Indian residents in many of the region's major cabeceras by the end of the colonial period. Also, with some justification, hacendados charged that the instigators of land and water disputes were strangers to the region and racial mongrels who had fled tribute payments and other obligations in their home communities. Although the haciendas clearly held formidable advantages in these struggles, the villagers were not completely powerless. In particular, they could easily vex an offending planter by tampering with his irrigation works. Dramatically phrased threats of violence often punctuated these conflicts, and actual blood-shed or property damage were not unknown.

A few examples will convey the flavor of these late colonial land and water disputes. The relations between Oaxtepec and Pantitlán clearly show the contest between peasant agriculture and sugar production. When Pedro Valiente rebuilt the ingenio and began milling in the early 1750s, he appropriated much of the water coming from a spring near the parish church of Oaxtepec. For more than forty years the villagers had enjoyed exclusive use of this water for the irrigation of their fruit, vegetable, and sugarcane crops. Although the villagers viewed Valiente's projects with apprehension, they struck a compromise, whereby in return for his promise to leave them enough water for their fields, the Indians rented him a portion of their lands. Evidently Valiente and his successors used this land, called Patláhuac, to expand his cultivation of sugar; hacienda records for 1766 mention cane growing in the *campo nuevo de Patláhuac*. By 1776, however, the compromise proved unworkable; the hacienda's owner charged that the villagers had seized more than their fair share of water, halting his ingenio at the height of the milling season.

Over the next two decades, protracted litigation and several attempted out-of-court settlements failed to produce lasting accord between the village and the hacienda. In 1797, a militant faction of villagers tried to secure exclusive use of the water for the town. The alcalde mayor of Cuernavaca rejected the villagers' petition but was able to enforce his decision only after local hacendados, in a rare gesture of unanimity, mustered a force of sixty armed men to subdue the angry villagers. Meanwhile, hacendados circulated the unfounded but alarming rumor that the Indians of Oaxtepec were planning a general uprising with other pueblos in the region. Perhaps fear of such a tumult lay behind the willingness of Pantitlán's owners to reach yet another compromise, which constituted at least a temporary victory for the villagers. The owners agreed to construct a new aqueduct to draw water from the Yautepec River rather than from the disputed spring; the villagers' only apparent concession was to allow a portion of the conduit to cross their land. This agreement did not end the controversy over the spring, however. Litigation on its disposition was still in progress during the first decade of the nineteenth century.[38]

While carrying on their contest with Pantitlán, the villagers of Oaxtepec also argued with the owners of Cocoyoc over water rights. The conflict evidently intensified after Antonio Velasco de la Torre acquired the hacienda in 1786. Prior to that time, Agustín de Aresti's widow had allowed the Indians to use a portion of the water drawn by Cocoyoc's conduits from the Yautepec River. Velasco resolved to end this concession, which he said deprived the hacienda of the share of river water guaranteed to it by governmental decree more than a century earlier.[39] According to Velasco, Cocoyoc's aqueducts were large enough only to carry the water rightfully allocated to the hacienda. Moreover, the villagers had damaged his aqueducts, making additional apertures in them to divert still more water to crops cultivated by the Indians and to the thousands of banana plants grown by the town surgeon, the parish priest, and other gente de razón who rented community lands. As a result, Velasco reported in March 1788 that he lacked sufficient water to continue milling operations. Indeed, he suspected that the villagers persistently and maliciously took increased amounts of water whenever they learned he was about to begin processing cane.

The intensity of this dispute can be attributed not only to the ambitious Velasco de la Torre's purchase of Cocoyoc, but also to the high maize prices prevailing after the crop failure of 1785 and the anticipation of future famines. Irrigated maize, produced during the winter dry season, had long been an important staple cultivated by the Indians of Oaxtepec. In January 1786 the Indians had received an emergency provisional allocation of water in order to irrigate their current crop of winter maize. In return, the Marqués del Valle required that they make a formal application for the continued use of the water, for which they were to pay the Marquesado an annual pension of 250 pesos. The Indians harvested their 1786 crop without making that application or paying the stipend. In 1788, Velasco de la Torre secured from the Audiencia of Mexico a decree overruling the Marquesado's allocation of additional water to the villagers of Oaxtepec.[40] This ruling served merely to deflect the Indians' anger toward the owner of Pantitlán, with whom they renewed their water dispute in the 1790s.

Features evident in Oaxtepec's conflicts with neighboring haciendas also appear in other late colonial disputes. In 1793 the owner of Miacatlán charged that Indians and gente de razón residing in the village of the same name had made more than twenty apertures in his main aqueduct, causing his mill to stop. The villagers retorted that the haci-

enda had appropriated the water they needed for their fruits and vegetables.[41] In November 1807, a similar conflict between the village of
Atlacholoaya and ascendant hacendado Vicente Eguía, owner of San
Vicente, sparked a confrontation that resulted in injury to one of Eguía's
employees. Three years later, Eguía and Atlacholoaya reached a compromise somewhat reminiscent of the Oaxtepec-Pantitlán accords. Eguía
agreed to sacrifice a small portion of canefield in order to build an aqueduct to serve the villagers' needs, with the understanding that they
were to pay him an annual pension of fifteen pesos for this concession.[42]

Already surrounded by such long-established haciendas as Cuahuixtla, Casasano, Calderón, and Hospital, the villagers of Cuautla suffered added vexation after the establishment of Buenavista, adjacent
to the very center of town. Even while at worship villagers could not
escape reminders of the hacienda's presence; from inside the parish
church they could clearly hear the voices of hacienda administrators
admonishing their workers. In 1800, the hacienda's owner, Martín
Angel Michaus, made plans for the construction of a new aqueduct.
Although one faction of villagers endorsed the hacendado's proposal,
perhaps because he promised to build public fountains and laundry
facilities for the villagers' convenience, others protested, arguing that
the conduit could easily overflow, at great peril to lives and property.
Despite these objections, Michaus won viceregal permission to build
his aqueduct. Those who had fought the project proved correct in their
grim forecasts. In 1801, shortly after its completion, the aqueduct
overflowed, inundating one of the town's barrios and causing considerable property damage. Shortly thereafter, a portion of the conduit
collapsed, killing a pregnant woman and injuring several other persons.[43]

The hacienda's intrusions into the daily lives of villagers are also evident in the experiences of Marcos Mariano, an Indian who cultivated
bananas and other fruits on lands he had rented for many years from
the town's *cofradía* (sodality) of Nuestra Señora del Rosario. Unfortu-
nately for Marcos Mariano, his orchard lay immediately adjacent to
canefields of Buenavista. In 1804 he complained that the hacienda's
administrator had extracted earth from his orchard in order to make
adobe for the hacienda's buildings. In the process, the administrator
had destroyed several of Marcos Mariano's banana plants.[44]

Meanwhile, the villagers of Cuautla were battling with the haciendas Cuahuixtla, Hospital, and Santa Inés, as well as with Buenavista,

for land that the haciendas had claimed inside the six hundred varas of land alloted to the town. The hacendados, particularly the Dominicans of Cuahuixtla, repeatedly chided the villagers for their pretensions to the prerogatives accorded to "Indian" communities and declared that the villagers' alleged land shortage was due to the fact that they had rented out most of their community lands to gente de razón. In fact, claimed Cuahuixtla's owners, the Indians enjoyed abundant lands.[45]

The most violent of the late colonial disputes involved a land conflict between Cuahuixtla and a barrio of Yecapixtla that had reestablished itself at its original, precongregación location, on land claimed by the hacienda. Evidently the Indians of Zahuatlán never fully relinquished their ancestral lands. Although they accepted incorporation into Yecapixtla as the barrio of Zahuatlán el Nuevo in 1603, they had requested and received permission to maintain their livestock at the old location.[46] During the second half of the seventeenth century they began cultivating maize and other crops at Zahuatlán el Viejo. Finally in the 1730s an Indian named Don Gregorio took his large family there to live permanently. Although the Dominicans repeatedly attempted to eject them, Don Gregorio and his numerous descendants and associates remained at the spot for more than half a century, numbering 48.5 tributaries in 1788. The Dominicans won several favorable rulings from the audiencia, but the Indians stubbornly ignored all court subpoenas. Finally, in 1793, the Dominicans persuaded local authorities to have the settlement burned to the ground.[47]

Although the Zahuatlán-Cuahuixtla dispute thus ended in a clearcut victory for the hacienda, not all sugar producers in the late colonial period were able to secure their objectives so decisively. Fear that angry villagers might damage their expensive equipment or tamper with their aqueducts at crucial points in the milling season gave landowners a powerful incentive to moderate their demands on neighboring communities. Moreover, by the end of the eighteenth century many hacendados encountered both economic and ecological obstacles that prevented them from expanding their output of sugar and other cash crops as much as they might have wished. Although the late colonial growth of mining and commerce produced surplus capital available for investment in commercial agriculture, sugar was still an expensive undertaking compared to other types of agricultural ventures. Several of those who developed sugar estates during the years after 1760 were prominent Mexico City merchants who had invested in sugar as a means of further diversifying their extensive holdings, but other hacienda owners had risen to their position from the ranks of local labradores. Such individuals often lacked the financial resources to sustain the profitability of their estates.

The careers of Rodrigo del Valle and José Vicente de Urueta, successive owners of Atlihuayan in the 1770s and 1780s, evidently followed such a pattern. Del Valle had been a small-scale merchant and labrador in Yautepec since at least 1746; in the 1750s he began renting the hacienda that he would later own. In the same decade, he became a compadre of Francisco de Urueta, father of José Vicente and an ambitious labrador who later succeeded in purchasing and developing the run-down haciendas Apanquesalco and Apisaco.[48] In 1788, the younger Urueta was the subject of a concurso de acreedores, an experience far less common for late colonial hacendados than for their predecessors in the late seventeenth and early eighteenth centuries.[49] By the 1790s, according to the census published by Manuel Mazari, sugar was no longer manufactured at Atlihuayan.[50] Some of the hacienda's difficulties may have been due to increased diversion of water from the Yautepec River by hacendados further upstream.

Even some of the wealthiest and most powerful of Morelos's hacendados were stymied in realizing all of their ambitions by the fact that they occupied relatively inferior positions within the larger elite of New Spain. Few claimed kinship with the burgeoning titled nobility of the late colonial era. Many failed to achieve the extensive diversification of enterprises that characterized the investment patterns of the colony's most powerful entrepreneurs. In particular, with a few notable exceptions, most hacendados of Morelos did not control the wholesale distribution of their product. Such vertical integration of enterprise was, according to John Kicza's recent work, a feature that distinguished the truly powerful families of late colonial Mexico from all others.[51]

Even Gabriel de Yermo, who built an imposing agricultural empire in western Morelos and in adjoining areas now in the state of Mexico, found himself snubbed by top members of the late colonial elite. John Tutino has pointed out that Yermo's relations with the powerful and titled Santiago family illustrate his relatively marginal position within the colony's elite. Only after considerable pressure from Yermo did the Santiagos allow him to drive herds of cattle across their estates en route to Mexico City markets. Moreover, the Santiagos exacted from Yermo a heavy fee for this concession, even though they routinely granted similar favors, with no charge, to elite members whom they considered their peers. Difficulties of the sort experienced by Yermo, according to Tutino, characterized the careers of persons "still climbing toward elite status."[52]

If even the richest of Morelos's hacendados failed to achieve all of their objectives, more frustrating still was the plight of small-scale agriculturalists. Throughout the region and particularly in the fertile Yautepec Valley, the aspirations of labradores further compounded the complexity of social conflict in the late colonial period. Like hacendados and Indian villagers, these individuals hoped to capitalize on the growing market for agricultural produce. Labradores rarely owned their land; they remained dependent on the hacendados or Indian communities from whom they rented their ranchos. Many experienced a perceptible deterioration in their situation as competition for land and water intensified in the late colonial period. Rents rose and some lost their lands.

For example, a humble ranchero who hoped to reap exceptional profits in 1786 found that his landlord, owner of the hacienda Nuestra Señora de Guadalupe, terminated his lease and made the property available to a higher bidder.[53] In 1810, another year of agricultural crisis, labrador Anastasio Figueroa complained that the Indians of Cuernavaca had not only raised his rent beyond what he could afford but had also refused to compensate him for improvements he had made during the many years he had occupied a small piece of property on the town's outskirts. The Indians had ejected him in order to make the land available to the holder of the *abasto*, or meat supply monopoly, of Cuernavaca.[54] Indian leaders of Yautepec also raised rents on land leased to gente de razón during the second decade of the nineteenth century.[55]

The revival of the sugar industry also brought difficulties for Joaquín de Albear, a mulatto or castizo ranchero in western Morelos. In 1782, Albear lost, at least temporarily, the lands he rented from the Indians of Coatlán del Rio. Site of an abandoned trapiche named Cocoyotla, the lands became the object of controversy between two rival sugar growers who both wished to force out Albear. Although Marquesado officials ruled in Albear's favor, it is uncertain whether he succeeded in retaining indefinite access to the land.[56] Many other rancheros were

simply overtaken by the burgeoning hacendados of the late colonial
period. The census of the 1790s, published by Manuel Mazari, refers
to the numerous ranchos absorbed by Gabriel de Yermo's emerging
agricultural empire.[57]

The difficulties of Gregorio Trinidad Fierro, set forth in a lawsuit
of 1815, provide another interesting example of changing patterns of
land use and their detrimental effect on small agriculturalists. Fierro
claimed rights to the site of the long-defunct trapiche San Nicolás
Tolentino, near Cuernavaca. The trapiche was one of many founded
in western Morelos during the late seventeenth century. In 1692, Tomás
González de Rebolledo had secured a license to build a sugar mill, for
which he and his successors incurred the obligation to pay an annual
stipend of ten pesos to the Marquesado, in addition to the seventy pesos
they paid each year for the use of the land. Following González de
Rebolledo's death, his daughters inherited the hacienda. By the mid-
eighteenth century, sugar production had ceased at San Nicolás Tolentino, as at so many other haciendas in the region. The property had
even changed names; in 1754 it was known simply as the Rancho de
Solís, probably named after one of the tenants to whom González de
Rebolledo's last surviving daughter rented it. At some unspecified date,
she simply turned the property over to Salvador del Fierro, grandfather of Gregorio, who assumed responsibility for the annual payments
to the Marquesado. Fierro continued the practice, begun by earlier
tenants, of subletting it in small parcels to various parties, including
Indians from the pueblo of Atlacholoaya. Later witnesses, both for
Gregorio Fierro and against him, agreed that in the mid-eighteenth
century the land had been of little value.

Salvador Fierro, who evidently spent much of his working life as a
mayordomo, or overseer, on such haciendas as Sayula and San Gaspar,
earned scant reward for his hard work. He died insolvent, unable to
continue the censo payments to the Marquesado. His son José therefore ceded the rancho to Juan Barrón, who lent him money to cover
his many debts. Barrón passed it, in turn, to Manuel del Villar, who
by 1782 became the owner of the sugar hacienda Chiconcoac. In time
Antonio Baldovinos Neri, owner of the nearby hacienda Treinta Pesos,
asserted that he was a direct descendant of Tomás González de Rebolledo and therefore had a better claim than Villar. Although Villar
eventually surrendered the property to Baldovinos, the matter was still

the subject of litigation between their heirs in the second decade of the nineteenth century. Meanwhile, the claim of Gregorio Fierro, grandson of the humble ranchero Salvador, foundered amid the rivalry between the two hacendados, each anxious to add the property to his sugar estate. Mariano Baldovinos Blanco, son of Antonio, argued that Fierro's claim had been prompted by Vicente de Eguía, who had married Villar's widow. Eguía had shown little sympathy for the pretensions of humbler agriculturalists. Although the outcome of this dispute remains unclear, claimants such as Gregorio Fierro seldom had great chances of winning their cases in the intensely fought land and water struggles of the late colonial era.[58]

Other frustrations also plagued even those labradores who retained access to lands. While some were able to finance the planting and cultivation of their own crops, and a fortunate few lent money for such purposes to other labradores, many others were unable to capitalize fully on the rising food prices of the late colonial period. Many labradores depended on hacendados and prosperous merchants for credit to finance their production costs, and therefore profited considerably less from changing economic conditions.[59] In Cuautla in the early 1770s, merchants and other moneylenders required farmers to sell to them, at harvest-season prices, a carga (two fanegas) of maize for each peso they had received in credit. Moneylenders thus received a more or less fixed amount of maize each year, while the farmer's surplus varied. In times of abundant harvests and low prices, he retained a greater supply of grain for sale than in years of scarcity and consequent high prices.[60]

Toward the end of the eighteenth century, local political officials began taking a more active role in grain speculation, at the expense of labradores and moneylenders. Manuel de Porras, teniente of Yautepec during the first decade of the nineteenth century, allegedly bought maize from farmers even though they had already contracted to sell their crops to others. Porras then shipped the grain out of Morelos to regions where it would fetch a higher price, thus creating an artificial shortage in his jurisdiction.[61]

Prolonged droughts and resultant poor harvests throughout New Spain in 1808 and 1809 gave agricultural entrepreneurs in Morelos new prospects for profit.[62] In the fall of 1809 the cura of Tetecala reported that wealthy people from Cuernavaca cultivated crops in the

area bounded by his parish. Immediately after the harvest, these cultivators husked the maize and sold it in Cuernavaca, leaving Tetecala
with insufficient grain for its sustenance. The alcalde mayor of Cuernavaca collaborated actively in the extraction of grain from subordinate communities throughout his jurisdiction. Even when Indians from
surrounding communities managed to sell their own grain in the markets of Cuernavaca and other towns, the alcalde mayor or one of his
tenientes charged them fees ranging from a half to a full real for this
privilege.[63]

By the opening decade of the nineteenth century, local officials and
the region's more substantial agriculturalists had had ample opportunity to devise means of turning agricultural crises to their own advantage. Nonetheless, peasants and other small cultivators still tried, with
occasional limited success, to profit from sale of their surplus produce.
Profitable cash crop production may explain the two thousand pesos
that the Indians of Tetecala admitted to having in their community
chest in 1809, funds which they intended to invest in a new roof for
their parish church.[64]

Regardless of the deteriorating prospects for peasants and small-scale

Table 5.5
Origins of Men Marrying in Yautepec, 1750–1789

Place	1750–59 #	% of total	1770–79 #	% of total	1780–89 #	% of total
Atlatlauca	3	1.0	1	0.2	2	0.4
Tlalnepantla	5	1.7	2	0.4	3	0.6
Tlayacapan	1	0.3	7	1.6	8	1.6
Totolapa	5	1.7	9	2.0	3	0.6
Chalco	7	2.3	45	10.0	17	3.4
Xochimilco	6	2.0	6	1.3	10	2.0
Coyoacán	2	0.7	1	0.2	2	0.4
Mexico City	3	1.0	5	1.1	3	0.6
Tacuba	2	0.7	0	—	0	—
Puebla-Tlaxcala	4	1.3	15	3.3	9	1.8
Elsewhere in Mexico	0	—	7	1.6	10	2.0
Total	38	12.5[a]	98	21.9[a]	67	13.2[a]

Source: Yautepec Parish Registers, GSU, microfilm, roll 655–851.
[a]Due to rounding, totals differ slightly from sums of columns.

labradores, the region's benign climate, fertile soil, and demand for labor continued to attract new settlers from less favored areas, especially from the highland communities to the immediate north. Marriage registers from Yautepec, summarized in Tables 5.5 and 5.6, suggest that this migration was particularly heavy during the 1760s and 1770s. Nearly 22 percent of the men and almost 16 percent of the women who married in Yautepec between 1770 and 1779 were identified as immigrants to the area. Data for the 1760s are omitted from the tables because marriage records for Indians are missing for that decade, but a significant number of the migrants who married in the 1770s must have settled in Yautepec before 1770. Of 105 men who specified how long they had lived at their current locations, 50 responded that they had done so since childhood.[65] These newcomers not only expanded the pool of labor available to the ascendant hacendados of the late colonial period. Their presence further taxed the communities' increasingly scarce resources, seriously disrupted village political life, and contributed to the intensification of social tensions in the towns and villages of the region.

During the course of the seventeenth and eighteenth centuries, the

Table 5.6
Origins of Women Marrying in Yautepec, 1750–1789

Place	1750–59 #	1750–59 % of total	1770–79 #	1770–79 % of total	1780–89 #	1780–89 % of total
Atlatlauca	0	—	0	—	3	0.6
Tlalnepantla	0	—	0	—	1	0.2
Tlayacapan	2	0.7	8	1.8	8	1.6
Totolapa	5	1.7	7	1.6	5	1.0
Chalco	4	1.3	23	5.1	15	3.0
Xochimilco	5	1.7	13	2.9	11	2.2
Coyoacán	3	1.0	4	0.9	1	0.2
Mexico City	2	0.7	3	0.7	3	0.6
Puebla-Tlaxcala	3	1.0	5	1.1	3	0.6
Elsewhere in Mexico	2	0.7	8	1.8	9	1.8
Total	26	8.6[a]	71	15.8[a]	59	11.6[a]

Source: Yautepec Parish Registers, GSU, microfilm, roll 655–851.
[a]Due to rounding, totals differ slightly from sums of columns.

fortunes of the sugar haciendas of Morelos fluctuated dramatically, producing corresponding changes in the region's structure of agricultural production, in the character of its social relations, and in prevailing patterns of settlement. Meanwhile, the haciendas themselves were experiencing important internal changes, in the composition of their labor forces as well as in the basic rhythms of life and labor. Chapter 6 surveys these developments in greater detail.

6
Life and Labor on
the Haciendas

Provision of adequate labor to perform the many tasks associated with the cultivation and milling of sugarcane was a perennial concern for the hacendados of colonial Morelos. As in most sugar colonies established by Europeans in the New World, planters in Morelos relied on slave labor for a significant portion of their labor needs. The example set by Fernando Cortés, Bernardino del Castillo, and Antonio Serrano de Cardona in the sixteenth century firmly established the connection between sugar production and African slavery. During the period of the industry's rapid expansion in the late sixteenth and early seventeenth centuries, several other factors induced aspiring hacendados to acquire African or Afro-Mexican slaves. Many Spaniards in the New World believed that Africans were stronger and able to work harder than Indians, and that slaves could be more easily disciplined and trained in the specialized techniques of sugar manufacture than could free Indians. Furthermore, the expansion of sugar production after 1580 coincided not only with the nadir of the Indian population in New Spain, but also with the union of the Spanish and Portuguese crowns, which, in turn, enabled Portuguese slave traders to increase their shipments of human cargoes to Spanish America.[1] Finally, governmental restrictions on the employment of Indians in sugar manufacture provided some added incentive for hacendados to acquire slaves. Therefore, a slave force quickly became a prerequisite for anyone aspiring to become a major producer of sugar in Morelos.

The hacendados never secured slaves in sufficient numbers to cover all of their labor needs, however. From the earliest days of the industry, Indians supplemented the slave forces, either as permanent workers who made their homes on the haciendas, or as unskilled laborers recruited on a temporary basis to meet seasonally heavy needs. The close association of Afro-Mexican slaves and Indian workers on the sugar haciendas not only accelerated the pace of racial mixture and acculturation; it also modified the institution of slavery in such a way that the condition of slaves in Morelos scarcely resembled that of their counterparts in other New World sugar colonies.

The trend toward Indian settlement on the haciendas is evident as early as the 1620s. A survey conducted in 1627 revealed the origins and extent of such migration to the haciendas near Yautepec. No fewer than 304 Indians from other jurisdictions lived on the estates or in the households of Spaniards in Yautepec. These migrants came from at least forty-one different locations, most of them within the boundaries of the present-day state of Morelos, including other villages in the lowlands as well as highland villages immediately to the north of Yautepec. Forty-two persons were from Tepoztlán and nineteen from Tlayacapan, while others came from Cuernavaca (twenty-one) and Pazulco (thirty-two). Many of these early migrations may have been temporary in nature; the owner of Atlihuayan stated in 1629 that none of the Indian migrants found on his hacienda two years earlier were still present.[2] Nevertheless, the haciendas became increasingly powerful magnets attracting Indians dissatisfied with the quality of their lives in their native villages.[3]

Transitory at first, Indian hacienda residence assumed greater permanence by the mid-seventeenth century. Peter Gerhard has estimated that by 1646 Indian hacienda residents, not counted on tribute rolls, numbered 3,090 in the state of Morelos.[4] Most Indian migrants to the haciendas were young adults, either couples with small children, or single people.[5] Therefore, it is not surprising that evidence of the Indians' presence on the haciendas begins to appear in Yautepec's baptismal registers by 1650. Although most haciendas had chapels, almost none had resident priests. The parish priest of Yautepec consequently administered and recorded all baptisms, marriages, and burials, even if he sometimes performed the ceremony at a hacienda chapel.

Table 6.1 shows hacienda residents baptized by the cura of Yautepec between 1650 and 1798. Baptismal records before 1650 do not give residences sufficiently often to permit their inclusion in the table, although they do indicate that a total of seventeen Indian hacienda residents, ten of them from Guajoyuca, were baptized between 1632 and 1649. Registers for non-Indians begin only in 1648. Data for the years after 1650 indicate that the migration of young Indian adults increased sharply in the 1650s and even more in the following decade. The number of Indian hacienda baptisms remained high at least until 1690. Gaps in the registers make it impossible to continue the analysis through the final decade of the seventeenth century, but by the quinquennium 1705–9 both the absolute number of Indian baptisms on the haciendas and their relative share of hacienda baptisms had dropped substantially, probably as a result of the epidemics and economic circumstances discussed in Chapters 3 and 4. Tables 6.2 and 6.3 show baptismal trends, respectively, at Atlihuayan and at Guausopán and Suchiquesalco, the two mills of the Brothers of San Hipólito.

Movement of Indians to the haciendas coincided with and accelerated major changes in the composition of the estates' slave forces. The most obvious of these changes was the decrease in the number of African-born slaves, due primarily to changes in the international slave trade and the severance of Portugal from Spanish rule after 1640.[6] Ward Barrett has noted that managers of the Cortés mill bought few new African slaves after 1650.[7] Similarly, the Jesuits of Xochimancas made few slave purchases after 1664.[8] Evidently many other hacendados followed suit. Slave inventories from several haciendas reveal the declining numbers of African-born *bozales* and the advancing ages of those who remained. Table 6.4 summarizes information on the slave force at Atlihuayan, for which the greatest number of successive inventories is available; while Table 6.5 gives data from other haciendas' inventories. At Atlihuayan, bozales comprised over one-fourth of the slave force in 1672; their numbers dwindled steadily for the next thirty years, leaving a lone African-born slave by 1701. Fourteen years later, no bozales were to be found among the hacienda's slaves. Other haciendas also showed a decline in the numbers of African born, although the timing of this process varied from one estate to another. At the

Table 6.1
Baptisms of All Hacienda Residents, Yautepec Parish, 1650–1798

Period	Unspecified		Indians		Negroes		Mulattoes		Mestizos		Other	
	#	%	#	%	#	%	#	%	#	%	#	%
1650–59	13	20.6	39	61.9	3	4.8	7	11.1	1	1.6	0	0
1660–69	32	18.4	72	41.4	15	8.6	45	25.9	8	4.6	2	1.1
1670–79	17	11.9	64	44.8	10	7.0	35	24.5	3	2.1	14	9.8
1680–89	32	16.6	67	34.7	9	4.7	72	37.3	5	2.6	8	4.1
1705–9	7	8.0	14	16.1	13	14.9	36	41.4	10	11.5	7	8.0
1710–19	5	2.8	31	17.4	12	6.7	93	52.2	16	9.0	21	11.8
1720–29	2	1.1	61	32.4	4	2.1	93	49.5	17	9.0	11	5.9
1730–39	13	5.3	82	33.5	2	0.8	115	46.9	17	6.9	16	6.5
1740–49	14	4.1	92	26.9	4	1.2	174	50.9	40	11.7	18	5.3
1750–59	5	2.0	68	27.9	2	0.8	138	56.6	21	8.6	10	4.1
1760–69	25	8.1	80	25.8	2	0.6	145	46.8	36	11.6	22	7.1
1770–79	25	5.2	175	36.6	0	0	195	40.8	64	13.4	19	4.0
1780–86	8	3.6	98	44.5	0	0	77	35.0	23	10.5	14	6.4
1787–96[a]	2	1.5	62	45.9	0	0	57	42.2	9	6.7	5	3.7
1797–98	5	3.8	46	35.4	0	0	65	50.0	6	4.6	8	6.2

Source: Yautepec Parish Registers, GSU, microfilm, rolls 655–833, 655–834, 655–835, 655–836, 655–837.
[a]Large numbers of baptismal entries for these years do not record places of residence.

125

Table 6.2
Baptisms, Residents of Atlihuayan, By Ethnic Group, 1650–1719

Period	Unspecified #	%	Indians #	%	Negroes #	%	Mulattoes #	%	Mestizos #	%	Other #	%
1650–59	1	16.7	4	66.7	0	0	1	16.7	0	0	0	0
1660–69	3	16.7	6	33.3	3	16.7	5	27.8	1	5.6	0	0
1670–79	3	23.1	3	23.1	2	15.4	5	38.5	0	0	0	0
1680–89	9	15.8	9	15.8	8	14.0	28	49.1	0	0	3	5.3
1705–9	3	7.5	5	12.5	6	15.0	18	45.0	7	17.5	1	2.5
1710–19	2	2.5	10	12.3	8	9.9	52	64.2	4	4.9	5	6.2

Source: Yautepec Parish Registers, GSU, microfilm, rolls 655–833, 655–834, 655–835.

Table 6.3
Baptisms, Residents of Suchiquesalco and Guausopán, by Ethnic Group, 1650–1719

Period	Unspecified		Indians		Negroes		Mulattoes		Mestizos		Other	
	#	%	#	%	#	%	#	%	#	%	#	%
1650–59	3	10.7	21	75.0	1	3.6	2	7.1	1	3.6	0	0
1660–69	13	20.3	28	43.8	4	6.3	11	17.2	6	9.4	2	3.1
1670–79	8	11.1	39	54.2	5	6.9	13	18.1	1	1.4	6	8.3
1680–89	14	14.6	44	45.8	0	0	32	33.3	5	5.2	1	1.0
1705–9	1	8.3	4	33.3	3	25.0	3	25.0	1	8.3	0	0
1710–19	2	3.6	14	25.5	1	1.8	22	40.0	10	18.2	6	10.9

Source: Yautepec Parish Registers, GSU, microfilm, rolls 655–833, 655–834,655–835.

Cortés mill, there were only two bozales by 1678, down from thirty-seven, or just under 40 percent of the total slave force, in 1625. However, in the mid-1680s the number of bozales at Atlacomulco probably increased, presumably as the result of a few additional purchases. Parish registers from Cuernavaca show the baptisms of eight adult slaves belonging to the hacienda in May 1684.[9] It is likely that these persons were African born, since creole slaves were almost always baptized in early infancy. Cocoyoc still had twenty bozales as late as 1714.[10]

As the numbers of bozales declined, the proportion of *negros criollos*, natives of the New World, increased among the slave forces on the haciendas of Morelos. Natural increase among slaves already resident on the haciendas accounted for a relatively small portion of this movement. As the figures in Table 6.1 show, Negroes usually accounted for less than 10 percent of all hacienda baptisms, except for the period from 1705–9, when their share increased to 14.9 percent. Throughout the seventeenth century, infant mortality among slaves remained quite high.[11] Landowners therefore supplemented the numbers of creole slaves born on their haciendas with purchases of new slaves from elsewhere in New Spain. Such phrases as *"negro criollo de Texcoco"* or *"negro criollo de Puebla"* frequently appear in slave inventories.

While the numbers of African-born slaves declined, Indian movement to the haciendas brought a dramatic increase in the number of mulattoes, evident in the figures for baptisms of all hacienda residents and in inventories of slave forces. Without question this change was due primarily to increased racial mixture between Indians and blacks. Although the English word mulatto usually refers to persons of white and Negro ancestry, in colonial Mexico the offspring of African-Indian unions were also known as mulattoes. The words *zambaigo* and *zambo*, while also denoting African-Indian mixture, were seldom used.[12] For example, Ward Barrett found only one person so designated among approximately nine hundred slaves listed in various inventories and other records of the Cortés estate.[13] Use of the term *lobo* to describe persons of African and Indian origin was much more common, but by far the greatest number of Afro-Indians were simply called *mulatos*.

Frequently the term mulato was modified by an adjective denoting the person's racial ancestry, real or supposed, or his physical appearance. Slave inventories from Morelos haciendas include such terms as *mulatos alobados*, who shared the physical characteristics of lobos, and

Table 6.4
Composition of Slave Force, Atlihuayan, 1672–1732

Date	African-born			Negros criollos			Mulattoes			Indeterminate		
	#	%	Avg. Age	#	%	Avg. Age	#	%	Avg. Age	#	%	Avg. Age
1672	23	26.1	66	42	47.7	23.9	17	19.3	12.5	6	6.8	44.8
1684	10	8.1	81	62	50.4	34.3	44	35.8	17.5	7	5.7	N.A.
1689	4	3.4	71.5	63	53.8	31.2	48	41.0	17.3	2	1.7	36
1701	1	1.1	39	45	47.4	29.9	49	51.6	23.4	0	—	—
1715	0	—	—	35	39.8	N.A.	38	43.2	N.A.	15	17.0	N.A.
1732	0	—	—	30	34.9	34.7	52	60.5	19.8	4	4.7	50

Sources: AGNT, Vol. 114, pt. 1, fols. 204v–206; AGNT, Vol. 2051, exp. 1; AGNC, Vol. 251, exp. 5; AGNT, Vol. 239, fol. 253; AGNT, Vol. 522, exp. 5.

Table 6.5
Slave Forces, Other Haciendas, 1625–1738

Hacienda	Date	African-born			Negros criollos			Mulattoes			Indeterminate			Source
		#	%	Avg. Age	#	%	Avg. Age	#	%	Avg. Age	#	%	Avg. Age	
Tenango	1693	10	20.0	63.8	27	54.0	37.2	12	24.0	14.5	1	2.0	73.0	AGNT, vol. 1980, exp. 2.
Barreto	1676	9	20.0	61.1	28	62.2	24.8	8	17.8	26.3	0	—	—	AGNT, vol. 1742, fol. 153v.
Guajoyuca	1680	2	3.1	60.0	32	50.0	30.4	30	46.9	14.4	0	—	—	AGNT, vol. 239, fol. 84v.
Cocoyoc	1714	20	35.7	52.2	17	30.4	34.0	17	30.4	22.0	2	3.6	4.5	AGNT, vol. 1564, fol. 69v.
Cocoyoc	1738	0	—	—	28	31.8	49.6	53	60.2	31.6	7	8.0	37.4	AGNT, vol. 1938, exp. 5.
Tlaltenango (Cortés Mill)	1625	37	39.4	43.5	51	54.3	16.9	6	6.4	19.8	0	—	—	AGNHJ, vol. 50 (leg. 28), exp. 9.
Atlacomulco (Cortés Mill)	1678	2	3.1	69.0	18	27.7	40.3	31	47.7	22.4	14	21.5	43.6	AGNHJ, leg. 93, exp. 2.
Suchiquesalco	1669	1	2.8	57.0	22	61.1	27.2	12	33.3	17.1	1	2.8	36.0	AGNT, vol. 1735, exp. 1, fol. 64v.

mulatos cochos, who were also presumed to be of African and Indian mixture. *Mulatos blancos* were of lighter pigmentation and probably had some European ancestry, while *mulatos prietos* and *mulatos atesados* were darker than other mulattoes. More often, however, slaves were merely identified as mulattoes, without any of these qualifying adjectives. Terms such as *negro atesado* (dark Negro) and *negro claro* (light Negro) were also used to describe the physical appearance of particular slaves.

It must be emphasized, of course, that the racial designations recorded in slave inventories are not precise indicators of the actual racial genealogy of persons described. Designations depended primarily on the physiognomy of the individual, as perceived by those recording their presence, supplemented by anything the recorder might have known of an individual's parentage. Individuals in the same family often appeared in different racial categories. In an inventory taken at Temisco in the early eighteenth century, a mulato prieto and his wife, a negra atesada, were listed as having four children: two mulatos cochos, one mulato prieto, and one negra atesada.[14] In some cases, of course, if a slave woman had children of several different racial classifications, the easiest explanation is that the children had different fathers. Nevertheless, we must be careful not to overestimate the precision of slave inventories as indicators of racial genealogy. Taken together, however, they do provide a guide to the changing physiognomy of slave forces in the region.

As the figures in Table 6.1 indicate, mulattoes already accounted for 11 percent of hacienda baptisms in Yautepec by the 1650s, the decade for which the first reasonably complete registers of non-Indian baptisms are available. The mulattoes' proportional share of hacienda baptisms more than doubled during the following decade, a period when many Indians were becoming permanent hacienda residents. By the second decade of the eighteenth century, mulattoes accounted for over half of the hacienda residents baptized by the cura of Yautepec. At Atlihuayan, the mulatto share of baptisms gained more than 10 percentage points each decade from the 1660s through the 1680s, while the Indians' proportion steadily declined. Meanwhile, at Guausopán and Suchiquesalco the mulatto share also rose during the second half of the seventeenth century, although not quite as dramatically as at Atlihuayan. Given the consistently high rate of endogamy among Indians who formally married (see below, Chapter 7), it is likely that many of these Afro-Indians were born outside of church-sanctified wedlock.

Inventories of slaves at Temisco and San Gaspar, taken in 1728 and 1738, respectively, show the variety of terms used to describe mulattoes, as well as the extent of interracial mixture among slaves by the early eighteenth century. Tables 6.6 and 6.7 show the number of persons in each racial category among these haciendas' slave forces. Average ages are also noted for each racial category at Temisco. The *negro chino* at San Gaspar, and the three *mulatos achinados* at Temisco were probably descendants of Filipino or other oriental slaves. According to J. I. Israel, perhaps as many as six thousand orientals per decade were brought to New Spain as slaves during the first half of the seventeenth century.[15] The relatively high percentage of mulatos prietos among Temisco's forces may have been due to a perceptible "re-Africanization," in racial but not cultural terms, of the slave forces after the demographic crisis of the 1690s. As the influx of Indians to the haciendas halted temporarily, mulattoes and Negroes were more likely to choose mates from among their Afro-Mexican neighbors. The average age of the mulatos prietos suggests the validity of such a hypothesis.

The presence of increasing numbers of Indian and free mulatto hacienda residents greatly altered the institution of slavery. Slaves in colonial Morelos lived surrounded by free persons of every imaginable racial combination, and they readily formed ties of concubinage, marriage,

Table 6.6
Racial Designations of Slaves, Temisco, 1728

Category	Number	Percentage	Average Age
Negro	16	19.5	36.6
Negro atesado	7	8.5	36.0
Negro cocho	1	1.2	45.0
Mulato blanco	6	7.3	25.0
Mulato cocho	23	28.0	18.5
Mulato alobado	5	6.1	11.2
Mulato prieto	19	23.2	20.9
Mulato acoyotado	1	1.2	3.0
Mulato achinado	3	3.7	14.0
Unspecified	1	1.2	85.0
	82	99.9[a]	

Source: AGNT, vol. 3428, exp. 1.
[a]Due to rounding, total is less than 100.

Table 6.7
Racial Designations of Slaves, San Gaspar, 1738

Category	Number	Percent
Negro atesado	7	9.0
Negro	20	25.6
Mulato cocho	25	32.1
Negro claro	1	1.3
Mulato	6	7.7
Mulato alobado	6	7.7
Cocho	1	1.3
Mulato lobo	1	1.3
Mulato blanco	2	2.6
Morisco	1	1.3
Mulato prieto	1	1.3
Negro chino	1	1.3
Mulato morisco	1	1.3
Lobo	4	5.1
Unspecified	1	1.3
	78	100.2[a]

Source: AGNT, vol. 2420, exp. 1.
[a]Due to rounding, total exceeds 100.

and compadrazgo (co-godparenthood) with these free persons. With a few exceptions, especially that of Xochimancas in the seventeenth century,[16] inventories that indicate slaves' marital status list one or more persons with free spouses. Proportions of slaves married to free persons varied over time and also from hacienda to hacienda. At the Order of San Hipólito's ingenio in 1690, for example, there were nineteen adult males, of whom six were married to free women, and two to slaves. The remaining eleven were bachelors. Five of the men with free wives were mulattoes; the sixth was probably a negro criollo. Among the hacienda's adult women, six were unmarried, three were widows, two were married to free men, and two had slave husbands.[17] At Cocoyoc in 1738, nine men and one woman had free spouses.[18] Other records indicate that slave women were just as likely as their male counterparts to have free spouses; by 1749 four of Cocoyoc's female slaves had free husbands, while three males were married to free women.[19] At Miacatlán and San Gaspar, in 1738, five female slaves were listed as being *casada con libre*, while only two males were so designated.[20] Records from later in the eighteenth century indicate that slaves' liberty to marry free persons continued. Of Hacienda Santa Ana Tenango's 141 slaves in 1768, 14 were married to free persons. On the adjoining hacienda, Santa Clara Montefalco, an even greater proportion—fifteen of eighty-five—had free spouses. At least two others were widowers of free women, entrusted with the guardianship of their free children.[21] Baptismal information from Atlihuayan points in the same direction, as the figures in Table 6.8 show. There, unions between slaves and free persons multiplied most notably in the late 1760s, when over a third of the slave children born at the hacienda had free fathers. Slaves married to free persons thus constituted an enduring minority on the haciendas of Morelos.

Baptismal records for the hacienda Cocoyoc, summarized in Table 6.9, reveal the close familial ties formed between slaves and free persons. Twenty percent of the slave children born at the hacienda between 1748 and 1753 were the legitimate offspring of slave women and free men. Of course a far greater proportion, over two-thirds, of the

Table 6.8
Offspring of Slave-Free Unions, Atlihuayan,
1730–1779

Period	Free father, slave mother	Slave father, free mother
1730–34	0	3
1735–39	0	2
1740–44	1	2
1745–49	2	0
1750–54	1	0
1755–59	5	5
1760–64	3	2
1765–69	11	13
1770–74	7	3
1775–79	2	1

Sources: Yautepec Parish Registers, GSU, microfilm, rolls 655–835, 655–836, 655–837.

slaves born at the hacienda during that period were illegitimate. It is quite possible that many of them also had free fathers, some of whom may have recognized and cared for their offspring. The case of Hermenegilda Susana, a mulatta slave of Cocoyoc, was typical of the haciendas of eighteenth-century Morelos. Her father, Vicente Ferrer, was a free mulatto, while her mother, Andrea Gertrudis, was a slave. In 1769, Hermenegilda Susana married a free Negro resident of Cocoyoc.[22] The data in Table 6.9 also document the eventual decline in slavery at Cocoyoc, to be discussed at greater length below.

Continuity in family life was a notable feature of slave life on the sugar haciendas of colonial Morelos. Most slaves had little reason to fear that their families might be disrupted by the sale of loved ones to other owners. On the rare occasions when slaveowners did sell any of their human chattels, the buyers were most often neighboring landowners. Colonial Mexico witnessed nothing comparable to the massive transfer of slaves from older plantation areas to the rapidly developing

Table 6.9
Baptisms, Hacienda Cocoyoc, 1748–1753; 1774–1775

	March 1748–April 1753		February 1774–August 1775	
	#	% of total	#	% of total
Mulatto Slaves				
Father unknown	17	32.7	0	—
Father slave	3	5.8	0	—
Father free	5	9.6	1	3.6
Negro slaves	0	—	1	3.6
Free Mulattoes				
Father unknown	7	13.5	2	7.1
Father slave	1	1.9	0	—
Father free	6	11.5	10	35.7
Indians	9	17.3	9	32.1
Lobos	1	1.9	0	—
Mestizos	3	5.8	3	10.7
Españoles	0	—	1	3.6
Indeterminate	0	—	1	3.6
Total	52	100	28	100

Source: Oaxtepec Parish Registers, GSU, microfilm, roll 606–326.

"Old Southwest" of the nineteenth-century United States. The economic growth of eighteenth-century New Spain, which did involve heavy migration to burgeoning mining and commercial centers of the north, depended almost completely on free workers. At worst, slaves might experience temporary separation from their homes and families if they were embargoed pending their owners' satisfaction of outstanding debts.

The inventory of Cocoyoc from 1749 is quite complete in its designation of the family relationships of slaves listed. While several single adults are mentioned, the youngest person living alone was a fourteen-year-old girl. All other children resided at least with their mothers, many of whom were unmarried but who may have formed stable common-law unions. Some slave households contained three generations. A six-month-old infant, for example, lived with his unmarried mother, three young aunts and uncles, his slave grandmother and free grandfather, as well as a great-grandmother, a great aunt, and two second cousins. The four children of another slave woman and her free husband lived with their parents and maternal grandmother.[23]

Ties of compadrazgo also bound slaves to their free neighbors, including Indians. In 1719, for example, two Indians served as godparents for a mulatto slave child born at Cocoyoc, while in 1749 two Indians who lived at Atlihuayan invited a slave couple to serve as godparents for their daughter. Slaves living on haciendas might even become *compadres* of Indians living in towns. For example, in 1765, two slaves of Atlihuayan became godparents of María Gregoria, daughter of Vicente Ferrer and Michaela Andrea, Indians of the barrio of San Juan in Yautepec.[24]

By the eighteenth century, slavery on the sugar haciendas of Morelos was, quite literally, an accident of birth, a condition inherited from one's mother. If anything, slaves enjoyed certain security and privileges not always shared by free hacienda residents. This privileged position derived primarily from the self-interest of hacienda owners and tenants. Rental contracts almost always stipulated that tenants would be held liable for half the value of any slave, except those explicitly excluded because of age or infirmity, who died during their tenure. Tenants also received compensation for half the value of any slaves born during the term of their rental and still alive at the termination of their lease.[25] Tenants as well as owners thus had a vested interest in the health and procreation of slaves. Except in times of dire financial troubles, hacendados evidently attempted to provide their slaves with an adequate diet and other perquisites necessary to maintain their health and strength.

The consistency of customary maize allocations suggests that certain standards of diet came to be expected by masters and slaves alike. Records from the Jesuit hacienda Xochimancas show that in 1664 each adult slave received 1 *almud* (4.6 liters) of maize per week, while children received half that amount.[26] Scattered evidence from other haciendas suggests that these rations remained at least constant during the eighteenth century. If anything, allotments may have risen somewhat, perhaps because some slaves now shared their rations with free children and other dependents. At Atlihuayan, in the early eighteenth century, slaves consumed 72 fanegas, an average of 6.7 liters per person, per week.[27] Accounts kept by the administrator of Cocoyoc in the early 1750s indicate that a typical week's total maize allocation for the forty adults and twenty-five children among the hacienda's slaves was about 5.25 fanegas. Again, the figures show remarkable consistency; adults received about 5.6 liters, and children 2.8 liters, per week.[28] Finally, in a report prepared in 1765, the administrator of Casasano stated that the weekly maize ration for slaves was one-eighth fanega, or 6.9 liters, for adults, and half that amount for children.[29]

Slaves also received regular allocations of other foods, including meat, salt, and chilis. At Atlacomulco, slaves over ten years of age received 4.6 kilograms of beef per week, while the ration for children was half that amount.[30] In some cases, hacendados gave their slaves cash or chits with which to purchase such commodities.[31] At Guadalupe in the 1730s, and probably on other estates as well, slaves purchased food from Indians in nearby villages. Whenever hacienda administrators lacked sufficient resources to provide slaves with their accustomed rations, slaves evidently expected relief from their duties in the fields and mills so that they could obtain their sustenance in some other way.[32] As we saw in Chapter 4, in times when the sugar industry came close to collapse, slaves and free hacienda residents alike simply reverted to subsistence agriculture on hacienda lands.

Hacendados also provided simple clothing and rudimentary shelter for their slaves. Hacienda inventories note the *jacales*, or huts, in which slaves lived, but offer little descriptive comment about these dwellings. The number of jacales suggest that each family probably had a hut to itself. At Cocoyoc in 1749, for example, there were twenty-nine dwellings for a total of sixty-five slaves.[33] Atlihuayan had thirty-three jacales and eighty-five slaves in 1676, and fifty-one dwellings for eighty-eight slaves in 1715.[34] At Tenango in 1693, there were twenty dwellings, all said to be in poor condition, for fifty slaves.[35] References from Hospital in 1685 and Casasano in 1719 indicate that slave families shared a common kitchen.[36]

The more conscientious owners and tenants provided regular medical care for their slaves. Accounts kept by hacienda administrators show regular if modest expenditures for doctors and medicine for their slaves. An inventory of Atlihuayan in 1701 noted numerous remedies purchased by an outgoing tenant for the slaves' needs.[37] In 1765, the administrator of Casasano paid fifty-four pesos to a surgeon, and eleven pesos, four reales to a midwife, both of whom had attended slaves of the hacienda.[38] Occasionally, administrators of the Cortés estate sent a slave from Atlacomulco to the Hospital de Jesús in Mexico City for treatment.[39] The inventory taken at Temisco in 1728 listed a slave woman then being cared for at the Hospital de San Antonio Abad, also in Mexico City.[40]

At least in theory, slaves also enjoyed certain guarantees against abusive treatment. Some slaves attempted to purchase their freedom, usually with the help of free relatives or benefactors, in order to escape intolerable conditions. In 1671, for example, the family and friends of a Negro slave of Atlacomulco bought his freedom, at a cost of 350 pesos, to spare him the heavy labor which they said endangered his already precarious health.[41] Such purchases evidently became more common by the end of the eighteenth century. However, the amounts paid often represented substantial sums, beyond the reach of most slaves, and well above current market prices.[42] Slaves also could request transfer to other owners if their masters mistreated them, but this recourse was seldom used, and almost never beneficial. In 1733, a free mulatto named Antonio de Sarantes sought slave wife removed from Atlacomulco. The administrator of the hacienda ignored Sarantes's request. Instead, he placed a pair of *grillos* (shackles) on the woman and threatened to send her to a hacienda where she would suffer more arduous conditions than at Atlacomulco. Her husband appealed to the governor of the Marquesado del Valle, who denied the request on the grounds that its approval might subvert slave discipline on haciendas throughout the region.[43]

Marquesado officials were no more sympathetic to similar requests advanced by slaves belonging to others. In 1777, for example, José Alberto, a slave belonging to Rodrigo del Valle, owner of Atlihuayan, approached the governor seeking a transfer because del Valle worked him too hard. The slave alleged that his owner had frustrated his attempts to gain the transfer by declaring his value at the exorbitant rate of eight hundred pesos, nearly three times the normal price for adult slaves in the eighteenth century. The governor paid little attention to José Alberto's petition. He ordered the slave returned to del Valle, whom he simply instructed to treat his chattel more humanely.[44] In 1764 a slave couple who succeeded in moving to another hacienda found that while their petition was pending the executor of their late master's estate had sold their two small children to a third party.[45]

Slaves could, and occasionally did, protest to local authorities when their masters failed to provide customary allocations of food and clothing,[46] but their material standard of living remained for the most part dependent on the goodwill, financial resources, and enlightened self-interest of their masters. Thus the formal and informal guarantees of the Spanish legal and social system, once thought to have contributed substantially toward assuring Iberian slaves a more satisfactory life than their counterparts in other societies,[47] brought few concrete benefits to the slaves of colonial Morelos. Nevertheless, most slaves enjoyed a degree of material security equal to, or greater than, free hacienda residents. They could usually count on being supported by their masters, even in their old age. In times of economic recession for the haciendas, slaves and free residents simply devoted their energies to subsistence agriculture.

Slaves derived added security from the fact that they were often more likely than their free cohorts to possess the specialized skills of sugar manufacture. Whenever possible, hacendados preferred to train slaves rather than free workers for these demanding and highly skilled jobs. The most prestigious of all jobs associated directly with sugar manufacture was that of *maestro de azúcar*, or sugar master, who oversaw all operations in the processing of cane into sugar. So important was this position that when exercised by free persons it was a highly paid occupation.[48] On most haciendas the job of sugar master remained reserved for slaves until late in the eighteenth century. At Casasano in 1765, the positions of *purgador* (purger), *mandador del molino* (mill supervisor), and *mayordomo* (general overseer) had passed to free workers, but a slave still held the job of maestro de azúcar.[49] Although in 1786 Cocoyoc's slave force included only six adult males, one of them was the sugar master.[50] Miacatlán's slaves in 1800 numbered only eleven: three adult women, six children, and two men, both of whom were *trapicheros*, or skilled mill workers.[51]

In addition to the position of maestro de azúcar, slaves also held other key skilled or supervisory jobs. Such posts entitled them to benefits not enjoyed by fellow slaves or unskilled free workers. At Casasano in the 1760s, most slaves received a half-real each week with which to buy salt and chilis, but the maestro de azúcar and other skilled slaves received as much as two reales. At Cocoyoc the maestro de azúcar received a full peso each week for these commodities, while other slaves' allowances varied in accord with their skills and responsibilities.[52] Slaves of the hacienda Guadalupe who complained of ill treatment in 1732 explained that the slave mayordomo had not joined their protest because his position afforded him greater material comforts than other slaves received.[53] For a minority of specially privileged individuals, then, slavery offered the opportunity to acquire skills which assured them greater security and a modicum of prestige within the hierarchy of hacienda workers. As time passed and the proportion of slaves among workers on most haciendas declined, the odds that a male slave might achieve such an enviable niche increased correspondingly.

The eighteenth century witnessed a gradual decline in the number of slaves in New Spain, thanks primarily to the growth in the Indian population and the consequent reduction in slave imports. Claude Morin has noted the shift from slave to free labor that characterized the history of sugar haciendas in the tierra caliente of Michoacán during the eighteenth century.[54] A similar development occurred in Morelos, although the timing and rate of this change varied from one estate to another, and occasionally a hacendado might increase the size of his slave force by purchasing additional workers. (See Table 6.10.) During the first two-thirds of the eighteenth century the slaves themselves played major roles in the eventual decline of the institution. References to flights by slaves were quite common during this period. The deterioration of the haciendas and consequent lapses in supervision gave slaves ample opportunity for flight.[55]

The growing importance of free workers is reflected in a statement

Table 6.10
Slave Forces, Major Haciendas, 1630–1800

Hacienda	Date	Number of Slaves	Source
Cocoyoc	1714	56	AGNT, vol. 1564, fol. 69v.
	1738	88	AGNT, vol. 1938, exp. 5.
	1749	65	AGNT, vol. 1974, exp. 2.
	1786	21	AGNT, vol. 1938, exp. 7.
Barreto	1676	45	AGNT, vol. 1742, fol. 153v.
	1702	20	AGNT, vol. 1742, fol. 175v.
Guajoyuca	1630	80	AGNT, vol. 239, fol. 43v.
	1680	64	AGNT, vol. 239, fol. 84v.
Calderón	1763	105	AGNT, vol. 1935, exp. 7.
	1791	56	AGNP, vol. 8.
Xochimancas	1653	246	Berthe, "Xochimancas," 110.
	1660	216	Berthe, "Xochimancas," 110.
	1664	217	Berthe, "Xochimancas," 110.
	1674	217	Berthe, "Xochimancas," 110.
	1705	157	Berthe, "Xochimancas," 110.
	1728	147	Berthe, "Xochimancas," 110.
	1750	150	Berthe, "Xochimancas," 110.
Miacatlán	1737	94	AGNT, vol. 1972, exp. 2.
	1776	17	AGNT, vol. 1950, cuaderno 2.
	1800	11	AGNT, vol. 1371, exp. 1, fol. 111v.
Tenango	1693	50	AGNT, vol. 1980, exp. 2.
	1768	141	GSU, microfilm, roll 641–723.
San Vicente-Matlapán	1740	65	AGNT, vol. 1951, cuaderno 10, fol. 171v.
	1754	54	AGNT, vol. 1951, cuaderno 1, fol. 10.
	1756	60	AGNT, vol. 1951, cuaderno 3.
	1760	22	AGNT, vol. 1952, cuaderno 4, fol. 12.
	1774	36	AGNT, vol. 1977, exp. 1, fol. 64v.
	1778	31	AGNT, vol. 1977, exp. 3, fol. 81v.
San Gaspar	1738	75	AGNT, vol. 2420, exp. 1.
	1796	2	AGNT, vol. 1945, fol. 10v.
Temilpa	1704	23	AGNT, vol. 1761, fol. 228.
	1759	34	AGNT, vol. 1962, fol. 11v.

of hacendado José Luque Galisteo in 1741, protesting regulations concerning the meat supply contract (abasto) of Cuernavaca. Only hacendados with slaves were allowed to slaughter animals to feed their labor forces; free hacienda servants were expected to buy their meat at markets provisioned by the holder of the abasto. Galisteo argued that the rule ignored the growing presence of nonslave hacienda residents.[56] One suspects that the source of Galisteo's opposition lay primarily in the hacendados' reluctance or inability to give their workers the cash necessary to buy meat.

The gradual transition from slave to free labor is graphically documented in records of the hacienda Cocoyoc from the mid-eighteenth century. This hacienda's slave force expanded from fifty-six to eighty-eight between 1714 and 1738. At least part of this increase was probably due to Pedro Carbajal Machado's transfer of slaves from Apanquesalco to Cocoyoc and Oacalco during the time that he owned the latter two haciendas and served as court-appointed depositario of the former.[57] After 1738, the slave force at Cocoyoc declined steadily, numbering sixty-five in 1749 and twenty-one in 1786. The decline in the slave forces at Cocoyoc is further confirmed by records of baptisms of Cocoyoc residents for two sample periods, summarized in Table 6.9 above. The figures reflect the hacienda's growing population; baptisms per month averaged .84 between 1748 and 1753 and 1.47 for the years 1774–75. While slaves comprised nearly half of the baptisms between 1748 and 1753, they accounted for less then 10 percent in 1774–75. The percentage of Indians nearly doubled, reflecting increased Indian migration to Cocoyoc and other haciendas of the region during the 1760s and 1770s.

Cocoyoc's administrators developed managerial strategies to mesh its free and slave work forces. During the harvest and milling seasons, male slaves performed the mill work while female slaves and temporary workers cut cane.[58] One by one positions demanding particular skill or responsibility passed from slaves to free hacienda residents. For example, in 1752, the slave who had customarily tended Cocoyoc's livestock became too ill to work. A free worker named Vicente Ferrer took his place, receiving six pesos per month and a ration of maize.[59] Vicente Ferrer may have been either a mestizo or a free mulatto. Baptismal registers from Oaxtepec list two men named Vicente Ferrer who were residents of the hacienda Cocoyoc and had children baptized in October 1749. The mestizo was married to a free woman of the same racial classification, while the free mulatto's wife was a slave (also mulatto) of the hacienda.[60]

In time, free workers learned the complicated techniques associated with sugar manufacture. Mulattoes, born and trained on the haciendas, were usually the first free workers to become maestros de azúcar and other skilled technicians, but eventually even some Indians overcame their ignorance and understandable fear of injury to learn the craft of sugar manufacture. San Carlos Borromeo, which never had more than a handful of slaves, had an Indian purger as early as 1767.[61] The sale of slaves belonging to Barreto and Xochimancas, following the expulsion of the Jesuits, forced those who eventually purchased these estates to build a new labor force based almost entirely on free workers. By 1801, an Indian originally from Tlayacapan occupied the coveted position of maestro de azúcar at Barreto. A mestizo from Izúcar assisted him as master purger, while several other workers, both mulatto and Indian, performed other skilled tasks.[62]

By the end of the eighteenth century the growing numbersof skilled and disciplined free workers had led most hacendados to abandon their seventeenth-century predecessors' preference for slave labor. Evidently, late colonial landowners found free workers more tractable than slaves. When a mysterious fire broke out at Matlapán in 1761, hacienda administrators and other witnesses dismissed the possibility that any of the estate's workers might have deliberately started the blaze. All of them were free, and, according to the witnesses, less likely than slaves to engage in such mischief.[63] The difficulty of maintaining order among slaves was often mentioned or implied by late colonial hacendados. In the 1760s, the heirs of Asencio González, late owner of Calderón, lamented that protracted legal battles over the disposition of his estate were tending to subvert discipline among the hacienda's slaves.[64] In 1789, the owner of San Gaspar gave the hacienda's tenant explicit permission to sell any slaves who undermined order. At the time of this contract, two of San Gaspar's thirteen remaining slaves had paid installments toward their eventual freedom. One suspects that their owner's willingness to accept these sums stemmed more from his desire to rid himself of potential troublemakers than from any magnanimous feeling.[65] The owner of Atlihuayan willingly forfeited the labor of two female slaves when he ordered their confinement in the jail at Yautepec as punishment for misbehavior.[66]

The most explicit indictment of slavery was penned by the accountant of the Marquesado del Valle in 1804. When Gabriel de Yermo offered to buy three male slaves who had fled from Atlacomulco to one of his haciendas, the accountant readily supported the sale. The five slaves still at Atlacomulco were so useless and bothersome that it would be best simply to free them all, wrote the *contador*. Two were too old or infirm to provide any useful labor, while another was a female cook who was then requesting her freedom because she, too, was gravely ill. The accountant suggested that granting her request would best serve the interests of the hacienda. Atlacomulco's most valuable slaves, fourteen in number, had all fled. At least two of the three who had gone to Yermo's estate were skilled operatives; one of them was currently serving as Yermo's maestro de azúcar. For his part, Yermo held few illusions regarding his ability to retain the three men, even if they became his slaves. To keep them, he said, he would have to pay them just as if they were free.[67] Although late colonial hacendados complained frequently of their difficulties in finding and retaining skilled and dependable free workers,[68] most had evidently abandoned any notions of slavery as an effective means of labor control. The fact that slave values listed in inventories of Atlacomulco and other haciendas remained constant or even declined during the course of the eighteenth century underscores the hacendados' growing disenchantment with the institution of slavery.[69] Many of them welcomed and even abetted its demise. Free hacienda residents, supplemented by temporary workers, provided a far more satisfactory source of labor.

Free hacienda workers received wages and other remuneration in accord with their strength and skills. Daily stipends ranged from one real for young boys, and two reales for unskilled adult peons, to more substantial salaries, often paid on a monthly basis, for skilled employees. At Pantitlán in 1766, *vaqueros* (cowboys) and certain other employees received a monthly salary of six pesos, the equivalent of the standard daily wage of two reales. The mayordomo and *caporal* (tender of livestock) received eight and nine pesos respectively, while the purger's monthly cash receipts totaled twenty-five pesos.[70] Resident workers also received maize rations or permission to cultivate small plots of land for their own subsistence. At Casasano in the 1760s, the free purgador and mayordomo each received two fanegas of maize per month; the caporal and other semiskilled workers got one and a half fanegas. Still others received one fanega or a half-fanega, the latter amount being equal to the ration given slaves. The purgador, the mandador del molino, and other skilled operatives were also invited to eat their meals with the hacienda administrator.[71] The owner of Atlihuayan treated skilled mill workers to extra rations of chocolate during the harvest season.[72]

Although resident workers had no formal claim to other perquisites, there is evidence that at least some hacendados provided them with certain amenities available also to their slaves. Church authorities expected hacendados to offer religious instruction for their free residents as well as for their slaves. Following a visit to the Yautepec area in 1715, the archbishop of Mexico reminded landowners of this obligation. While many may have ignored this injunction, the owner of Calderón sent twelve pesos to a local priest for hearing confessions of the hacienda's *gente libre* (literally, "free people") between March and August of 1763.[73] Some hacendados also paid for schoolmasters who provided basic instruction, primarily in Christian dogma, for children of both slave and free workers. In 1768, Santa Ana Tenango's *maestro de escuela* was a slave named Bernardo de la Cruz, while at Santa Clara Montefalco a free man performed this service.[74] Nicolás de Icazbalceta undertook a campaign to inoculate his workers against smallpox during the epidemic of 1797.[75] Other hacendados provided their resident workers with special foods and other supplies for the celebration of Christmas and other holidays. In December 1765, the administrator of Cocoyoc purchased olives, fruit, fresh fish, sweets, nuts, *cebiche* (marinated fish) from Veracruz, Spanish brandy, and white wine for his employees' customary Christmas Eve celebration.[76]

Highland Indian villages to the immediate north of the sugar-growing region supplied most of the Indian migrants who became permanent hacienda residents. Certain highland villages, as well as some towns in the lowlands, also provided substantial numbers of temporary workers who came to the haciendas during the harvesting and milling seasons. In 1786, for example, the owner of Atlihuayan reported that for the last six years he had procured workers from several sujetos of the highland village of Ozumba.[77] Accounts kept by the administrator of the same hacienda in 1799 show that he employed crews from the three upland communities of Xochimilco, Tlayacapan, and Atlatlauca, and from one lowland village, Tetelcingo, near Cuautla.[78] Indians from Tlayacapan also worked regularly at the haciendas San Carlos Borromeo and Oacalco in the second half of the eighteenth century.[79]

To recruit temporary workers most hacendados relied on intermediaries known locally as *capitanes de gañanes*, who were frequently gobernadores or other persons of importance in the villages. Hacendados paid the capitanes, evidently in advance, and the recruiters then distributed wages to the workers. The recruiters themselves might receive a commission, typically two reales per twenty man-days, for the laborers they supplied.[80] When a captain failed to deliver workers for whom he had already received advances, hacendados might apprehend the recruiter or seize his assets.[81] Hacendados sometimes made loans to village authorities and then required the Indians to perform labor until the debt was repaid. In the 1720s, for example, José Galisteo advanced 347 pesos to the Indian gobernadores of Tepoztlán, allegedly to assist them in meeting their tribute obligations. He then demanded that Indians from the village work for him, leaving half of their salaries toward repayment of the debt. Galisteo claimed that other landowners followed similar procedures in procuring labor.[82] Workers also received credit at the tiendas, or stores, maintained on most major estates. When workers settled accounts with their employers, credits received at the tienda and advances made in cash were deducted from their accumulated wages. In 1731, a worker at Cocoyoc received twenty-nine pesos, three reales in cash and cancellation of sixty-seven pesos' worth of debts incurred at the tienda during the ten-month period he worked at the hacienda.[83]

Loans to capitanes, gobernadores, and individual workers were a common but relatively ineffective means of forcing laborers to continue working for a particular employer against their will. Evidently, landowners in eighteenth-century Morelos regarded advances to workers and capitanes as normal costs of doing business, and expected to write off a certain portion of such sums as unrecoverable. In September 1739, Pedro Salgado, owner of Chiconcoac, lamented the financial risks involved in advancing funds to potential workers. Especially during the first half of the eighteenth century, even a liberal use of credit failed to hold workers; numerous operatives fled without settling their accounts.[84]

Recent research on several different regions in colonial Mexico has emphasized the degree to which "debt peonage" reflected the bargaining position of workers, rather than the compulsive power of employers.[85] As Herman Konrad has succinctly stated, the Jesuit administrators of Hacienda Santa Lucía "had less interest in having workers in debt than workers had in being in debt."[86] At Santa Lucía, workers who had earned their employers' trust received greater credits than others. Evidence from Morelos also suggests that some workers were in a decidedly better position to bargain with hacienda owners. In general, a person's level of indebtedness varied in direct proportion to the status of his occupation. For example, one of the largest amounts in a list of debts owed by Miacatlán's workers in 1735 was the 143-peso liability of a carpenter, whose relatively high occupational standing is indicated by the fact that he was paid on a monthly rather than a daily basis.[87] Accounts from other haciendas show a similar tendency. For unskilled workers, debts totaling ten pesos, and often much less, were the general rule. Most debts owed by Temilpa's workers in 1714 amounted to two pesos or less.[88] Sixty workers owed a total of 170 pesos, 5 reales, to Cocoyoc's tienda in 1732.[89] Almost a half-century later, the debts of most workers at Atlihuayan were under ten pesos.[90] In 1819, fifty-nine persons owed a total of 212 pesos to the store at Barreto; the highest single debt, 29 pesos, was that of a man who used the title "Don."[91]

The relatively constant levels of debt incurred by workers during the course of the eighteenth century stands in contrast to a tendency observed by Eric Van Young for haciendas in the Guadalajara region. There, the average debts of workers declined as the century advanced, as population growth brought a deterioration in the power of individual workers to bargain with their employers.[92] In Morelos, demographic increase, augmented by immigration, certainly produced a similar effect on workers' leverage in the late colonial period. The low levels of indebtedness prevailing earlier in the eighteenth century, despite the hacendados' oft-expressed need for labor, probably owed much to the financial difficulties of landowners, who lacked adequate amounts of cash or merchandise to advance to workers. Indeed, the recession left many hacendados unable to pay their workers for labor already performed. For example, when Francisco Rebolledo turned Santa Ana Tenango over to a tenant in 1693, he requested a 450-peso advance rental payment, to be used to pay overdue wages to his employees.[93] Ironically, such workers found far greater incentive to remain at their haciendas than those theoretically "bound" by debts. On more than one occasion, "creditor-peons" appealed to judicial authorities to recover wages owed to them.[94]

The inadequacy of "debt peonage" as a device for binding labor to the haciendas led some employers to experiment with the employment of prisoners convicted by the Real Sala del Crimen and then sold for stipulated periods of time to hacendados and others needing workers. The "purchase" price usually represented the fines incurred by a defendant; the length of service was considered the equivalent of the time needed to work off that amount. Local officials evidently played an active role in providing prisoners to serve terms as hacienda laborers. Such workers rarely amounted to more than about a half dozen on any one hacienda at any particular time. One exception was Pedro Carbajal Machado's new mill at Oacalco, which in 1729 included in its work force fourteen such *reos vendidos*.[95]

The hacendados' frustrations with credit as a means of labor recruitment, as well as the mutual distrust prevailing between workers and employers, is amply demonstrated in the willingness of some landowners to use debts as a means to harass their workers even if they could not bind them to their jobs. In 1744, José Luque Galisteo tried to force a worker who had injured his hand in a mill accident to remain working until he paid a hundred-peso debt. When the worker fled to Mexico City, Galisteo, a perpetual member of the city's municipal council, had him apprehended and sent to an *obraje*, or textile factory. A court ruling freed the worker and relieved him of the obligation to pay Galisteo.[96] In 1782, José Alvarado, an Indian from Yautepec, claimed that after working as a muleteer for hacendado Francisco de Urueta for more than nineteen years, he had left his job owing only twenty-two pesos. Although the governor of the Marquesado agreed that Alvarado should be allowed to pay off his debt at the rate of two reales per week, the teniente of Yautepec ignored the governor's directive and ordered Alvarado's imprisonment. Francisco de Urueta thus succeeded in making life unpleasant for this recalcitrant employee, but as long as Alvarado remained in jail, Urueta had no chance of using his labor.[97]

Other evidence also points to the harsh character of labor relations on the sugar haciendas. Whipping was a customary punishment for workers, slave or free, who showed signs of insubordination or neglect of duty. Workers sometimes suffered physical abuse for trivial breaches of labor discipline. In the 1790s, for example, the administrator of Hacienda Buenavista ordered a young worker beaten and then jailed for two days simply because the youth had urinated in the canefields.[98] Other administrators used stocks (*cepos*) and shackles (grillos) to restrain unruly workers.[99] Indians, less accustomed to the routine of sugar production, may have incurred such penalties more often than free mulattoes who had lived on the haciendas all of their lives.

Problems associated with labor recruitment and discipline gave hacendados ample reason to favor the growth of permanent resident populations on their estates. While such workers might also depart without paying debts owed to their employers, they probably had greater reason to remain at their jobs than did workers recruited on a temporary basis from outside the haciendas. Whatever the harsh nature of hacienda labor, resident workers usually identified themselves as vecinos of a particular estate, with much the same sense of permanence as village dwellers. Those descended from seventeenth-century slaves or Indian migrants often lived surrounded by kinfolk. Their lifelong familiarity with sugar manufacture gave them access to higher-paying, more prestigious positions than those occupied by temporary or recently arrived workers. Finally, residents of at least some estates enjoyed the benefits of a limited form of paternalism that extended to free workers as well as to slaves. References to such benevolent gestures are few in number and readily attributable to the self-interest of the hacendados. Nevertheless, they contributed in some small way to the quality of life among hacienda residents.

To encourage the growth of resident populations on their estates, late colonial hacendados needed only to let current demographic trends take their course. Population growth in Morelos and throughout New Spain in the eighteenth century provided a steady stream of migrants to the haciendas. The figures in Table 6.1, showing the ethnic distribution of hacienda residents baptized in Yautepec between 1650 and 1798 reveal that the years from 1650 to 1690, the 1720s and 1730s, and the final three decades of the eighteenth century, all periods of notable population increase in New Spain, were also periods when Indian migration to the haciendas was especially marked. After 1760, the "push" of population pressure was reinforced by the "pull" of a resurgent sugar industry.

As a result of these combined demographic and economic forces, the typical hacienda of late eighteenth-century Morelos had a resident population numbering as many as five hundred or more persons, including those too young, too old, or too infirm to be counted in the active labor force. The proportions of resident Indians and mulattoes varied according to the particular hacienda's history. Those estates which had once had large slave populations, or were located adjacent to other haciendas with such histories, had higher percentages of mulattoes. Other haciendas' labor forces contained more substantial proportions of Indians.

Sources for determining the size and ethnic composition of late colonial hacienda populations include several ecclesiastical censuses, which list persons of all racial categories old enough to be communicants in the church—that is, adults and children over about the age of ten. Two such censuses for haciendas within the ecclesiastical jurisdiction of Cuautla, summarized in Table 6.11, show the size of hacienda populations and changes that occurred between 1777 and 1797. Rates of population change in that interval varied considerably from one hacienda to another. In several cases, figures based on the ecclesiastical census of 1797 correspond well with those derived from the military *padrón* of 1791–92 (see the final column of Table 6.11), especially when we keep in mind that the latter count excluded Indians but included young children. Thus Buenavista had 155 non-Indians of all ages in 1791 and 157 non-Indian communicants six years later, while for Santa Inés the respective figures are 220 and 201. The counts for Calderón and Tenextepango show similar correspondence.

Other haciendas, however, showed greater divergence between the two censuses of the 1790s. These discrepancies may have been due either to errors of the census-takers or to internal changes on the haciendas in question. It is possible that Casasano, Hospital, and Cuahuixtla lost population during the decade. The owners of the latter two haciendas engaged in bitter land disputes with neighboring villages, a factor which may have induced their residents to seek more peaceful abodes on other haciendas.

Data from haciendas outside the Cuautla district also show differences in the rates of resident population growth in the late colonial era. Table 6.12 gives figures for three haciendas south of Cuernavaca, according to a listing of communicants in the parish of Xochitepec in 1779, and the Mazari census, conducted in the 1790s, which evidently included persons of all ages and racial classifications. Still other figures, given in Table 6.13, show the remarkable population growth on the two most important haciendas of eastern Morelos, Santa Ana Tenango and Santa Clara Montefalco, as well as the continuing importance of slavery on these estates as late as 1768.

Table 6.11
Hacienda Populations, Communicants, Cuautla, 1777–1797

Hacienda	Date	Españoles #	%	Indians #	%	Mulattoes, Lobos Negroes #	%	Mestizos #	%	Indeterminate and Other #	%	Total	% change 1777–1797	Military Padrón Population, 1791 (non-Indians)
Buenavista	1777	9	9.2	0	—	89	90.8	0	—	0	—	98	—	155
	1797	10	5.4	27	14.7	108	58.7	11	6.0	28	15.2	184	+ 87.8	
Calderón	1777	9	4.0	19	8.4	199	87.7	0	—	0	—	227	—	256
	1797	11	3.7	61	20.6	174	58.8	18	6.1	32	10.8	296	+ 30.4	
Casasano	1777	12	5.7	34	16.2	117	55.7	47	22.4	0	—	210	—	561
	1797	15	3.3	29	6.5	354	78.8	28	6.2	23	5.1	449	+113.8	
Cuahuixtla	1777	8	2.4	85	25.4	195	58.2	47	14.0	0	—	335	—	512
	1797	9	2.2	24	6.0	270	67.2	63	15.7	36	9.0	402	+ 20.0	
Hospital	1777	6	2.0	45	14.8	201	66.1	52	17.1	0	—	304	—	419
	1797	26	9.3	40	14.3	139	49.8	34	12.2	40	14.3	279	– 8.2	
Santa Inés	1777	2	2.5	25	31.6	37	46.8	15	19.0	0	—	79	—	220
	1797	11	4.6	39	16.3	158	65.8	27	11.3	5	2.1	240	+203.8	
Tenextepango	1777	29	6.0	144	30.0	128	26.7	76	15.8	103	21.5	480	—	462
	1797	17	2.8	153	25.0	333	54.4	54	8.8	55	9.0	612	+ 27.5	

Sources: 1777: AGNBN, leg. 403, exp. 20; 1797: GSU, microfilm, roll 641–728.

150

Table 6.12

Hacienda Populations, Parish of Xochitepec, 1779–1790s

Hacienda	Communicants, 1779								Popu- lation 1790s
	Españoles		Indians		Mulattoes & Lobos		Mestizos		
	#	%	#	%	#	%	#	%	Total	
El Puente	31	8.7	129	36.1	180	50.4	17	4.8	357	615
Chiconcoac	17	8.5	99	49.5	84	42.0	0	0	200	172
Temisco	14	4.2	92	27.5	208	62.3	20	6.0	334	624

Sources: GSU, microfilm, roll 641–733; Mazari, "Un antiguo padrón."

It is impossible to measure precisely the proportion of their labor needs that hacendados could cover by employing persons already residing on their estates. Surviving account books usually do not indicate whether or not individual workers were hacienda residents. Ward Barrett has calculated the productive capacities of major haciendas in the 1790s and the number of field and mill workers, each contributing 315 workdays per year, required to produce those amounts. These figures are indicated in Table 6.14. However, the seasonal nature of the sugar industry, requiring particularly heavy labor inputs during the harvest and milling season, permits only tentative conclusions to be drawn from these estimates. If they hoped to produce at capacity levels, most late colonial hacendados had to continue seeking temporary workers during peak periods. Nevertheless, it is possible to conclude that on such haciendas as Hospital, Casasano, Tenextepango, and Cuahuixtla the number of adult male residents permitted owners to meet a significant portion of their labor requirements from within the bounds of their estates. Of course, some of these residents probably did not work in sugar production. On the other hand, it is quite likely that some female residents performed field labor and other chores; certainly female slaves were so employed on a routine basis. Children also worked in the fields, usually beginning about the age of eight.[100]

The presence of growing resident labor forces, together with the persistent tendency of highland Indians to migrate temporarily or permanently to the sugar haciendas, reduced the hacendados' dependence on neighboring lowland villages for workers. The Indian communities of the sugar region could not avoid other types of relationships

Table 6.13
Hacienda Populations, Eastern Morelos, 1768–1790s

| | Communicants, 1768 | | | | | | | | | | | | Population, 1790s |
| | Slaves | | Free Mulattoes and Lobos | | Mestizos | | Indians | | Other | | Total | |
Hacienda	#	%	#	%	#	%	#	%	#	%		
Santa Ana Tenango	141	38.5	154	42.1	37	10.1	28	7.7	6	1.6	366	660
Santa Clara Montefalco	88	23.9	165	44.8	45	12.2	65	17.7	5	1.4	368	998

Sources: GSU, microfilm, roll 641–723; Mazari, "Un antiguo padrón."

Table 6.14
Hacienda Labor Needs and Resident Labor Forces, Late Eighteenth Century

Hacienda	Productive Capacity, 1790s, Tons	Estimated Field/Mill Workers Required	Adult Males, 1770s	Adult Males, 1790s	Population, 1790s
Atlacomulco	265	233	—	72[c]	230[a]
Barreto	155	136	—	—	416[a]
Apanquesalco	115	101	—	30[c]	70[a]
Buenavista	125	111	40	85	184[b]
Calderón	175	156	81	113	296[b]
Casasano	175	156	75	154	449[b]
Chiconcoac	125	111	66	44[c]	172[a]
Cocoyoc	230	202	—	56[c]	181[a]
Cuahuixtla	175	156	114	175	402[b]
Dolores	145	128	—	—	44[a]
Hospital	175	156	95	137	278[b]
El Puente	195	174	139	167[c]	616[b]
San Gaspar	178	157	—	100[c]	284[a]
San Carlos	95	84	—	77[c]	240[a]
Pantitlán	155	136	—	139[c]	373[a]
Santa Clara Montefalco	400	352	—	178[c]	998[a]
Santa Ana Tenango	400	352	—	211[c]	660[a]
Santa Inés	175	156	23	109	220[b]
Tenextepango	175	156	163	257	602[b]
Temisco	365	325	90	159[c]	624[a]

Sources: Barrett, "Morelos," 163, 168; GSU, microfilm, rolls 641–728, 641–733; Mazari, "Un antiguo padrón"; AGNBN, leg. 403, exp. 20.
[a]From Mazari census; includes all ages and ethnic groups.
[b]From ecclesiastical padrón; excludes children under approximately age ten.
[c]Number of vecinos, according to Mazari census.

with neighboring haciendas, however. These relationships profoundly affected the history of the lowland villages. Chapter 7 surveys the process of internal political and social change within major Indian communities of the lowlands, especially in the Cuautla and Yautepec Valleys, where local leaders had long experience in adapting to the presence of sugar haciendas and other forms of commercial agriculture.

7

The Indian Villages of Late Colonial Morelos

As Ward Barrett has observed, Morelos was unique among sugar-producing regions in the Western Hemisphere in that it remained an important center of indigenous population even after the establishment of sugar estates.[1] In Brazil, the islands of the Caribbean, and even other parts of Mexico, European colonists built sugar plantations in tropical lowlands whose native population had been virtually obliterated by the combined effects of exotic diseases and the rigors of conquest. In Morelos, some villages indeed disappeared as a result of governmentally ordered resettlement, land appropriations by sugar hacendados, or the continued scourge of epidemic disease. However, other communities dating from before the Spanish—or even the Aztec—conquests endured as Indian pueblos for hundreds of years following the establishment of the sugar industry on lands once used by the villages.

Nevertheless, the presence of the haciendas and other forms of commercial agriculture profoundly affected the social and political development of these villages. Most obviously, hacendados and labradores in periods of economic expansion attempted to encroach on land and water vital to the economic base of the villages. Moreover, sugar estates and labradores' farms attracted migrants of every racial category to the region. Hacendados imported large numbers of African slaves, whose

Afro-Mexican descendants moved into the Indian towns when opportunities arose. Indian newcomers often increased the tribute liabilities
of their host communities, as the experience of Yautepec in the early
seventeenth century, discussed in Chapter 3, illustrates. When they
settled in the pueblos, Indian migrants might demand allocations of
community land or challenge long-established bargains with neighboring landowners. Finally, the major Indian cabeceras became important centers of local trade and artisan activity, providing a wide range
of services to the surrounding haciendas and ranchos.

The present chapter analyzes social processes and deliberate strategies that enabled towns situated in the heart of the sugar-producing
region to survive as "Indian" communities for hundreds of years despite
the multiple influences of sugar haciendas and other threats to their
economic base and their political and social identity. By the end of the
colonial period the leaders of each village had formulated their own
distinctive stance toward non-Indian residents, toward others with
whom villagers competed for land and water, and toward Indian commoners living in the villages. Although gobernadores often compro-
mised their communities' identities as "Indian" villages by making
intricate and extensive bargains with hacendados and other gente de
razón, these same leaders might initiate or sustain conflicts with non-
Indians when it served their interests. The particular posture of each
village often reflected the specific pattern of social and agricultural
development in its immediately surrounding area. The most complex
patterns of adaptation appeared in the Yautepec and Cuautla valleys,
where the influence of non-Indians and of sugar haciendas had been
longer and more pervasive than anywhere else in Morelos.

By the end of the colonial period, non-Indian residents outnumbered
Indians in virtually every major town in Morelos, as the figures in Table
7.1 indicate. In communities such as Oaxtepec, Yautepec, and Cuautla,
gente de razón had comprised an important sector of town population
for over two hundred years. Documents dating from the late sixteenth
and early seventeenth centuries are replete with references to españoles
and mestizos who identified themselves as vecinos of these pueblos.[2]
As the colonial period advanced, more and more mulattoes joined
them in the towns. While many of these gente de razón were farmers,
others occupied important economic niches providing products and
services to the haciendas and to their fellow townsmen. A typical towns-

Table 7.1
Non-Indian Residents of Selected Towns, Circa 1795

Town	Total population	No. of non-Indians	% of total population
Jantetelco	890	666	74.8
Cuernavaca	2,722	1,985	72.9
Tlaltizapán	591	404	68.4
Oaxtepec	323	213	65.9
Miacatlán	267	172	64.4
Yautepec	1,570	908	57.8
Jonacatepec	1,850	956	51.7
Yecapixtla	1,717	740	43.1
Tepoztlán	2,851	223	7.8

Source: Mazari, "Un antiguo padrón."

man was Nicolás de León, a *calderero*, or maker of cauldrons used in the sugar haciendas, who lived in Cuautla in the late seventeenth century.[3] The military census of Cuautla's non-Indian population, taken in 1791, records the presence of numerous artisans and specialized tradesmen in the town. An ethnic and occupational breakdown of the census is given in Table 7.2.

The numbers of non-Indian residents in the towns evidently grew slowly but steadily in the seventeenth century and more rapidly during the final century of colonial rule. Baptismal registers from Yautepec show that the proportion of non-Indians living in the villa of Yautepec or in one of its Indian barrios remained relatively small until after 1670, when the gente de razón began to multiply at a faster rate. Table 7.3 shows the numbers of children baptized in Yautepec and listed as residents of the villa or one of the barrios. The Indians' share of baptisms dropped sharply in the 1690s, probably as a result of that decade's epidemics. Although the Indian population apparently recovered somewhat after 1710, its share of baptisms in the town of Yautepec never returned to the levels prevailing before 1690. The figures for Indians again declined in the 1740s, rose briefly in the 1760s as a result of Indian migration into Yautepec, and then continued to fall. Meanwhile, the number of mulatto town residents increased steadily from the seven-

Table 7.2
Ethnic and Occupational Structure, Adult Males in Cuautla, 1792

Category	Españoles #	% of category	Mestizos and Castizos #	% of category	Pardos #	% of category
Merchants (traficantes, tenderos comerciantes)	19	90.5	1	4.8	1	4.8
Priests, Clerics	13	100.0	0	0	0	0
Misc. "Literate" Occupations	17	81.0	2	9.5	2	9.5
Skilled or Specialized Trades						
Carpenters	11	57.9	4	21.1	4	21.1
Tailors	13	61.9	0	0	8	38.1
Silversmiths	4	80.0	1	20.0	0	0
Blacksmiths	5	35.7	3	21.4	6	42.9
Masons	0	0	3	30.0	7	70.0
Teamsters	2	18.2	3	27.3	6	54.5
Bakers	4	25.0	5	31.3	7	43.8
Makers, Suppliers of Misc. Consumer Goods	4	14.8	7	25.9	16	59.3
Misc.	3	25.0	3	25.0	6	50.0
Total Trades	46	34.1	29	21.5	60	44.4
Sirvientes	6	35.3	4	23.5	7	41.2
Trabajadores	44	20.8	53	25.0	115	54.2
Total Adult Males	145	34.6	89	21.2	185	44.2

Source: AGNP, vol. 8.

teenth century forward with the exception of the 1760s and 1770s. From the 1770s until the end of the century, Indians accounted for between 36 and 43 percent of baptisms of Yautepec residents. This proportion corresponds well with the census of circa 1795, summarized in Table 7.1, according to which Indians comprised just over 42 percent of the town's population. That census, which counted 662 Indians in Yautepec, corroborates, in turn, an ecclesiastical padrón of 1807, which recorded 620 Indian communicants in the town.[4]

Table 7.3
Baptisms, Residents of the Villa and Barrios of Yautepec, 1660–1798

Period	Indians		Españoles		Mestizos and Castizos		Mulattoes, Moriscos, and Lobos		Indeterminate or other	
	#	%	#	%	#	%	#	%	#	%
1660–69	247	89.8	14	5.1	4	1.5	5	1.8	5	1.8
1670–79	194	75.2	23	8.9	6	2.3	15	5.8	20	7.8
1680–89	263	76.0	18	5.2	14	4.0	19	5.5	32	9.2
1705–9	124	47.7	36	13.8	33	12.7	24	9.2	43	16.5
1710–19	316	56.5	51	9.1	88	15.7	81	14.5	23	4.1
1720–29	358	55.8	32	5.0	98	15.3	139	21.7	15	2.3
1730–39	425	56.9	36	4.8	92	12.3	177	23.7	17	2.3
1740–49	406	50.1	49	6.0	102	12.6	210	25.9	43	5.3
1750–59	346	48.7	56	7.9	104	14.6	192	27.0	13	1.8
1760–69	377	56.6	37	5.6	85	12.8	134	20.1	33	5.0
1770–79	286	43.3	34	5.2	151	22.9	169	25.6	20	3.0
1780–86	178	40.8	26	6.0	65	14.9	154	35.3	13	3.0
1797–98	44	36.4	8	6.6	12	9.9	56	46.3	1	0.8

Source: Yautepec Parish Registers, GSU, microfilm, rolls 655–833, 655–834, 655–835, 655–836, 655–837, 655–838.

Other communities showed similar declines in their Indian populations during the eighteenth century. Indians accounted for about half
of the residents of Oaxtepec, according to samples taken of baptismal
registers of 1719–20, 1740, and the late 1780s.[5] By the final decade of
the century, however, census counts revealed only 110 Indian residents,
or about a third of the village's population. (See above, Table 7.1.)
Another count, made in 1807, found 137 Indians living in Oaxtepec.[6]
Two late colonial ecclesiastical censuses of Cuautla also reveal the extent
of non-Indian residence in that cabecera. While a wide discrepancy
appears in the numbers of españoles in the two censuses, they nonetheless document the decline in the Indian population and the corresponding increase in the numbers of mulattoes. Table 7.4 summarizes the
results of these two padrones.

Evidence from the Cuautla censuses, combined with other information, indicates that the Indian population of some towns declined in
absolute as well as proportional terms during the course of the eighteenth century. Counts of Indian tributaries in Oaxtepec offer a particularly striking example. That town's tributaries numbered 98 in 1627.[7]
Sixty years later, in 1686, that number had declined to 53. By 1729,
the total of tributaries had expanded to 65, a perceptible but hardly

Table 7.4
Communicants in Cuautla Cabecera, By Ethnic Group,
1777 and 1797

Category	1777		1797	
	#	%	#	%
Españoles	274	21.4	140	11.8
Indians	280	21.8	196	16.5
Mestizos	374	29.2	305	25.6
Castizos	44	3.4	36	3.0
Moriscos	49	3.8	19	1.6
Negroes	5	0.4	6	0.5
Lobos	52	4.1	36	3.0
Mulattoes	205	16.0	402	33.8
Indeterminate	0	—	50	4.2
Total	1283	101.1[a]	1190	100

Sources: 1777: AGNBN, leg. 403, exp. 20; 1797: GSU, microfilm, roll 641–728.
[a]Due to rounding, total exceeds 100.

surprising increase in an era of rapid Indian population growth.[8] The town's Indian tributary population declined substantially during the next half-century, numbering only 41 in 1785.[9] Furthermore, the census taken in the 1790s revealed the presence of 44 Indian vecinos, or householders, while the assessment of 1796 counted 37.5 Indian tributaries in Oaxtepec.[10] Similarly, the tributary population of Yautepec and the four towns that were its sujetos for tributary purposes (Itzamatitlán, Oacalco, Istoluca, and Tlaltizapán) expanded rapidly during the first quarter of the eighteenth century but climbed only minimally thereafter. From a count of 391.5 in 1707, the towns' total rose to 527 in 1729 and to 533 in 1785.[11]

Several factors account for these limitations on Indian population increase, despite substantial immigration of Indians into the region during the eighteenth century. As the figures in Appendix 2 demonstrate, heavy Indian mortality often canceled out rising numbers of Indian baptisms in Yautepec. In particular, epidemics of matlazáhuatl, smallpox, and measles influenced both the rate of population growth and its ethnic composition, because for whatever reason these diseases usually took heavier tolls among Indians than among gente de razón. Thus Indian burials in Yautepec often show a proportionate rise in those years when excessive mortality indicates the occurrence of an epidemic.

Moreover, fluctuations in the proportion of Indians among all children baptized in Yautepec confirm at least indirectly the importance of late colonial epidemics in limiting Indian population growth. (See Appendix 2.) At first glance these fluctuations appear so erratic that one is tempted to discount the figures' validity. Yet, on closer inspection, one can discern a definite rhythm that gives a clue to the origins of the fluctuations. The percentage of Indian baptisms dropped sharply at intervals of about seventeen years after major epidemics. For example, Indian baptisms first fell below 50 percent in 1754, exactly seventeen years after the matlazáhuatl epidemic of 1737. Their percentage again dropped sharply in 1764, seventeen years after the first of the major smallpox epidemics of the eighteenth century. In 1779, again seventeen years after the smallpox outbreak of 1762, baptisms of Indians fell under 40 percent for the first time. The sharp rise in the number of Indian baptisms in 1781, when Indians accounted for 56.9 percent of all baptisms, was itself a response to the severity of the smallpox epidemic of 1779–80. The Indians' share then hovered around 50 percent until it fell precipitously in 1796—again, seventeen years after the deadly epidemic of 1779.

Available evidence indicates that Indians in eighteenth-century Mexico married young, usually before entering their twenties.[12] Therefore, the deaths of many infants and small children could be expected to produce a drop in baptisms approximately seventeen years after an epidemic. Although infant deaths were often offset by high birth rates during the year following a major epidemic, deaths of children already weaned produced no compensatory increase in their mothers' fertility. Epidemics of these "childhood diseases" resulted in what Elsa Malvido has called *generaciones huecas*, or lost generations.[13] The marked severity of measles and smallpox in Morelos served to contain Indian population growth despite heavy migration into the region.

The importance of smallpox, measles, and other causes of infant and child mortality in limiting Indian population growth might also be inferred from the fact that in most Morelos communities Indian households contained fewer persons than those of gente de razón. Table 7.5 shows the number of *almas* (literally, "souls") per householder, or vecino, in towns listed in the census of the 1790s published by Manuel

Table 7.5
Household Size, Circa 1795

Town	Persons Per Household	
	Indians	Non-Indians
Jiutepec	2.73	2.38
Tepoztlán	2.97	4.05
Yautepec	2.40	3.43
Yecapixtla	2.78	4.28
Oaxtepec	2.50	3.87
Jonacatepec	3.21	6.73
Jantetelco	2.24	4.01
Tlaquiltenango	2.67	4.30
Tlaltizapán	3.02	3.88
Miacatlán	2.07	4.00
Achichipico	2.46	3.64
San Mateo Tetecala	2.28	3.21

Source: Mazari, "Un antiguo padrón."

Mazari. Only in Jiutepec did the number of Indian persons per vecino exceed the ratio for gente de razón. The figures for Oaxtepec and Yautepec are corroborated by the census of those towns' Indian population taken in 1807. The average Indian household sizes recorded in that census are listed in Table 7.6. Although further research is necessary to determine the extent to which cultural factors may have influenced household sizes among various ethnic groups in colonial Mexico, it is reasonable, for the time being, to assume that heavier mortality among Indian children accounted for a significant portion of the difference between Indian and non-Indian households.

The sharply limited growth in the number of Indian tributaries in Yautepec, Oaxtepec, and Cuautla cannot be attributed exclusively to the effects of disease, however. Other pueblos in Morelos, subject to the same epidemiological influences, showed increases in the numbers of their Indian tributaries during the course of the eighteenth century. In what is now western Morelos, Tlatenchi and Panchimalco experienced considerable growth in their Indian tributary populations. According to Villaseñor y Sánchez's survey of the 1740s, Tlatenchi's population numbered 74 Indian families, while Panchimalco had 26; neither town reported any non-Indian residents.[14] An ecclesiastical census of 1779 listed 106 Indian families for Tlatenchi, 62 for Panchimalco, and still no gente de razón for either pueblo.[15] In eastern Morelos, the Indian populations of both Jantetelco and Jonacatepec increased by nearly 50 percent between 1729 and 1785. Jantetelco's tributary count rose from 53.5 to 78.5, that of Jonacatepec from 159.5 to 231.[16]

The limited growth of the Indian tributary population in such com-

Table 7.6
Indian Household Size, 1807

Place	Persons per Household
Yautepec, barrio de Santiago	2.48
Yautepec, barrio de San Juan	2.44
Pueblo of Oacalco	2.09
Pueblo of Itzamatitlán	2.34
Oaxtepec	2.40

Source: AGNHJ, leg. 356, exp. 8.

munities as Oaxtepec, Yautepec, and Cuautla owed as much to deliberate political decisions made by village leaders as to the continued
effects of epidemic disease. In 1806, the teniente of Yautepec commented that the gobernador of Oaxtepec and his close associates had
carefully controlled allocation of the community's lands, reserving the
best plots for themselves or for favored non-Indian tenants. Indian
immigrants received at most a house site and a single fruit tree to
sustain their families. These meager resources proved inadequate to
satisfy the many exactions demanded by the gobernador. Not surprisingly, the unwelcomed migrants soon departed Oaxtepec. Similar
favoritism characterized the distribution of land in Yautepec and other
communities.[17]

Indian leaders had ample reason to deny community agricultural
lands and even house sites to Indian commoners in order to rent them
to gente de razón. They used the funds paid by tenants of these resources for a variety of purposes, selfish and public spirited. For example, rental of Jiutepec's community lands to the hacienda San Gaspar
paid the one-hundred peso annual salary of the village schoolmaster.[18]
The principales of Oaxtepec rented a portion of land to the hacienda
Cocoyoc between 1797 and 1805. Part of the proceeds underwrote
repairs on the parish church and the costs of the community's continuing water dispute with Pantitlán, but the gobernador and at least six
other Indian leaders found a way to appropriate the remainder of the
money for themselves. They claimed that the land in question was
really their personal property, inherited from their ancestors. Although
documents from the early and mid-eighteenth century do not support
this contention, the audiencia upheld their position in a decision rendered in 1810. The principales then divided more than 4,200 pesos
among themselves. In their own defense, the leaders pointed out that
they had often dipped into their own pockets to pay for church repairs
and other community needs.[19]

Not all tenants of village lands provided such substantial funds to
serve either the public needs of the community or the private desires
of local leaders. By the late colonial period the legal bases by which
gente de razón occupied house sites had long been obscured by the
passage of time and the evolution of custom. Although those who
acquired solares in the late sixteenth and early seventeenth centuries
often did so by promising to pay annual stipends to the Indian com-

munities, with time many gente de razón found ways to claim virtual ownership of their plots. An incident in Cuautla provides one example of how such transfers occurred. Don Pedro de la Cruz, gobernador of the town in 1721, claimed as his personal property a vacant lot at the edge of the pueblo. He had inherited the plot from his father-in-law, who had in turn purchased it from its previous owner for one hundred pesos. When de la Cruz needed funds to pay tributes and the expenses of his wife's funeral, he borrowed sixty pesos from Mateo Ramírez, a Spanish vecino of Cuautla. Because he was unable to repay Ramírez, the land was placed on public auction in 1725, with the understanding that de la Cruz would use the proceeds to satisfy his debt. Because no Indian entered a bid, Ramírez was allowed to take possession of the land.[20]

By the end of the eighteenth century non-Indian vecinos of Cuautla reported a variety of bases for their occupation of solares. Several claimed outright ownership of their plots, while others rented from individual Indians rather than from the community. At least ten persons paid rents, ranging from ten reales to twelve pesos per year, to the community of Cuautla. The total amount paid by these ten tenants was forty-two pesos, two reales per year. Others, including three men sharing the surname Rebolledo, simply occupied house sites without either claiming ownership or paying rent. Moreover, at least two individuals occupied solares by virtue of rents paid annually to a cofradía, a practice well established for at least a century. Still other gente de razón, such as the mulatto Antonio Reyes, received allotments from the Indian community because they were married to Indian women. Some of Cuautla's non-Indian residents were evidently so long established in the town that local landmarks were named after them. For example, an español named José Manso, who paid the Indians four pesos per year for the use of a solar, lived on the street known locally as the "Calle de los Mansos."[21]

The occupation of community lands by gente de razón could spark considerable confusion and controversy, particularly as land values rose during the late colonial period. An example from Yautepec illustrates the complicated nature of non-Indian tenure in the Indian towns. In 1798 an Indian named María Luisa Suasa ceded her solar to a mulatto, Juan Tilapa, who paid her a lump sum of forty or fifty pesos. The two parties evidently viewed their transaction as a sale, rather than a lease.

Nonetheless, Tilapa, and later his widow, Rita Valero, paid the town's Indian gobernador four pesos per year as interest on a censo perpetuo imposed on the solar. Tilapa and Valero did not use the land themselves; instead they rented it to a succession of modest mestizo and mulatto sugarcane cultivators, each of whom paid fifteen pesos per year in rent. In 1808, the newly elected gobernador of Yautepec, Vicente Bejarano, who was also the nephew of the now deceased María Luisa Suasa, seized the solar and declared it communal property, but in fact appropriated it for his own use.

During the next several years, Rita Valero attempted to regain control of the site through legal action. Don Vicente Gil, a former gobernador of Yautepec and avowed opponent of Bejarano, supported Valero's claim. His testimony revealed his understanding of the complicated legal status of non-Indian landholdings in the town. He conceded that the solar in question, as well as other property used by both Indians and gente de razón, could not in fact be bought or sold because, he believed, they belonged to the entailed estate (*vínculo*) of the Marqués del Valle. Nonetheless, in Yautepec the custom had developed by which gente de razón were allowed to plant community lands in maize, indigo, and other crops. In return, they paid stipends, like those paid by Rita Valero, to the native gobernadores, who used the money to meet community expenses, including the support of a primary school. Holders of such plots freely bought and sold usufruct rights to the land, together with improvements such as houses, corrals, and orchards. Despite the claim of Valero's opponents, that only Indians should have use of solares within the *fundo legal*, or six hundred-vara radius of Indian towns, the Audiencia of Mexico upheld her case.[22]

Although individual leaders might attempt to withdraw specific concessions to particular gente de razón, late colonial caciques of many communities had developed intricate networks of compromise—tempered by conflict when it served their interests—with hacendados and other holders of political and economic power. Don Alberto Reymundo de Alva, gobernador of Yautepec in the 1760s and 1770s, cultivated bonds of economic alliance, friendship, and even compadrazgo (ritual kinship) with influential gente de razón. He and his wife, who was a mulatta, chose local officials and hacienda administrators to be godparents for several of their children. Cayetano Ortega, teniente of Yautepec in the early 1770s and tenant of the haciendas Pantitlán and Oacalco a decade later, thus became Alva's compadre in 1778. Manuel Pellón, a gachupín and professional hacienda administrator, served as godfather for two other children born to the couple. Sometime after 1768, Don Alberto even attempted briefly to join the hacendado ranks himself, building a trapiche on lands he rented from the community at sixty pesos per year. Meanwhile he borrowed funds from hacendado Rodrigo del Valle, in order to purchase a new bell for the town's church and to finance his personal agricultural ventures. Unable to repay, Don Alberto evidently ceded to del Valle title to the land on which he had built his trapiche. After del Valle's death, in the early 1780s, Alva drew on his friendship with the current teniente, Manuel Francisco del Cerro, to avoid paying other debts he owed to the hacendado's estate.[23]

Leaders in such communities as Yautepec, Oaxtepec, and Cuautla found strong reason to cooperate with the gente de razón living in their midst as well as with landholders in the surrounding region. Tenants of community lands provided much-needed cash, while alliances with hacendados and local officials might help leaders attain some of their personal ends. Yet other factors worked to undermine such compromises in the late colonial period. Chief among these forces was the rising value of land and water, which sparked the kind of confrontations discussed in Chapter 5. The arrival of Indian migrants also made it more difficult for village leaders to maintain long-standing agreements, even if they so wished. Immigrants and other commoners to whom leaders were unwilling or unable to allocate sufficient lands found little reason to support existing accommodations with hacendados and labradores. Their unsatisfied demands provided an excuse to question the legitimacy of incumbent village officials and to challenge their real or apparent bargains with hacendados or local officials.

For example, in the 1790s one faction in Cuautla's outlying barrio of Ahuehuepa accused former gobernador Anastasio Antonio of having been an ally of the alcalde mayor and other officials and of having been too subservient to the owners of neighboring haciendas, paying them rent and offering other concessions in order to use lands that belonged by right to the pueblo. It is likely, too, that Anastasio Antonio was not an Indian; a mestizo of that name was listed as a resident of Ahuehuepa in the Cuautla military census of 1791.[24] For their part, Anastasio Antonio and his adherents argued that the opposing faction, though headed by a former gobernador, was comprised largely of immigrants who had settled in Ahuehuepa after a recent agricultural crisis, presumably that of 1785–86. Their efforts to secure the barrio's elevation to the status of an independent pueblo, and with it the corresponding land allotments, threatened long-established bargains with local landowners.[25] A similar dispute also divided the cabecera of Cuautla during the first decade of the nineteenth century. Again, a faction of alleged outsiders accused their opponents of catering to the interests of hacendados and favored instead a more aggressive stance.[26]

The growing resident populations on the haciendas also contributed indirectly and unwittingly to an aggravation of hacienda-village conflict in the late colonial period. By this time, hacendados were increasingly able to draw on their resident populations to fill a major portion of their labor needs. Moreover, when they did need workers to supplement their resident labor forces, landowners found an ample supply of prospective employees in nearby highland communities. With these villages the sugar haciendas developed relationships approaching the kind of symbiosis identified by John Tutino elsewhere in central Mexico in the late colonial period. Central to the maintenance of those relationships, according to Tutino, was the communities' retention of enough land to meet their residents' needs for much of the year, but not so much that they could subsist without temporary recourse to hacienda labor. Income derived from hacienda jobs helped communities pay tributes and support religious functions that reinforced community identities. Thus, writes Tutino, haciendas and Indian pueblos in many of Mexico's central valleys grudgingly tolerated each other's existence.[27] So deeply entrenched was this symbiosis between highland villages and lowlands sugar haciendas that many of its features endured to the twentieth century.[28]

Sugar hacendados were less willing to maintain this kind of symbiotic relationship with communities in the lowlands, where the value of land and water provided powerful inducement to remove these resources from the control of villagers, whenever possible. In some instances, hacendados simply engulfed neighboring villages, seizing virtually all of their lands and forcing villagers to pay rent for the use of the expropriated land and to earn additional income from hacienda jobs. That hacendados were not averse to enlarging their resident populations in this manner can be inferred from a concession temporarily offered by the Dominicans of Cuahuixtla to the troublesome community of Zahuatlán El Viejo. (See above, Chapter 5.) The Dominicans expressed their willingness to allow the villagers to remain on lands claimed by Cuahuixtla, as long as they did so as tenants of the hacienda rather than as residents of a settlement claiming to be a corporate village.[29]

This process occurred most readily in small villages that were predominantly Indian in population, often located on the fringes of the sugar-growing region, where the interests of few gente de razón were likely to impede either the growth of the Indian population or the haciendas' encroachments on community lands. In eastern Morelos, Nicolás de Icazbalceta, owner of the enormous haciendas Santa Clara Montefalco and Santa Ana Tenango, moved blatantly in the late eighteenth century to appropriate virtually all of the land belonging to neighboring villages. Few prosperous gente de razón rented lands from these communities.[30] A comparable development took place in southwestern Morelos in the 1770s and 1780s, when Miguel Ascárate Gastelu, then owner of Hacienda Guadalupe, seized lands claimed by Panchimalco and forced the Indians to rent from him.[31]

In the Cuautla Valley, predominantly Indian communities such as Tetelcingo and Anenecuilco resisted complete absorption by the haciendas but still lost most of their lands to the estates. Village residents therefore had to seek hacienda jobs to supplement their earnings from subsistence agriculture.[32] Yet these villages' relationships with the haciendas hardly resembled the kind of symbiosis prevailing elsewhere in central Mexico. Hacendados showed little enthusiasm for these villagers' retention of lands sufficient for their support during a portion of the year.

Towns such as Cuautla, Oaxtepec, and Yautepec worked out different patterns of coexistence with neighboring haciendas. Hacendados had little choice but to accept these communities' retention of lands, but for reasons quite different from those of estate owners elsewhere in central Mexico. As long as a particular piece of land remained under the control of a town's Indian leaders, competing hacendados and labradores might hope to rent it by persuading the gobernador to terminate any existing lease. Certainly, Indian leaders were usually willing to accommodate a prospective tenant who made a tempting offer. Rather than creating a coherent and enduring symbiosis, compromises between sugar haciendas and neighboring Indian villages often assumed the character of makeshift arrangements, subject to modification with changes in village politics or in the value of local resources.

Deals made by leaders of major lowlands cabeceras with neighboring hacendados usually revolved around land, water, and special favors, and less often around labor recruitment. In any case, the towns' limited Indian populations hardly offered a large pool of potential workers. While many of the gente de razón living in these towns—such as the 212 men listed as *trabajadores* (workers) or *trabajadores del campo* (field workers) in Cuautla's census of 1791—probably worked on the haciendas, they almost certainly contracted independently with their employers, without use of the brokerage services usually performed when Indian leaders arranged jobs for their villagers.[33] Cuautla's Indian leaders therefore held no direct claim on wages earned by these gente de razón.

Whatever their specific adjustments to the presence of gente de razón and commercial estates, villages throughout Morelos faced powerful threats to their continued juridical and cultural identity as "Indian" communities. For some smaller, predominantly Indian villages, the danger lay in the possibility that surrounding haciendas would simply absorb them, converting them into settlements of resident peons. For major lowlands cabeceras, on the other hand, the limitations on Indian population growth seemed to augur their de facto conversion to Spanish and mestizo farming communities in which well acculturated Indian leaders served as intermediaries in allocating land and other resources among Indian villagers and non-Indian tenants. Most lowlands village leaders were proficient in Spanish, able to make court depositions without any assistance from an interpreter. Many, like the *"sumamente ladino"* ("highly fluent in Spanish") Alberto Reymundo de Alva of Yautepec, were married to gente de razón; others were themselves mestizos or mulattoes.

Late colonial gobernadores readily alienated community lands to hacendados and labradores, seriously undermining the villages' capability to provide for the subsistence needs of Indian residents. Even when confronted with the prospect of losing all of their community lands to neighboring estates, some Indian leaders were willing to cooperate with hacendados in order to salvage a certain amount of gain for themselves and their friends. Gobernadores of the pueblos that lost their lands to Nicolás de Icazbalceta found that if they agreed to the rental arrangement they could at least control the allocation of the lands in question, reserving the best portions for themselves and their allies.[34]

At the same time, late colonial gobernadores consciously cultivated the form, if not the substance, of the traditional Indian community, protected by law against encroachments on its community lands and against other harassments by gente de razón. Allusions to the legally mandated, if often ignored, privileges and rights of Indian communities gave these leaders a recognized basis on which to advance their lawsuits against non-Indian rivals. Often with considerable justification, their adversaries discounted such claims, arguing that gobernadores who secured land or water concessions in the name of their communities appropriated those resources for themselves or ceded them to gente de razón rather than dedicating them to strengthening the economic base of their villages.

There can be no doubt that the Indian leaders of the late colonial period violated the spirit of laws designed to protect the landholdings of their communities. Yet their allusions to the "Indian" character of the villages were not always as cynical as their adversaries implied. Despite the pervasive influence of gente de razón and the self-serving behavior of highly acculturated native officals, the villages retained core populations still identifiably Indian in racial, cultural, and linguistic terms. Two factors, neither of them actively encouraged by village leaders, account for this phenomenon.

First, the available evidence suggests a remarkable tendency toward endogamy among Indian commoners, in marked contrast to their leaders. Table 7.7 shows percentages of Indian men and women marrying in Yautepec from 1680 to 1799 who selected Indian partners. Even amid the rapid social and economic change that occurred between 1770 and 1799, well over 80 percent of Indian women, and more than 90 percent of Indian men, married within their racial group. In contrast, mulattoes, while still quite endogamous, were more likely to choose mates of other classifications, usually mestizos. Even in Cuautla, where Indians were even more thoroughly surrounded by gente de razón than in Yautepec, they nonetheless demonstrated a persistent tendency toward endogamy, as revealed in the ecclesiastical padrón of 1797, summarized in Table 7.8. Without doubt, extensive racial mixture was an important feature in the social history of colonial Morelos, as the presence of so many mulattoes and mestizos clearly indicates. But the con-

Table 7.7
Endogamy Rates, Yautepec, 1680–1799

Period	Indians		Mulattoes	
	Men	Women	Men	Women
1680–89	98.5	89.1	29.2	53.8
1690–99	92.6	87.9	52.4	52.4
1700–9	95.7	91.7	73.3	50.0
1710–19	92.6	89.3	45.7	55.2
1720–29	98.6	96.3	63.6	58.3
1730–39	95.6	93.5	79.4	64.3
1737–44	86.5	90.1	68.6	66.7
1740–49	—	—	72.7	58.2
1750–59	99.1	91.0	72.5	76.7
1760–69	—	—	72.4	70.7
1770–79	91.9	85.1	55.6	50.5
1780–89	91.3	92.5	50.0	56.7
1790–99	91.0	84.6	62.7	69.3

Source: Yautepec Parish Registers, GSU, microfilm, rolls 655–850, 655–851.

sistency of Indian endogamy suggests that when Indians did form unions with gente de razón, they did so outside of church-sanctioned wedlock. Those who chose to have their relationships formally ratified by the church most often selected Indian partners, helping preserve, to some extent, the indigenous racial and cultural identity of their communities.

The second tendency contributing to the maintenance of the villages' "Indian" character was the continued migration of Indians from highland communities to the lowlands. Such migration persisted despite the gobernadores' attempts to discourage newcomers by denying them resources adequate to support their families. Nevertheless, when Indian migrants did manage to secure permanent homes and land allotments in their adopted villages, their presence enhanced to some degree the plausibility of the gobernadores' claims that their communities still merited special treatment as "Indian" villages. Moreover, migrants were often single young adults who reinforced the tendency toward endogamy by increasing the pool of eligible Indian mates for Indian natives of the lowlands villages. Finally, the migrants' poverty, their lack of

Table 7.8
Endogamy Rates, Cuautla, 1797

Category	Town of Cuautla	Haciendas in Cuautla Jurisdiction
Indian Men	79.4%	82.0%
Indian Women	90.9%	91.9%
Mulatto Men	66.6%	79.4%
Mulatto Women	81.1%	77.9%

Source: Archivo General de la Curia Metropolitana de Mexico, Padrón de las familias del partido de Cuautla Amilpas en el año de 1797, GSU, microfilm, roll 641–728.

sophistication, and their inability to speak Spanish placed a premium on the acculturated leaders' fluency in communicating, both literally and figuratively, with local holders of political and economic power. Whatever the gobernadores' conscious attitudes and actions toward Indian migrants, the presence of these newcomers was not wholly detrimental to the leaders' interests.

Without question the Indian leaders of late colonial Morelos abused their power and appropriated community resources for themselves, their close associates, or favored gente de razón. The very survival of their villages as "Indian" communities depended in part on social processes which they were powerless to prevent and even tried to discourage. Few if any village leaders could claim that they owed their positions to the operation of any sort of "grass roots democracy" in which the majority of community residents found their interests represented. Dissident factions complained repeatedly that priests, alcaldes mayores, tenientes, and hacendados interfered in village elections.[35] Despite governmental orders forbidding reelection to community posts, the same persons served as gobernadores year after year in many pueblos, or the positions rotated regularly among a small group of individuals.[36]

Yet the positions of late colonial village leaders were hardly enviable. They possessed no hereditary holdings comparable to those attached to the cacicazgos (cacique estates) of Oaxaca.[37] Whatever personal fortunes they enjoyed they held largely by virtue of their own skill at converting community assets into private patrimony and cultivating

alliances with persons in positions to do them favors. Their hold on
such assets often proved tenuous; their goods could be seized at any
time if they failed to meet tribute payments or other monetary obligations. The leaders themselves might be punished or jailed if they did
not pay their tributes or if they advanced community claims too asser-
tively. Their desire to evade such strictures helps explain their interest
in becoming compadres and friends of local officials.

These leaders' positions and their fortunes depended on a delicate
and judicious mix of conflict and compromise with hacendados and
other gente de razón. They stood ready to make continued adjustments
in this balance as changing circumstances warranted. A gobernador
might initiate a lawsuit against a neighboring landowner while invit-
ing the hacendado's administrator to become a compadre. Another
might condone a violent confrontation in defense of village water rights
while renting lands to the very hacendado who threatened their continued access to the same water. Then too, a village leader might form
economic alliances with local alcaldes mayores or tenientes while com-
plaining to higher authorities that those officials misused the prerogatives of their offices. Rectification of specific abuses may have been
less important to them than the simple need to remind local gente de
razón that there were limits to the Indians' patience.

Despite their rather precarious position, gobernadores of major cabeceras in Morelos nonetheless commanded a crucial balance of local
power. Even though for centuries the region had attracted sizable numbers of gente de razón, there were no Spanish municipal councils to
articulate, coordinate, and advance the interests of any segment of the
non-Indian community or to claim any voice in the distribution of land
and water resources. Aside from the two alcaldes mayores and their
handful of tenientes, Indian gobernadores and their councils held the
only duly constituted political authority in the region. They therefore
assumed roles as political and economic brokers that might not have
been theirs if local gente de razón had possessed well-defined vehicles
for settling disputes and allocating resources.

By the end of the colonial period the major Indian cabeceras of the
sugar-growing region hardly resembled the Indian villages envisioned
in colonial law. Instead they had become highly hispanized towns
where non-Indian vecinos outnumbered Indians. These towns provided
important support services for the sugar haciendas and ranchos of the

surrounding region. Despite the absence of formal political vehicles through which provincial merchants and labradores could articulate their concerns, such individuals played increasingly vocal roles in local affairs. Yet these communities still remained "Indian villages" in their formal political structure and in the strategies adopted by gobernadores to protect personal and community resources.

The accelerating pressure on regional land and water resources, the concurrent economic and political changes, the deteriorating position and resultant frustrations of labradores, and the ever-changing adaptations of Indian leadership combined to create a volatile political climate in many communities during the final decades of colonial rule. An additional source of tension lay in the fact that the colonial political order, based on the delegation of local government to Indian leaders under the supervision of the alcaldes mayores and their lieutenants, had become patently anachronistic. Indian officials and Spanish alcaldes mayores and tenientes proved increasingly able to handle the competing demands of the ethnically and occupationally diverse groups that comprised the villages' populations. The contradictions between the formal political institutions and the socioeconomic realities of the late colonial period are nowhere better illustrated than in a remarkable series of disputes that erupted in Yautepec after 1790. Chapter 8 turns to a detailed analysis of these controversies.

8

Political and Economic Struggle in Late Colonial Yautepec

As the preceding chapters have shown, the economic and demographic changes of the late colonial period had a significant impact on Morelos. Social tensions rose with the value of the region's land and water, as poorer labradores, Indian villagers, and even some hacendados found themselves at a disadvantage in the competition for those resources. Meanwhile, the region continued to attract immigrants whose arrival further complicated its social history. Yet the late colonial period witnessed other changes beyond the economic and demographic forces already considered. In response to the growing power of England following the Seven Years' War (1756-1763), King Charles III and his ministers fashioned a series of governmental changes designed to buttress what seemed to be Spain's increasingly precarious hold on its American colonies. Peninsulares quickly replaced creoles on audiencias and in other posts throughout the hemisphere, while the creation of local militia units symbolized the crown's mounting preoccupation with colonial defense. Regalist bureaucrats, with some cooperation from like-minded churchmen, introduced major changes in ecclesiastical administration, including the secularization of many parishes still under control of the regular clergy, limitations on certain forms of clerical privilege, and the sudden and spectacular expulsion of the Jesuits in 1767. Finally, reorganization of local government, implemented tardily in New Spain in 1786, brought the appearance if not the substance of change to virtually every provincial town in the realm.[1]

These so-called Bourbon Reforms added subtle but significant dimensions to the mounting social conflicts of late colonial Morelos. In particular, the transfer of parish administration from the regular to the secular clergy generated confusion and conflict over the disposition of property once designated for ecclesiastical purposes. New priests, sharing their parishioners' enthusiasm for profitable ventures in commercial agriculture, were not above exploiting the prerogatives of their positions to advance their own interests. Meanwhile, changes in local government, though producing few improvements in the conduct of officials, nonetheless served to raise popular dissatisfaction with continuing abuses.

Controversy surrounding these administrative changes combined with the concurrent economic and demographic changes to produce a volatile political situation. Nowhere is the interplay between political, social, and economic change better demonstrated than in Yautepec, where articulate but increasingly vulnerable labradores, a bitterly divided Indian community, and a handful of ambitious clerics and civil officials vied with one another and with owners of surrounding haciendas for control of land and of water for irrigation.

Much of Yautepec's conflict centered around water from a small stream originating in two *ojos*, or springs, called Ocopetlatla and Las Peñuelas. From the seventeenth century forward the town's Spanish and Indian vecinos had jealously guarded their claim to the spring water, which they said was "sweeter" than that drawn from the Yautepec River.[2] Evidently they enjoyed exclusive use of this water more or less continuously from the 1730s until the last quarter of the century, when enterprising labradores and hacendados in the surrounding area began diverting it to their own lands. A principal culprit was Father Manuel de Agüero, a secular priest who had set out to capitalize on the fruitful prospects for commercial agriculture immediately after his appointment as curate of Yautepec in 1772. The centerpiece of the padre's agricultural empire was the hacienda San Carlos Borromeo, which he acquired in the 1780s. However, Agüero also cultivated indigo and other crops on a piece of property called the Rancho de la Virgen, a portion of which bordered the conduit that carried water to the barrio of Santiago from Ocopetlatla and Las Peñuelas.[3]

Manuel Francisco del Cerro, teniente of the district between 1782 and 1792, emerged as the most powerful and vocal of Agüero's many competitors for the water. Beginning at least as early as 1786, Cerro cultivated indigo and sugarcane at Guausopán and later at ranchos rented from the owners of Pantitlán, diverting to these properties a portion of the water flowing from the ojos.[4] As a result, the Indians of Yautepec's barrio of Santiago, located downstream from both Agüero's Rancho de la Virgen and Cerro's lands, found their water supply sharply curtailed. In 1795 the Indians of the barrio, together with those gente de razón who also depended on the use of this water, formally protested Cerro's action. However, the former teniente's growing economic power, stemming from his commercial ventures, his ability to extend credit to local farmers, and his agricultural pursuits, gave him considerable leverage in defending his interests. He succeeded in persuading the townsfolk to allow him continued use of the water until he harvested his current crops. In return Cerro agreed to build a public fountain for the use of Yautepec's residents.[5]

Not content with this concession, early in the following year Cerro approached the vecinos of Yautepec, requesting access to the water for two additional seasons in return for his building a much-needed new prison, at an estimated cost of nine hundred pesos. Cerro promised to take only the amount absolutely necessary for his crops, allowing the surplus to flow to the barrio of Santiago. The array of witnesses who appeared before teniente Luis Antonio de Mesa y Herrera to testify for or against Cerro's proposal reveals the intense factionalization of local politics in Yautepec. Those who endorsed Cerro's plan included the local collectors of tithes and alcabalas, several labradores, the current Indian gobernador, a past gobernador, and the town's Indian notary (escribano). The Indians' stance is explained by the fact that these officials lived in the barrio of San Juan, located across the river from the villa of Yautepec and the barrio of Santiago. Residents of San Juan were therefore unable to use the water from Ocopetlatla and Las Peñuelas; they depended exclusively on the river for their agricultural and domestic needs. In addition to the fact that they had no vested interest in the water from the two ojos, the leaders of San Juan had other reasons for supporting Cerro. Sometime during 1796 Cerro lent them

Villa de Yautepec in the Eighteenth Century

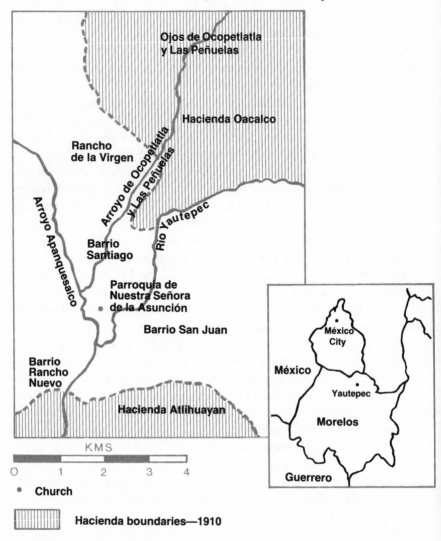

Church

Hacienda boundaries—1910

Sources: AGNHJ, vol. 73 (leg. 38), exp. 3; Yautepec Parish Registers, GSU, micro-film, roll 655-835, book 2, fols. 65, 81; Christopher R. Rounds, "From Hacienda to Ejido: Land Reform and Economic Development in Yautepec, Morelos, 1920–1970," Ph.D. diss., State University of New York, Stony Brook, 1977.

Dominican church of La Natividad at Tepoztlán, Morelos. Beginning in the late 1520s, the Dominicans built their first Indian mission in Morelos in Oaxtepec and then undertook the conversion of such surrounding communities as Yautepec and Tepoztlan. (Photograph by Michael Grizzard)

money for the payment of their tributes. In return they agreed to rent him an additional portion of community land, on which he cultivated indigo for at least the next ten years.

The Indians of Santiago, however, vigorously protested Cerro's proposition. They maintained that the town's prosperity depended on its continued access to the contested water. Probably with some justification, Cerro's supporters retorted that there would be enough water for him and for the townsfolk if the Indians of Santiago had not rented so much land to non-Indian labradores, who consumed great amounts of water.[6]

Cerro evidently failed to obtain as much water as he desired. Not only did he face the opposition from the Indians of Santiago, but Father Agüero also moved behind the scenes to secure additional water for irrigating the Rancho de la Virgen. On 3 March 1797, Agüero secured a decree from the Audiencia of Mexico permitting him to use the controverted water, provided that he permit a stipulated amount to flow into Yautepec for the domestic needs of the townspeople.[7] However, Cerro then persuaded the current teniente to ignore the audiencia's order. At the same time, local citizens, probably incited by Cerro, brought charges against Agüero for neglecting his clerical duties, for exacting excessive fees for those services he did perform, and for improperly administering the assets of the Cofradía de Nuestra Señora del Rosario, chief of which was the Rancho de la Virgen. While the Indians of Santiago and their tenants had blamed Cerro for the lack of sufficient water in the town, Cerro's allies now made similar accusations against Agüero, even charging that Agüero had contaminated the water which the town did receive. As a result, they said, several cases of leprosy (*mal de San Lázaro*) had been reported in Yautepec.[8]

The combined charges against Agüero brought him a lengthy suspension from his parish duties while ecclesiastical authorities conducted an investigation.[9] Agüero himself had mixed feelings about his forced removal to Mexico City. In 1799, he requested permission to return to Yautepec. Two years later, however, he penned an extraordinary appeal to his superiors, in which he vented his bitter feelings against his parishioners and begged for reassignment to a comfortable position in some other parish. He began his memorandum by describing the beauty of Yautepec and the fertility of its soil—the latter a subject with which he could certainly claim considerable firsthand experience. For much of his tenure in Yautepec, his parishioners had shown him nothing but love and obedience, asserted Father Agüero; donations from his flock had even enabled him to construct a new sugar mill at San Carlos Borromeo. In recent years, however, newcomers (*avenedizos*) to the parish had fomented opposition to their curate. As a result, Father Agüero had suffered *"la horrible tormenta de aquel lugar"* ("the horrible torment of that place"), from which he now asked relief. Until 1805, however, Agüero remained the nominal curate of Yautepec, though exiled in Mexico City. Meanwhile, his nephew, Nicolás Gómez, supervised his business affairs in Yautepec, including construction of a new aqueduct at San Carlos Borromeo.[10]

Father Agüero's protracted absence did not end the controversies surrounding the parish's administration or the disposition of its assets. Father Domingo Sancho Yerto, named coadjutor of Yautepec in 1797, proved no more popular with the town's disgruntled vecinos than his predecessor. Parishioners chided him for failure to adhere to published schedules stipulating fees for clerical services, and for maintaining a female companion, rumored to be his mistress. Finally in 1802, he resigned from his position in Yautepec, pleading reasons of health.[11] At least two other priests also ministered in Yautepec between 1797 and 1802. One of them, Bachiller Francisco de Urueta, was a relative of a locally prominent landowning family. Both he and his fellow assistant, Licenciado José Luis Núñez de Ibarra, became embroiled in the bitter factional divisions of Yautepec. In November 1797 a visiting priest named Cristóbal Gómez, curate of Tetela del Volcán and possibly a relative of Father Agüero, delivered a sermon in which he reportedly urged the local citizenry to live in peace with one another. Gómez's exhortations evidently served to arouse rather than calm the troubled community. A few days after the sermon, an anonymous broadside accusing Agüero, Urueta, and Núñez de Ibarra of atheism, Lutheranism, and other heresies appeared on the door of the church.[12]

Meanwhile, former teniente Cerro and his associates took advantage of Agüero's absence to seize the Rancho de la Virgen and the water used for its irrigation. In the spring of 1798, two labradores, both enemies of Agüero, prepared to plant crops at the rancho. One of them, Andrés Payes de San Julián, had been a prominent figure in Yautepec for at least forty years; his career aptly illustrates the pretensions and frustrations of modest labradores in late colonial Yautepec. As early as

1758 he and a partner had sublet 40 fanegas de sembradura (or about 350 acres) at Apanquesalco from Pedro Valiente, tenant of that hacienda and owner of Pantitlán. When his contract expired six years later, Payes de San Julián rented the badly deteriorated hacienda Temilpa for a mere three hundred pesos per year. According to his own account, he invested considerable sums in renovating the hacienda during the succeeding decade. Rather than resume sugar production, however, Payes de San Julián concentrated on indigo, which required less capital than sugar. Nevertheless, he claimed in 1775 that his hard work and expenditures had brought virtually no profit, leaving him with insufficient funds even to finance the coming year's planting.

In subsequent years Payes de San Julián pursued more modest agricultural ventures, while nurturing his political connections. In 1779, for example, he served as an aide to alcalde mayor Luis Francisco de Esparza. A decade later he was working as administrator of the hacienda Oacalco. In a dispute with Don Pedro Flores, a Mexico City merchant, tenant of the hacienda and his employer, Payes de San Julián accused teniente Cerro of trying to persuade Flores to terminate his contract two years before its stipulated expiration. In the late 1790s Payes de San Julián intermittently served as collector of alcabalas in Yautepec. Despite his earlier disagreement with teniente Cerro, Payes de San Julián was a well-known enemy of Father Agüero; according to local gossip he was the author of the scurrilous anticlerical broadside of 1797. His farming companion at the Rancho de la Virgen was a young labrador and merchant named Francisco del Soto, who was to play a significant role in town affairs during the coming decade.[13]

As Soto and Payes de San Julián plowed the rancho in the spring of 1798, Father Agüero's nephew, Nicolás Gómez, together with a number of armed men, tried to seize the property from them.[14] Although Cerro and his associates evidently thwarted Agüero on this occasion, they decided to strengthen their hold on the Rancho de la Virgen, hoping to keep the land, and, more important, its water, forever beyond the priest's grasp. Cerro's principal tactic was to revive interest in the long-defunct Cofradía de Nuestra Señora del Rosario, whose activities the rancho in theory supported. Since at least 1780, the cofradía had existed in name only. A close ally of Father Agüero had served continuously as its nominal mayordomo; even the pretext of his annual reelection was abandoned after 1787. In the spring of 1800, with encouragement from both Cerro and the current teniente, a faction of the town's Spanish vecinos, all claiming to be cofradía members, met to choose new officers for the organization. It should come as no surprise that they selected Cerro to be mayordomo. The two other officers elected were among those who had testified in favor of Cerro's jail proposal in 1796 and against Father Agüero's conduct the following year. Meanwhile, the audiencia upheld the reassertion of the cofradía's control over its assets by overruling Agüero's claim that with the organization's de facto abolition ownership of the lands reverted to the parish. For the next several years Cerro's ally Francisco del Soto farmed the Rancho de la Virgen, while presumably Cerro appropriated for himself an increased share of water from the contested ojos.[15]

In 1804 Father Agüero tried unsuccessfully to regain control of the rancho when Bachiller Manuel Muñoz, in charge of the parish for twenty-two months following Sancho Yerto's resignation, was transferred to Achichipico. Aguero then lobbied to have the parish entrusted to Father Antonio Caballero, who had agreed to make the Rancho de la Virgen available to him. Once in Yautepec, however, Caballero ignored his commitment to Agüero and even failed to insure that the exiled priest received his allotted monthly stipend from parish revenues.[16]

In the clash between Cerro and Agüero there surfaced a number of issues which sprang from the concurrent bureaucratic reorganization and economic growth of late colonial New Spain. Local opposition to Father Agüero focused on his enviable ability to turn current administrative and economic change to his own advantage. His success in appropriating cofradía assets for his own use owed much to the disruption in parish administration following its secularization in 1756.[17] In addition, Father Agüero associated himself with the state monopolies for the distribution of tobacco, playing cards, and gunpowder, another program designed by the Bourbon monarchy to generate increased colonial revenues. The local concessions for these commodities operated out of Agüero's residence. Although Agüero insisted that his controversial nephew, Nicolás Gómez, was the official holder of the distributorships, the angry vecinos of Yautepec viewed these activities as just another of the opportunistic curate's many schemes for self-enrichment.[18]

Manuel Francisco del Cerro was as typical a figure of the age as his clerical nemesis. Serving as teniente of Yautepec from 1782 to 1792,

Cerro survived the introduction of reforms in local government in 1786 with little apparent need to change his mode of operations. The reorganization divided the viceroyalty of New Spain into twelve districts, each supervised by an intendant. Magistrates in the old alcalde mayor seats now became subordinates of their respective intendants and adopted the new title of subdelegados. They continued as before to appoint lieutenants in principal towns in their jurisdictions. Those who formulated the reform hoped that its enactment would streamline local administration and curtail some of the abuses long associated with the alcaldes mayores and their tenientes, especially the repartimientos, or distributive monopolies of various commodities, which were usually viewed as a perquisite of local office.[19]

Although the reform placed the jurisdictions of Cuernavaca and, after 1793, Cuautla, under the general supervision of the intendant of Mexico, Marquesado territories were declared exempt from actual implementation of the change and in Cuernavaca the old title of alcalde mayor remained in use.[20] However, persons living in Manuel Francisco del Cerro's jurisdiction evidently hoped that he would modify his acquisitive behavior to conform to the stricter codes of official conduct advocated by the framers of the intendant system. In 1791, one of the teniente's bitter enemies observed that "with the establishment of the intendancies, the alcaldes mayores and their lieutenants have been forbidden to engage in any type of repartimiento." Nevertheless, like many of his counterparts in local government throughout late colonial New Spain, Cerro continued his commercial dealings virtually unchanged after 1786. His only concession to the "reform" was the occasional use of intermediaries in the conduct of his business affairs.[21]

The mutual antagonism between Agüero and Cerro went far beyond their contest for control of land and water. Aguero felt keenly the deterioration of clerical prestige that William B. Taylor has identified as an important social tendency in many localities during the late colonial period.[22] According to Agüero's embittered account, Cerro's supporters regularly feted their patron with banquets and comedies, evidently showing him a deference reserved in former times to the clergy. Father Agüero also pointed out Cerro's preponderant economic role in Yautepec. The former teniente's numerous loans to local farmers had given him liens on virtually all of their crops.[23]

Indeed, by the first decade of the nineteenth century at least one hacendado even found himself at the former teniente's mercy. Ignacio García Menocal, owner of Pantitlán, faced mounting debts, probably due in part to the growing competition for water among the agriculturalists of the Yautepec Valley. In 1797 he formed a partnership with Cerro, who paid several of his outstanding debts, supplied additional funds for the hacienda's daily operation, and took over its management. Cerro also agreed to forward a regular allowance to García Menocal and his two sons, all residing in Mexico City. During the next several years, Cerro invested heavily in the hacienda's operation and upkeep, particularly after a fire severely damaged the mill and the current crop in April 1801. When García Menocal's debts passed 94,000 pesos, Cerro demanded that he repay in full within five years or surrender ownership of the hacienda to him. Although Cerro ultimately failed to realize his bid for membership in the hacendado elite, he reduced García Menocal to the point of begging for increased stipends to enable him and his sons to live in a style befitting their social standing.[24]

With a once-powerful hacendado at his mercy, Cerro had secured an enviable position in the socioeconomic hierarchy of late colonial Yautepec. His triumph appears to have been short-lived, however; after about 1807 he seems to have disappeared from the area. Father Agüero returned there in 1805, but continued as before to devote more time to his business affairs in Mexico City than to his clerical duties in his parish. Finally, in July 1807, he retired permanently from Yautepec, this time to accept a comfortable sinecure as a prebendary in the Mexico City cathedral.[25]

Retreat of both men from Yautepec brought no end to the town's internal squabbles, although the arrival of a new curate in the fall of 1807 seemed at first to signal a more peaceful era in local politics. On 27 November, the town's two Indian barrios, in a rare gesture of harmony, united to welcome a governmental decree restoring the water of Ocopetlatla and Las Peñuelas to the town. The decree posed an immediate threat to the interests of Francisco del Soto, the partisan of Cerro who had succeeded in cultivating the Rancho de la Virgen. Soto had recently irrigated the rancho, perhaps because Cerro no longer needed the water he had once disputed so bitterly with Father Agüero. The new curate, José Mariano Ruíz Calado, was able to bring about a compromise between Soto and the two Indian barrios. The Indians allowed Soto to use half the water during nighttime hours until he harvested his current crop, valued at eight thousand pesos. In gratitude, Soto gave them two hundred pesos in cash.[26]

Within less than a year the persistent competition among all agriculturalists in the area, together with the chronic divisions within the Indian community, shattered this brief accord. The continuing ambitions of Francisco del Soto sparked a new round of controversy, which took on added intensity during the politically charged year of 1808. Evidently Soto was not satisfied with the temporary concession given him by the Indians in the fall of 1807. He hoped to continue farming indefinitely at the Rancho de la Virgen, which reportedly brought him gross annual receipts of more than twelve thousand pesos. Soto's enmity focused on Manuel de Porras, teniente of Yautepec since 1806, who had supported a move to grant exclusive use of the water from Ocopetlatla and Las Peñuelas to the Indians of Santiago and their tenants. Moreover, Porras had removed Soto from his position as collector of alcabalas and charged him with mishandling royal funds. Porras had also enraged Soto and other labradores by forcing them to sell him their maize at low prices, even though they had already contracted to sell to others. He had then marketed the maize outside the region where it fetched higher prices, depriving the labradores of their chances for profit and creating artificial local shortages.

During 1808, Porras's enemies undertook a concerted campaign to remove him from office, citing his dealings in maize and other alleged abuses. Father Ruíz Calado, a close friend of Soto, played an active role in promoting the cause against the teniente. In return, Soto and his allies flattered their new priest, trying to insure that he did not suffer the same deterioration of clerical prestige so lamented by Father Aguero. On one occasion they staged an elaborate reception, complete with music and fireworks, to greet Ruíz Calado when he returned from a trip to Mexico City. Moreover, the priest formed a partnership with Soto for the cultivation of the Rancho de la Virgen.

Chronic divisions within the Indian community, masked only temporarily in the unstable accord of 1807, further complicated local strife during the politically sensitive year of 1808. The stance of each barrio toward teniente Porras was determined by its position with regard to the disputed water of Ocopetlatla and Las Peñuelas, and by other political controversies among the Indians. Residents of the barrio of Santiago defended Porras in gratitude for his help in regaining for them control of water from the two ojos. The fact that Indians from San Juan joined the movement to oust Porras gave added incentive for those of Santiago to support him. A San Juan faction continued to dominate town government, ignoring the views of those from Santiago, slighting them in making land allocations and appropriating for themselves the rental income of land once claimed by Santiago.[27]

Grievances against gobernador Vicente Antonio Bejarano and other Indian officials in Yautepec also explain why residents of the town's two sujetos, Itzamatitlán and Oacalco, joined the barrio of Santiago in supporting Porras. For several months prior to the eruption of the anti-Porras campaign, the two sujetos had been attempting to escape from subjection to Yautepec, whose gobernadores had repeatedly exacted excessive labor and financial contributions from them. Indians from the two sujetos also complained that Father Ruíz Calado had similarly exploited them.[28]

Despite their enmity toward teniente Porras and toward the dissident Indians of Santiago, Oacalco, and Itzamatitlán, gobernador Vicente Antonio Bejarano and his associates in San Juan showed little enthusiasm for helping Porras's rival, Francisco del Soto, in achieving his designs. They maintained that they had been tricked into approving his temporary use of the water from the disputed ojos. Bejarano's opposition to Soto also stemmed from his interest in obtaining control over the Rancho de la Virgen for himself. In the fall of 1808, he announced his intention to prevent Soto from continuing to irrigate the property. Meanwhile, Bejarano tried to install a small farmer named Cirilo Mostacho on a portion of the disputed rancho. In this effort the gobernador probably enjoyed the active support of Father Ruíz Calado, for Mostacho was known to be an outspoken partisan of the cura; it was he who had arranged the festive welcome party for Ruíz Calado.[29]

Long-standing competition for resources, controversy surrounding the performance and relative prestige of civil and ecclesiastical officials, bitter divisions within the Indian community, and the absence of a Spanish cabildo that might have seized the initiative to resolve these issues in favor of one faction, all contributed to the creation of a politically tense atmosphere in Yautepec in 1808. Meanwhile, events in Europe and their reverberations in Mexico City supplied a fresh set of symbols for acting out old grievances. In March of that year Prince Ferdinand, son of King Charles IV, capitalized on popular dissatisfaction with both his father and with chief royal confidante Manuel Godoy. Ferdinand forced his father to abdicate and then ascended the throne himself as Ferdinand VII. At the same time the occupation of Spain by troops of French emperor Napoleon Bonaparte awakened strong feelings of patriotism in the Spanish people, expressed most openly in the popular uprising that began on 2 May, the famous *dos de mayo*. Also in early May, Ferdinand and his father met with Napoleon in Bayonne, where the new king renounced in favor of his father, who in turn abdicated. Less than a month later, on 6 June, Napoleon named his brother, Joseph Bonaparte, king of Spain. Both in Spain and in the colonies, citizens created local *juntas*, or committees, to govern in the absence of their rightful sovereign. Word of Ferdinand's abdication and subsequent political developments in Spain reached Mexico City in late July. While no junta was formed there, an important segment of public opinion began to favor the creation of some sort of autonomous provisional government. Leading peninsulares advocated instead a subordination to the junta of Seville until Ferdinand's restoration. Because of Viceroy José de Iturrigaray's alleged sympathy for the autonomist position and his connections to the hated Godoy, a group of peninsulares deposed him on 16 September, in a coup led by Gabriel de Yermo, a leading sugar planter of Morelos.[30]

Citizens of Yautepec quickly grafted current political controversies onto their own long-standing disputes. In August, Miguel Vázquez Rincón, a labrador and holder of the *asiento de gallos* (cockfighting monopoly) in Yautepec, proposed that funds be collected for a demonstration of loyalty to King Ferdinand VII, including a Mass for the prompt liberation of the young king from his French captors. Teniente Porras showed little enthusiasm for the plan. According to a deposition given by Vázquez Rincón, Porras explained that he opposed the Mass because he did not wish to fatten the pockets of the cura. Porras then confiscated from Vázquez Rincón a banner honoring King Ferdinand. As a result of the teniente's opposition, the planned festivities were cancelled. Vázquez Rincón then demanded that Marquesado authorities investigate Porras's alleged disloyalty to Ferdinand VII. He also charged that Porras had disregarded his religious obligations, setting a poor example for other townsfolk, and that he had allowed several recent murders and other crimes to go unpunished. Father Ruíz Calado corroborated the accusations of impiety, stating that Porras rarely attended church functions. Others testified that each year when Holy Week approached, the teniente departed for a holiday in Cuernavaca rather than remain in Yautepec for traditional religious observances. Francisco del Soto commented that the enmity between Porras and Ruíz Calado stemmed from the priest's attempts to persuade Porras to conform more closely to accepted religious practice.

To prove his loyalty to King Ferdinand, Porras summoned several witnesses who testified that he had in fact shown proper respect for the exiled sovereign. On learning of Ferdinand's accession to the throne of Spain, Porras reportedly had shouted "Viva Fernando Séptimo" several times and had immediately begun to plan a public demonstration in honor of the new monarch, complete with banners and music, but without a religious ceremony. He had also openly destroyed a portrait of Napoleon on hearing of the king's captivity in France. If Porras's witnesses were telling the truth, it would seem that the teniente's objections to the manifestation planned by Vázquez Rincón focused on the projected role of Father Ruíz Calado in the festivities.[31]

Faint traces of creole-peninsular rivalry surfaced in Yautepec's political struggles of 1808. Teniente Porras was European born, as were all of the individuals who swore to his loyalty to King Ferdinand VII. Many of his most outspoken enemies were creoles, but at least two, including the vocal Francisco del Soto, were gachupines. Economic rivalry, rather than any considerations of patriotism or nationalism, was the major cause of friction. With the exception of the Indians of Santiago, Itzamatitlán, and Oacalco, who had their own reasons for supporting the teniente, Porras's allies were closely associated with the sugar haciendas. Those who testified in his behalf all identified themselves as administrators of local estates. Porras himself had risen to his political appointment after a long career as a manager of hacienda stores and later as general administrator of several haciendas in the area.[32]

The teniente's adversaries, on the other hand, were frustrated labradores and provincial merchants who resented the petty tyranny of local officials and the formidable power of the region's more successful hacendados. Many evidently felt that the economic changes of the late colonial era had rendered their own situation more vulnerable. Indian leaders, though in command of the formal powers conceded them by colonial law, had much in common with the labradores who were their neighbors and tenants. Gobernadores and labradores alike cultivated ties with local officials when they could, but just as readily joined movements to demote tenientes and other power holders with whom they could not forge profitable alliances.

In seeking relief from their troubles, articulate labradores assumed a political importance far out of proportion to their numbers or their economic success. Unlike the owners of the larger haciendas, many of whom maintained their principal residences in Mexico City, the labradores were firmly rooted in Yautepec; local political struggles remained the only medium through which they might hope to better their situation. Yet no formal institutions existed to channel their grievances. Had there existed a Spanish cabildo in Yautepec, local hacendados or a handful of the most substantial labradores might easily have dominated such a body and used it to silence the complaints of other labradores and townsmen. In the political vacuum created by the absence of a municipal council, local affairs assumed a strident, free-for-all character.

In the two centuries since the establishment of the sugar industry in Yautepec's vicinity, the community had evolved from a major Indian cabecera, recipient of populations relocated in the congregación of 1603, to a provincial town in which hacendados, labradores, local merchants, and Indian leaders and commoners all identified themselves as vecinos. After independence, the creation of municipal governments in communities such as Yautepec finally gave non-Indian labradores and townsmen a formal position in local political life.[33] Political changes of the early national period, then, gave formal recognition to social processes much in evidence by the end of the colonial era.

Conclusion

The social and economic changes in late colonial Morelos generated a reservoir of discontent among those who failed to realize their aspirations for profit or personal advancement. Resulting economic and social tensions fused easily with political questions of the day, as the struggles of Yautepec in 1808 demonstrate. It is tempting, therefore, to draw connections between the land and water disputes of the late colonial period and the region's well-known involvement in the independence movement. That struggle was formally inaugurated with Father Miguel Hidalgo y Costilla's call to arms in September 1810.[1]

Certainly, the region figured prominently in the campaigns of Hidalgo's follower and successor, José María Morelos y Pavón, for whom it would one day be named. One of the most important military encounters of the independence period took place in Cuautla, where for nearly three months in the spring of 1812 royalist commander Félix María Calleja laid siege to insurgent forces led by Morelos. Moreover, at least two local men assumed places of honor in the pantheon of revolutionary martyrs. Mariano Matamoros, parish priest of Jantetelco, held a major military command in Morelos's forces until he was captured and executed in 1814. Francisco Ayala, proprietor of the hacienda Mapastlán, also joined Morelos, reportedly after being attacked by royalist soldiers who presumed he was related to another insurgent who shared his surname. He too was executed, together with his two sons, for his participation in the rebellion.[2]

The precise agendas that Hidalgo and Morelos might have pursued had they attained political power remain subject to debate. Nevertheless, their contemporaries, both adversaries and adherents alike, associated with the movements such objectives as independence from Spain, an end to the special privileges of peninsulares, some rectification of the glaring economic inequalities of the time, and abolition of slavery, tribute, and other distinctions based on racial considerations. Understandably, many sugar hacendados viewed these proposals with alarm, especially after Gabriel de Yermo's estates suffered an insurgent attack in the fall of 1810. As a result, Yermo and other landowners armed contingents of their resident workers and sent them into battle for the royalist cause.[3] Peter Gerhard has claimed, although without substantial evidence to document his statement, that many of these conscripts defected to the insurgents as soon as they found opportunities to do so.[4] It is certainly true that large numbers of people in the region gave assistance to the insurgents.[5] Without doubt, the reputed objectives of Morelos, whatever the imprecision of their articulation, held great appeal for the so-called lower classes of the region.

Some, however, calculated that their interests lay in supporting the royalist cause. The Indians of Yautepec's barrio of Santiago, for example, at least claimed to have guarded the entrance to the town in order to prevent its capture by troops of Morelos.[6] Countless others became martyrs to the revolutionary cause only because they stumbled into the cross fire as they went about their daily routines. Many died in the siege of Cuautla simply because their town lay athwart Morelos's route from Acapulco to Puebla. The troops defending the town had in large part followed Morelos there from earlier stops on his itinerary.

The social basis of the insurgency of 1810—who joined Hidalgo and Morelos, and why—remains a subject in need of exhaustive research. The territorial extent of the movement—its major episodes including Hidalgo's capture in Coahuila, his execution in Chihuahua, and Morelos's taking of Oaxaca in November 1812—suggests that a broad spectrum of specific local concerns fed the struggle and shaped its history.

An understanding of its social causes, then, demands an approach wider in geographical scope than that employed in the present work.

Whatever the direct connections between the social history of the area that became the state of Morelos and its role in the independence battles, the disruptions caused by military operations there gave those who harbored grudges against the hacendados opportunities to attack the estates. Damage to some hacienda facilities eased pressure on local resources, giving Indian communities and other small cultivators a chance to increase once again the amounts of land and water at the their disposal. For example, shortly before 1810 Juan José Irazábal established a new sugar mill on lands rented from the Indians of Nexpa and Tetecala. The Indians soon came to regret their concessions to Irazábal, after he received permission from Marquesado authorities to build a new aqueduct across additional lands belonging to the two towns. Sometime between 1810 and 1819, however, the hacienda was destroyed. All of its lands then reverted to the Indians' use.[7]

In addition to bringing physical damage to the haciendas, the decade of fighting after 1810 and the subsequent attainment of national independence in 1821 shattered the economic base on which the late colonial expansion of commercial agriculture had stood. John Tutino has concluded that the events of the independence period so weakened the financial position of the hacendado elite in Chalco that "the first half of the nineteenth century was a period of stagnation, if not actual regression, in the development of the great estate and of increased autonomy for the long-struggling Indian villagers."[8] It is likely that a comparable process occurred in Morelos. The agricultural empire of Gabriel de Yermo crumbled rapidly after independence, leaving his heirs to face repeated judicial proceedings resulting from their inability to pay the estate's accumulated debts.[9] The estate of Nicolás de Icazbalceta suffered comparable financial troubles by the mid-nineteenth century.[10]

Other evidence suggests that the haciendas showed significant population losses during the generation after independence. In 1848, the parish priest of Oaxtepec estimated that the haciendas Cocoyoc and Pantitlán each had about one hundred residents. It is possible that the cura underestimated the haciendas' populations; his own "very broken" ("*quebrantadísima*") state of health and the pressure of his many duties had prevented him from providing a breakdown of his parish's population by age, as his superiors had requested. Nevertheless, the figures he gave for Cocoyoc and Pantitlán are considerably lower than those reported in the census taken a half-century earlier, when Cocoyoc's residents had numbered 181 and Pantitlán's 373.[11]

Hacienda troubles during the first half of the nineteenth century evidently reversed, in part, the social and economic trends of the late colonial period, giving villagers and labradores more freedom to maneuver than they had enjoyed at any time since before 1760. Residents of Indian cabeceras such as Oaxtepec continued as before to cultivate the fruits and vegetables for which they had long been famous and on which their relative prosperity had long rested.[12] The continuing importance of orchards (huertas) to villagers' livelihoods is evident in an anecdote told of Emiliano Zapata's boyhood, according to which the youngster had watched his father shed tears after a hacendado seized an orchard belonging to the villagers of Anenecuilco. Young Emiliano had then vowed that he would one day recover the land for his fellow villagers.[13] Whatever the story's literal truth, it nonetheless reveals the enduring value that the villagers attached to their orchards.

Any vitality that peasant or labrador agriculture might have recovered during the early nineteenth century faced formidable pressures as the sugar industry entered a new phase of expansion after 1880. Competition for land and water intensified once again, especially after the introduction of steam-driven machinery and railroad lines. Many villages lost virtually all of the lands they had defended so tenaciously for centuries.[14]

Changes in the structure of local government and in the legal status of village landholding enacted during the course of the nineteenth century facilitated the transfer of village lands to hacendados. Following independence in 1821, state legislatures received authority to decide which communities in their jurisdictions warranted designation as *municipios*, with elected *ayuntamientos*, or town councils. According to Peter Gerhard, thousands of towns throughout the republic failed to meet the minimum population quotas required for municipio status. The result was, in effect, their "legal abolition." In Morelos, ninety-four cabeceras had existed in 1800, of which only twenty-two survived as municipios in 1870. Many others continued to survive as settlements, but, in Gerhard's words, "without juridical personality they could hardly defend themselves, much less when the ayuntamientos were dominated by mestizos or the adherents of the local prefect."[15]

The political philosophy of the Liberals, who assumed intermittent leadership in national politics after independence, further undermined the villages' continued survival. The Liberals believed that property ownership by ecclesiastical bodies and civil corporations, such as Indian villages, hampered economic growth. Following a few attempts at the state level to strip such bodies of their real estate, the Liberals who seized power in 1855 finally enacted their program on a nationwide basis with the passage of the Ley Lerdo in 1856 and the adoption of a new constitution the following year. In theory, property belonging to communities was to be divided among the residents, who as individual property owners would now presumably contribute in a progressive manner to the nation's economic development, with their personal initiative no longer stymied by conservative local chieftains. In practice, the new owners proved far more vulnerable than corporate communities to pressure from land-hungry neighbors. While the exact extent to which these measures accelerated the pace of land alienation is not known, hacendados found in them a cloak of legality with which to cover their encroachments on erstwhile community land.[16] The Porfirio Diaz regime gave added encouragement to the hacendados by staffing the executive and judicial arms of the government with persons friendly to their interests.

Sugar hacendados in Morelos during the Porfiriato thus benefited from a more sophisticated technology and a more unequivocal political support than their late colonial predecessors. Yet many of the social processes that accompanied the expansion of the sugar industry in Porfirian times had their parallels in the late colonial era. Late nineteenth-century estates became, in John Womack's words, virtual "company towns," with residents numbering in the hundreds or even thousands, for whom hacendados provided medical care, schools, stores, and religious observances, all presumably designed to lessen employees' dependence on persons and institutions off the haciendas.[17] Yet late colonial hacendados, as paternalistic as their descendants a century later, also supplied their workers with services similar in their intended purpose if not in their scope. More importantly, the sociopolitical outlook and objectives of the Porfirian planters bore surprisingly close resemblance to ideas articulated by their late colonial forebears. Hacendados in the late nineteenth century, who expressed their desire to see sugarcane growing in the very plazas of neighboring villages, merely echoed sentiments voiced by their counterparts a century before.[18] For well over a hundred years preceding the Revolution of 1910, hacendados in Morelos had worked toward the coming of a social order in which the corporate Indian villages had no place.

Landowners of the late nineteenth century enjoyed the added advantage of the liberal political program that had given formal legal sanction to the emergence of that new social order. Nevertheless, in Morelos the Liberals' Reforma served primarily to ratify sociopolitical changes already well advanced by the end of the eighteenth century. Villages in late colonial Morelos hardly resembled the Indian communities, isolated from the corrupt and exploitive influences of gente de razón, that were the intended beneficiaries of protective colonial legislation. Choice lands in the villages, occupied by gente de razón, supported ventures in specialized commercial agriculture rather than subsistence farming of Indian commoners. Indian community leaders of the late colonial period maneuvered constantly to protect their personal interests in light of ever-shifting demands on local resources. Except for their conscious invocation of prerogatives accorded by colonial law to indigenous villages, gobernadores' schemes for self-advancement differed little from those of modest non-Indian labradores. In short, they had already become, in a sense, the individualistic, hustling rural entrepreneurs envisioned by nineteenth-century Liberals as likely to promote national economic progress. Even the postindependence creation of ayuntamientos in the major cabeceras was foreshadowed in the late colonial period by the intense political involvement of labradores and townsmen in communities such as Yautepec. The political changes of the postindependence period, then, merely codified a set of social and economic processes already long in evidence in Morelos, and probably in other areas similarly subject to pervasive acculturation and the manifold effects of sugar cultivation or other forms of highly commercialized agriculture.[19]

Without question, the sugar haciendas exerted a profound influence on the social history of Morelos from 1580 forward. Most obviously, their very presence altered forever the region's physical landscape. The introduction of plows, draft animals, and other features of Old World agricultural practice brought dramatically new forms of land utilization.

The haciendas' aqueducts, though often built, to be sure, on the foundations of indigenous systems, nonetheless diverted water from age-old uses to the irrigation of an alien crop and to the operation of strange machinery. Some of the buildings that once sheltered hacienda personnel and equipment have survived to the twentieth century; a few have been refurbished as lavish resorts. The edifice that once housed the sugar mill at Cocoyoc is now a discotheque called El Trapiche; the magnificent aqueduct built there by Antonio Velasco de la Torre in the first decade of the nineteenth century still straddles the highway leading to Cuautla.

The establishment of the haciendas also brought social changes not readily apparent to twentieth-century eyes. Hacendados introduced not only an unfamiliar crop but also the quasi-industrial process needed for the conversion of raw cane into sugar. To the end of the colonial period, Indians looked upon the sugar mills, their steaming cauldrons of syrup and their complicated machinery, with apprehension and understandable fear of injury. The Indians' reluctance to work in the sugar mills gave hacendados added incentive, over and above that provided by the calamitous sixteenth-century decline in the indigenous population, to import slaves of African descent to serve as the estates' primary labor force. In addition to performing the many tasks associated with sugar manufacture, slaves and their free mulatto descendants tended livestock, served as blacksmiths and carpenters, and even learned certain managerial skills by working as mayordomos on the haciendas. Skilled mulattoes could count on steady employment in the sugar industry or as independent tradesmen living in the major towns in the region.

Slaves and their mulatto offspring also served as cultural and biological bridges between Indian and Spaniard, thus facilitating the extensive acculturation that marked the region's social development. Some Negroes and mulattoes evidently learned Náhuatl; in 1635 Hacienda Hospital employed a free black described as fluent in the indigenous tongue.[20] More often, however, black met Indian on the common ground of essentially hispanic culture. They conversed in Spanish as they worked together in the fields, applying European agricultural techniques in the cultivation of an imported crop. In time, they formed bonds of marriage and compadrazgo through the intermediary of the Spanish church. Association with Negro and mulatto hacienda residents therefore hastened the Indians' assimilation of certain aspects of hispanized culture.[21] Nonetheless, compared to the positions occupied by other racial groups, Indians remained at the periphery of the sugar industry and its related economic activities.

The impact of the sugar industry on the history of colonial Morelos can also be discerned in the region's marked sensitivity to changes in the broader economy of New Spain. Fluctuations in the availability of capital and in market conditions for sugar had perceptible repercussions on the structure of agricultural production and on corresponding settlement patterns. Prospects for labradores' or peasants' agricultural success varied inversely with the vitality of the sugar industry. Phases of contraction or expansion in that industry produced more abrupt alterations in patterns of land utilization and water consumption than might have been the case had the produce of commercial haciendas more closely replicated the subsistence crops of the local population.

Despite the great importance of the sugar haciendas, certain features of the region's social history would have emerged if for some reason the industry had never developed. The lowlands' climate and proximity to Mexico City assured commercial agriculture a dominant position in the structure of production while guaranteeing also that market fluctuations in the viceregal capital would exert powerful influences on the region's social and economic development. Prospects for profit in the production of fruits and vegetables would have in any case attracted significant numbers of non-Indian labradores to the "Indian" communities of Morelos. Without the haciendas' tremendous demands for water, labradores and the more fortunate of the region's Indians could have expanded their output of fruits, vegetables, maize, or indigo to their ecological limits. Conflict over land and water, though perhaps not quite as intense, would still have characterized social relations in Morelos, especially during periods when population growth or agricultural crisis elsewhere heightened demand for the region's produce. Meanwhile, its milder climate, fertility of soil, and relative good fortune in times of widespread epidemic or crop failure would have lured Indian migrants there from less favored parts of New Spain. The presence of sugar haciendas, then, accentuated social processes that would have taken place even in their absence.

Appendix 1

Geographic and Climatic Features, Selected Towns

Place	Elevation (meters)	Mean Annual Rainfall (mm)	Mean Annual Temperature
Cuernavaca	1,542	1,242.3	20.9
Cuautla	1,303	997.6	23.9
Jonacatepec	1,165	863.9	23.4
Jojutla de Juárez	891	976.1	25.3
Yautepec	1,250 (est.)	928.2	20.9
Jantetelco	1,430 (est.)	1,049.6	19.7
Tlaltizapán	990 (est.)	907.9	23.2
Ticumán	990 (est.)	816.9	23.2
Yecapixtla	1,600 (est.)	1,029.9	20.1
Tepoztlán	1,750 (est.)	N.A.	N.A.

Sources: Servicio Meteorológica Nacional, *Normales Climatológicas* (Mexico City, 1976); Secretaría de Programación y Presupuesto, *Carta de México—Topográfica 1:250,000* (Mexico City, 1982); *Atlas Nacional del Medio Fisico* (Mexico City, 1981).

Appendix 2

Baptisms and Burials in Yautepec Parish, 1689–1799

Year	Total Baptisms	Indian Baptisms #	% of Total	Total Burials	Indian Burials #	% of Total
1689	92	—	—	74	—	—
1690	125	—	—	102	—	—
1691	120	—	—	70	—	—
1692	118	68	57.6	193	—	—
1703	109	63	57.8	—	—	—
1704	104	61	58.7	—	—	—
1705	98	61	62.2	—	—	—
1706	95	50	52.6	—	—	—
1707	119	51	42.9	—	—	—
1708	103	53	51.5	—	—	—
1709	100	58	58.0	—	—	—
1710	99	60	60.6	87	—	—
1711	97	63	64.9	98	—	—
1712	82	60	73.2	86	—	—
1713	128	72	56.3	63	—	—
1714	101	64	63.4	52	—	—
1715	123	71	57.7	85	—	—
1716	106	62	58.5	108	—	—
1717	115	73	63.5	115	—	—

Year	Total Baptisms	Indian Baptisms #	Indian Baptisms % of Total	Total Burials	Indian Burials #	Indian Burials % of Total
1718	122	63	51.6	64	—	—
1719	124	76	61.3	78	—	—
1720	103	51	49.5	102	—	—
1721	136	81	59.6	114	—	—
1722	122	82	67.2	91	—	—
1723	101	55	54.5	61	—	—
1724	123	82	66.7	108	—	—
1725	114	66	57.9	141	100	70.9
1726	160	100	62.5	134	98	73.1
1727	141	82	58.2	265	206	77.7
1728	93	56	60.2	218	147	67.4
1729	141	85	60.3	92	65	70.7
1730	130	83	63.8	128	98	76.6
1731	155	100	64.5	60	51	85.0
1732	137	80	58.4	62	54	87.1
1733	119	62	52.1	93	62	66.7
1734	135	81	60.0	104	72	69.2
1735	158	107	67.7	59	—	—
1736	116	88	75.9	67	—	—
1737	176	110	62.5	273	229	83.9
1738	145	88	60.7	130	101	77.7
1739	177	101	57.1	79	61	77.2
1740	174	91	52.3	71	56	78.9
1741	225	132	58.7	83	62	74.7
1742	206	121	58.7	174	117	67.2
1743	195	111	56.9	117	83	70.9
1744	186	109	58.6	106	71	67.0
1745	176	96	54.5	80	57	71.3
1746	181	94	51.9	98	63	64.3
1747	162	90	55.6	211	148	70.1
1748	144	76	52.8	120	—	—
1749	156	96	61.5	77	—	—
1750	153	85	55.6	94	—	—
1751	147	81	55.1	—	—	—
1752	144	80	55.6	—	—	—
1753	159	85	53.5	—	—	—
1754	161	76	47.2	—	—	—
1755	161	77	47.8	—	—	—
1756	141	75	53.2	119	68	57.1
1757	160	76	47.5	162	90	55.6
1758	141	70	49.6	111	63	56.8
1759	167	85	50.9	113	59	52.2

Year	Total Baptisms	Indian Baptisms #	% of Total	Total Burials	Indian Burials #	% of Total
1760	161	84	52.2	95	62	65.3
1761	157	75	47.8	108	56	51.9
1762	151	81	53.6	361	249	69.0
1763	199	105	52.8	75	—	—
1764	173	75	43.4	84	—	—
1765	189	82	43.4	108	55	50.9
1766	192	86	44.8	99	52	52.5
1767	188	77	41.0	110	—	—
1768	157	76	48.4	214	—	—
1769	174	84	48.3	134	66	49.3
1770	204	91	44.6	166	—	—
1771	186	81	43.5	122	—	—
1772	216	110	50.9	192	112	58.3
1773	201	86	42.8	153	78	51.0
1774	207	84	40.6	99	54	54.5
1775	195	105	53.8	110	64	58.2
1776	197	90	45.7	85	—	—
1777	179	103	57.5	111	—	—
1778	219	100	45.7	144	73	50.7
1779	169	67	39.6	369	147	39.8
1780	183	82	44.8	396	197	49.7
1781	209	119	56.9	128	89	69.5
1782	128	53	41.4	91	59	64.8
1783	164	83	50.6	73	—	—
1784	191	92	48.2	154	—	—
1785	186	90	48.4	129	63	48.8
1786	167	81	48.5	109	69	63.3
1787	170	80	47.1	91	55	60.4
1788	151	75	49.7	—	—	—
1789	142	62	43.7	125	—	—
1790	178	91	51.1	116	—	—
1791	175	86	49.1	151	77	51.0
1792	185	96	51.9	107	57	53.3
1793	146	70	47.9	112	—	—
1794	165	84	50.9	208	—	—
1795	178	90	50.6	120	—	—
1796	188	69	36.7	129	63	48.8
1797	209	94	45.0	191	100	52.4
1798	175	69	39.4	347	197	56.8
1799	199	—	—	124	—	—

Source: Yautepec Parish Registers, GSU, microfilm, rolls 655–833, 655–834, 655–835, 655–836, 655–837, 655–838, 655–910, 655–911, 655–912.

Appendix 3

Hijos de Padres No Conocidos, Percentage of All Baptisms, Yautepec, 1680–1799

Period	Percent	Period	Percent	Period	Percent
1680–89	20.0	1701*	23.5	1745–49	12.2
1690	12.8	1702*	27.7	1750–54	14.6
1691	20.0	1703	18.3	1755–59	10.6
1692	17.8	1704	17.3	1760–64	8.3
1693*	7.1	1705–9	15.7	1765–69	8.8
1694*	2.4	1710–14	14.4	1770–74	7.7
1695*	30.5	1715–19	14.1	1775–79	7.0
1696*	26.6	1720–24	13.3	1780–84	9.1
1697*	25.1	1725–29	11.6	1785–89	9.8
1698*	12.2	1730–34	8.5	1790–94	12.0
1699*	31.1	1735–39	13.5	1795–99	12.9
1700*	41.5	1740–44	9.4		

Source: Yautepec Parish Registers, GSU, microfilm, rolls 655–833, 655–834, 655–835, 655–836, 655–837, 655–838.
*Non-Indians only.

209

Appendix 4

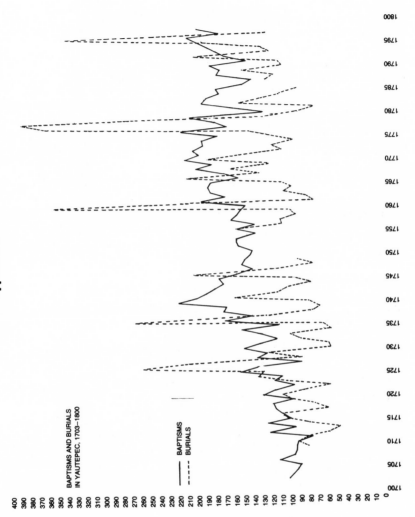

BAPTISMS AND BURIALS
IN YAUTEPEC, 1703–1800

———— BAPTISMS
------- BURIALS

List of Abbreviations

AGIM	Archivo General de Indias, Seville, *Ramo de Audiencia de México*
AGN	Archivo General de la Nación, Mexico City
AGNA	AGN, *Ramo de Albóndigas*
AGNBN	AGN, *Ramo de Bienes Nacionales*
AGNC	AGN, *Ramo de Civil*
AGNCo	AGN, *Ramo de Congregaciones*
AGNCRS	AGN, *Ramo de Clero Regular y Secular*
AGNCr	AGN, *Ramo de Criminal*
AGNE	AGN, *Ramo de Epidemias*
AGNH	AGN, *Ramo de Hospitales*
AGNHi	AGN, *Ramo de Historia*
AGNHJ	AGN, *Ramo de Hospital de Jesús*
AGNM	AGN, *Ramo de Mercedes*
AGNP	AGN, *Ramo de Padrones*
AGNT	AGN, *Ramo de Tierras*
CJD	Collection of photocopied documents in possession of Ing. Juan Dubernard, Cuernavaca, Morelos
GSU	Genealogical Society of Utah, Salt Lake City

Notes

Introduction

1. For discussions of Porfirian Morelos, see John Womack, *Zapata and the Mexican Revolution* (New York, 1969), 37–66; Arturo Warman, *"We Come to Object": The Peasants of Morelos and the National State* (Baltimore, 1981), 42–90; Roberto Melville, *Crecimiento y rebelión: El desarrollo económico de las haciendas azucareras en Morelos (1880–1910)* (Mexico City, 1979). The suggestion made to the villagers of Anenecuilco is quoted in Womack, *Zapata*, 63.

2. Womack, *Zapata*.

3. Ibid., ix.

4. Jesús Sotelo Inclán, *Raíz y razón de Zapata: Anenecuilco* (Mexico City, 1970).

5. Warman, *"We Come to Object."*

6. Womack, *Zapata*, 371.

7. Ward Barrett, *The Sugar Hacienda of the Marqueses del Valle* (Minneapolis, 1970).

8. For a fuller discussion of the geology and geography of the region, see Barrett, *Sugar Hacienda*, 25–26.

9. C. Langdon White and George T. Renner, *Human Geography: An Ecological Study of Society* (New York, 1948), 353; Robert C. West and John Augelli, *Middle America: Its Lands and Peoples* (Englewood Cliffs, N.J., 1966), 36–37.

10. Warman, *"We Come to Object,"* 13–19.

11. G. Michael Riley, *Fernando Cortés and the Marquesado in Morelos, 1522–1547* (Albuquerque, 1973), 1.

12. José Antonio Alzate y Ramírez, *Consejos útiles para socorrer a la necesidad de comestibles en tiempo que escasesen los comestibles* (Mexico City, 1786).

13. AGNBN, leg. 369, exps. 58, 60.

14. Frances Calderón de la Barca, *Life in Mexico* (New York, 1973), 298–327, passim.

15. Bernardo García Martínez, *El Marquesado del Valle: Tres siglos de régimen señorial en Nueva España* (Mexico City, 1969), 120–31; Peter Gerhard, *A Guide to the Historical Geography of New Spain* (Cambridge, 1972), 91–98; Peter Gerhard, "Continuity and Change in Morelos, Mexico," *Geographical Review* 65 (1975); Howard Cline, "Viceroyalty to Republics, 1786–1952: Historical Notes on the Evolution of Middle American Political Units," in *Handbook of Middle American Indians*, ed. Robert Wauchope, vol. 12, pt. 1 (Austin, 1972), passim.

16. Eric Van Young, *Hacienda and Market in Eighteenth-Century Mexico: The Rural Economy of the Guadalajara Region, 1675–1820* (Berkeley and Los Angeles, 1981), 4 and passim; see also Eric Van Young, "Urban Market and Hinterland: Guadalajara and Its Region in the Eighteenth Century," *Hispanic American Historical Review* 59 (1979).

17. The standard worldwide history of the sugar industry is Noel Deerr, *The History of Sugar*, 2 vols. (London, 1949).

18. Barrett, *Sugar Hacienda*, 4.

19. For discussions of the uses and limitations of parish registers in historical research, see Sherburne F. Cook and Woodrow Borah, "Materials for the Demographic History of Mexico, 1500–1960," in Cook and Borah, *Essays in Population History*, vol. 1 (Berkeley and Los Angeles, 1971–79), 1–72; David Brading and Celia Wu, "Population Growth and Crisis: León, 1720–1860," *Journal of Latin American Studies* 5 (1973).

Chapter 1

1. G. Michael Riley, *Fernando Cortés and the Marquesado in Morelos, 1522–1547* (Albuquerque, 1973), 3–21, 36–37; Bernal Díaz del Castillo, *The Conquest of New Spain* (Baltimore, 1963), 328–29, 338–40; for a general discussion of the encomienda, see Lesley Byrd Simpson, *The Encomienda in New Spain: The Beginning of Spanish Mexico* (Berkeley and Los Angeles, 1950); Silvio Zavala, *La encomienda indiana* (Madrid, 1935).

2. Riley, *Fernando Cortés*, 21–34; Bernardo García Martínez, *El Marquesado del Valle: Tres siglos de régimen señorial en Nueva España* (Mexico City, 1969), 33–58.

3. Riley, *Fernando Cortés*, 40–48.

4. Ward Barrett, *The Sugar Hacienda of the Marqueses del Valle* (Minneapolis, 1970), 11; Riley, *Fernando Cortés*, 59–60, 64.

5. Barrett, *Sugar Hacienda*, 11; Riley, *Fernando Cortés*, 42, 51, 64–65; Eric Van Young, "Tuxtla in the Sixteenth Century: A Study in Decline," unpublished ms., 1971.

6. AGNHJ, leg. 90, exp. 19.

7. Barrett, *Sugar Hacienda*, 11; Riley, *Fernando Cortés*, 49–66.

8. Sherburne F. Cook and Woodrow Borah, *The Aboriginal Population of Central Mexico on the Eve of the Spanish Conquest* (Berkeley and Los Angeles, 1963); Sherburne F. Cook and Woodrow Borah, *The Indian Population of Central Mexico, 1531–1610* (Berkeley and Los Angeles, 1960); Sherburne F. Cook and Woodrow Borah *The Indian Population of Central Mexico in 1548* (Berkeley and Los Angeles, 1960).

9. For views critical of the Cook-Borah population estimates, see David Henige, "On the Contact Population of Hispaniola: History as Higher Mathematics," *Hispanic American Historical Review* 58 (1978); Angel Rosenblat, *La población de América en 1492: Viejos y nuevos cálculos* (Mexico City, 1967); William T. Sanders, "The Population of the Central Mexican Symbiotic Region, the Basin of Mexico, and the Teotihuacán Valley in the Sixteenth Century," in *The Native Population of the Americas in 1492*, ed. William M. Denevan (Madison, 1976).

10. Riley, *Fernando Cortés*, 5, 116, 133.

11. Peter Gerhard, "Continuity and Change in Morelos, Mexico," *Geographical Review* 65 (1975), 343.

12. Riley, *Fernando Cortés*, 133.

13. Gerhard, "Continuity and Change," 345.

14. Riley, *Fernando Cortés*, 15–17, 100–109.

15. Riley, *Fernando Cortés*, 57–66, 153. A seventeen-acre tract near Yautepec, probably that known in later colonial times as the Rancho del Marqués, became Cortés's property through a slightly more complicated process. In 1526 or 1527, Diego de Ordaz, holder of Yautepec during the period of Cortés's suspension from his encomienda privileges, had purchased the land from the town's Indians. Later, in a compromise with Ordaz, Cortés traded the encomienda of Huejotzingo for those of Yautepec and Tepoztlán. The seventeen-acre plot, planted in fruit trees, was also included in the transfer. Riley, *Fernando Cortés*, 59.

16. AGNHJ, leg. 251, exp. 1.

17. Riley, *Fernando Cortés*, 153.

18. AGNHJ, leg. 90, exp. 19.

19. Riley, *Fernando Cortes*, 62.

20. François Chevalier, *La formation des grands domaines au Mexique, terre et société aux xvie–xviie siècles* (Paris, 1952), 57–85.

21. William B. Taylor has identified preemption of encomienda rights by the Marqués del Valle as a major factor in the slower pace of land acquisi-

tion by non-Indians in Oaxaca. William B. Taylor, *Landlord and Peasant in Colonial Oaxaca* (Stanford, 1972), 36.

22. García Martínez, *El Marquesado*, 73–81; Chevalier, *La formation*, 167–71.

23. Gerhard, "Continuity and Change," 344.

24. AGIM, leg. 130, fols. 47–50.

25. AGNHJ, leg. 90, exp. 2, fols. 73v, 144v, 152.

26. *Relación de Oaxtepec*, in Joaquín García Icazbalceta Collection, University of Texas Library, Austin, Texas.

27. For a general discussion of the hospitals operated by the Order of San Hipólito in the seventeenth century, see Cheryl English Martin, "The San Hipólito Hospitals of Colonial Mexico, 1566–1702" (Ph. D. diss., Tulane University, 1976).

28. AGIM, leg. 130, fols. 47–50.

29. Alonso Ponce, *Relación breve y verdadera de algunas cosas de las muchas que sucedieron al Padre Fray Alonso Ponce en las provincias de la Nueva España*, vol. 1 (Madrid, 1878), 202; Martin, "San Hipólito Hospitals," 12.

30. Silvio Zavala and María Castelo, eds., *Fuentes para la historia del trabajo en Nueva España*, vol. 3 (Mexico City, 1939–1945), 79–80.

31. See below, Chapter 2.

32. Charles Gibson, *The Aztecs under Spanish Rule: A History of the Indians of the Valley of Mexico, 1519–1819* (Stanford, 1964), 359.

33. *Relación de Oaxtepec*.

34. See Murdo J. MacLeod, *Spanish Central America: A Socio-Economic History, 1520–1710* (Berkeley and Los Angeles, 1973), 19, for evidence supporting the thesis that this was an epidemic of bubonic plague.

35. Cook and Borah, *Indian Population, 1531–1610*, 48.

36. *Relación de Oaxtepec*.

Chapter 2

1. For general discussions of the economic transitions in New Spain after 1580, see Woodrow Borah, *New Spain's Century of Depression* (Berkeley and Los Angeles, 1951); Peter J. Bakewell, *Silver Mining and Society in Colonial Mexico: Zacatecas, 1546–1700* (Cambridge, 1971), 221–36; Charles Gibson, *The Aztecs under Spaniah Rule: A History of the Indians of the Valley of Mexico, 1519–1819* (Stanford, 1964), 323–27; John TePaske and Herbert S. Klein, "The Seventeenth-Century Crisis in New Spain: Myth or Reality?," *Past and Present* 70 (1981); Alejandra Moreno Toscano, "Tres problemas en la geografía del maíz, 1600–1624," *Historia Mexicana* 14 (1965).

2. François Chevalier, *La formation des grands domaines au Mexique, terre et société aux xvie–xviie siècles* (Paris, 1952), 89.

3. Ward Barrett, *The Sugar Hacienda of the Marqueses del Valle* (Minneapolis, 1970), 19; Chevalier, *La formation*, 95.

4. Moreno Toscano, "Tres problemas."

5. Fernando B. Sandoval, *La industria del azúcar en la Nueva España* (Mexico City, 1951), 52–75; Richard E. Greenleaf, "Viceregal Power and the Obrajes of the Cortés Estate, 1595–1708," *Hispanic American Historical Review* 48 (1968).

6. Moreno Toscano, "Tres problemas"; Sandoval, *La industria*, 55–61.

7. AGNHJ, leg. 294, exp. 85.

8. AGNHJ, leg. 96, exp. 3, fol. 78.

9. AGNT, vol. 1955, fol. 263v.

10. AGIM, leg. 130, fol. 50.

11. Cheryl English Martin, "The San Hipólito Hospitals of Colonial Mexico, 1566–1702" (Ph.D. diss., Tulane University, 1976).

12. Moreno Toscano, "Tres problemas," 647–48.

13. Colin Palmer, *Slaves of the White God: Blacks in Mexico, 1570–1650* (Cambridge, Mass., 1976), 12.

14. AGNT, vol. 3428, exp. 1, fols. 34–35.

15. AGNM, vol. 11, fols. 31v, 74, 106v, 203; AGIM, legs. 111, 114; Carmen Venegas Ramírez, *Régimen hospitalario para indios en la Nueva España* (Mexico City, 1973), 92–93; Silvio Zavala and María Castelo, *Fuentes para la historia del trabajo en Nueva España* (Mexico City, 1939–1945), vol. 3, 165; vol. 4, 375.

16. AGNHJ, leg. 128, exp. 5.

17. AGIM, leg. 130, fols. 47–50.

18. AGNHJ, leg. 90, exp. 2, fols. 68v–80v.

19. AGNT, vol. 1501, exp. 6; vol. 1545, exp. 1.

20. AGNT, vol. 1825, exp. 1.

21. Howard Cline, "Civil Congregations of the Indians in New Spain," *Hispanic American Historical Review* 29 (1949).

22. Ibid.

23. AGNT, vol. 1513, exp. 7, fol. 16; Peter Gerhard, *A Guide to the Historical Geography of New Spain* (Cambridge, 1972), 91–98.

24. AGNT, vol. 150l, exp. 6; vol. 1545, exp. 1. Diego Caballero, founder of Hacienda Santa Inés, and the Brothers of San Hipólito also augmented the lands they had purchased by requesting mercedes for adjoining property. AGNT, vol. 1825, exp. 1; AGNHJ, leg. 90, exp. 2; leg. 128, exp. 5.

25. AGNT, vol. 1475, exp. 1, fol. 235 *bis*.

26. AGNT, vol. 1731, exp. 2.

27. For a general discussion of Pedro Cortés's land allocations and their

legal consequences, see Chevalier, *La formation*, 171–76.

28. AGNHJ, leg. 294, exp. 88.

29. AGNHJ, leg. 128, exp. 5; leg. 339, exp. 10.

30. Bernardo García Martínez, *El Marquesado del Valle: Tres siglos de régimen señorial en Nueva España* (Mexico City, 1969), 97.

31. AGNHJ, leg. 96, exp. 1, fol. 170.

32. García Martínez, *El Marquesado*, 97–99.

33. AGNHJ, leg. 96, exp. 4, fol. 418; AGNT, vol. 114, pt. l, fol. 67v; vol. 1955, fols. 212–18.

34. AGNT, vol. 2057, exp. 1, fol. 42v; AGNHJ, leg. 73 (vol. 38), exp. 8.

35. AGNT, vol. 1731, exp. 2, fol. 1; vol. 1608, exp. 2, cuaderno 3, fols. 20v–23; vol. 1973, exp. 1, fols. 65–67; vol. 2051, exp. 8; AGNHJ; leg. 447, exp. 59; AGNM, vol. 31, fol. 310v.

36. AGNT, vol. 1154, exp. 9; see also AGNHJ, leg. 93, exps. 23, 38.

37. AGNT, vol. 1944, cuaderno 3, fol. 120.

38. AGNHJ, leg. 312, exp. 19, fols. 28–29.

39. AGNT, vol. 1475, exp. 1; vol. 1954, exp. 1; vol. 2735, pt. l, exp. 4; AGNHJ, leg. 96, exp. 3, fols. 270–270v, 352; AGNM, vol. 26, fol. 216.

40. Ward Barrett, *The Sugar Hacienda of the Marqueses del Valle* (Minneapolis, 1970), 29–30, 39.

41. AGNHJ, leg. 90, exp. 2, fols. 88–88v; AGNM, vol. 28, fol. 233v.

42. AGNCRS, vol. 168, exp. 7; AGNM, vol. 34, fols. 149v–150.

43. AGNM, vol. 28, fol. 266v; vol. 34, fols. 148v–149; vol. 34, fols. 4, 9; vol. 37, fols. 37, 60; vol. 38, fol. 38.

44. AGNT, vol. 1545, exp. 1.

45. AGNT, vol. 239, fols. 41–44v.

46. AGNT, vol. 114, pt. 1, fol. 283.

47. AGNBN, leg. 1215, exp. 1.

48. Gisela von Wobeser, *San Carlos Borromeo: Endeudamiento de una hacienda colonial (1608–1729)* (Mexico City, 1980), 103–4.

49. AGNT, vol. 239, fols. 41–44v.

50. AGNT, vol. 114, pt. 1.

51. AGNBN, leg. 892, exp. 4; leg. 1116, exp. 2; leg. 1215, exp. 1, fols. 71–83; AGNCRS, vol. 168, exp. 7; Cheryl English Martin, "Crucible of Zapatismo: Hacienda *Hospital* in the Seventeenth Century," *The Americas* 38 (1981).

52. Chevalier, *La formation*, 348–63.

53. AGNM, vol. 45, fol. 260.

54. AGNHJ, leg. 96, exp. 2, fols. 491–98.

55. AGNHJ, leg. 96, exp. 1, fols. 202–208; exp. 3, fol. 46; AGNM, vol. 45, fols. 241–42.

56. AGNT, vol. 2157, exp. 1.

57. AGNHJ, leg. 96, exp. 3, fols. 58–78, 524; AGNM, vol. 45, fols. 241–42.

58. AGNT, vol. 114, pt. 1, fol. 61v.

59. AGNHJ, leg. 96, exp. 2, fols. 272, 291; exp. 3, fols. 364, 537–53.

60. Barrett, *Sugar Hacienda*, 19.

61. Von Wobeser, *San Carlos Borromeo*, 53.

62. Colin Palmer, *Slaves of the White God: Blacks in Mexico, 1570–1650* (Cambridge, Mass., 1976), 80–81.

63. Bakewell, *Silver Mining and Society*, 221–36; Te Paske and Klein, "Seventeeth-Century Crisis"; J. I. Israel, "Mexico and the 'General Crisis' of the Seventeenth Century," *Past and Present* 63 (1974).

64. Ward Barrett, "The Meat Supply of Colonial Cuernavaca," *Annals of the Association of American Geographers* 64 (1974), 536.

65. AGNHJ, leg. 96, exp. 2, fols, 272, 291; exp. 3, fols. 364, 537–53.

66. AGNHJ, leg. 96, exp. 1, fols. 175v–179.

67. AGNHJ, leg. 312, exp. 10.

68. AGNHJ, leg. 294, exp. 102.

69. AGNHJ, leg. 96, exp. 3, fol. 264v.

70. AGNHJ, leg. 312, exp. 10.

71. AGNHJ, leg. 294, exps. 106, 107.

72. AGNT, vol. 1731, exp. 2; vol. 1760, exp. 6.

73. AGNHJ, leg. 96, exp. 1, fols. 279–332.

74. AGNHJ, leg. 312, exp. 10.

75. AGNHJ, leg. 294, exp. 95.

76. GSU, microfilm, roll 655–833.

77. AGNHJ, leg. 96, exp. 3, fol. 566.

Chapter 3

1. Howard Cline, "Civil Congregations of the Indians in New Spain," *Hispanic American Historical Review* 29 (1949).

2. AGNCo, fol. 61v; AGNT, vol. 1513, exp. 7.

3. AGNCo, fol. 53.

4. AGNCo, fol. 119; AGNT, vol. 1958, exp. 1.

5. AGNCo, fol. 10v.

6. Peter Gerhard, *A Guide to the Historical Geography of New Spain* (Cambridge, 1972), 47.

7. AGNCo, fols. 55, 104, 125v.

8. AGNHJ, vol. 49 (leg. 28), exp. 8. For a discussion of Indian response

to Spanish-imposed settlement patterns in Yucatán, see N. M. Farriss, "Nucleation versus Dispersal: The Dynamics of Population Movement in Colonial Yucatán," *Hispanic American Historical Review* 58 (1978).

9. José Antonio Villaseñor y Sánchez, *Teatro americano: Descripción general de los reynos y provincias de la Nueva España, y sus jurisdicciones*, vol. 1 (Mexico City, 1746), 172.

10. AGNT, vol. 1475, exp. 1.

11. AGNT, vol. 2763, exp. 28.

12. See, for example, J. I. Israel's comments on the depletion of the local ruling class in Texcoco, in Israel, *Race, Class and Politics in Colonial Mexico, 1610–1670* (London, 1975), 44–45.

13. AGNT, vol. 2353, exp. 3.

14. AGNT, vol. 2756, exp. 2.

15. AGNT, vol. 2353, exp. 3.

16. AGNT, vol. 185, exps. 7, 8; AGNHJ, leg. 96, exp. 1, fols. 175v–190.

17. AGNM, vol. 35, fols. 10–10v.

18. AGNH, vol. 32, exp. 15; AGNCRS, vol. 98, exp. 1; AGNT, vol. 3082, exp. 2.

19. AGNHJ, vol. 52 (leg. 29), exps. 3, 4, 5, 8, 12, 14; leg. 447, exp. 12.

20. Ward Barrett, *The Sugar Hacienda of the Marqueses del Valle* (Minneapolis, 1970), 29; AGNHJ, leg. 447, exp. 2.

21. AGNHJ, leg. 96, exp. 1, fol. 468.

22. AGNHJ, vol. 52 (leg. 29), exps. 1, 2.

23. AGNHJ, leg. 312, exp. 11.

24. AGNHJ, leg. 447, exp. 12.

25. AGNT, vol. 2684, exp. 4.

26. AGNHJ, leg. 312, exp. 10.

27. AGNHJ, leg. 251, exp. 21; AGNT, vol. 1475, exp. 1, fol. 233v.

28. AGNHJ, leg. 312, exp. 10.

29. AGNHJ, leg. 312, exp. 13.

30. JoséMiranda, "La población indígena de México en el siglo xvii," *Historia Mexicana* 12 (1962).

31. William H. McNeill, *Plagues and Peoples* (New York, 1976), 58.

32. José Carlos Chiaramonte, "En torno a la recuperación demográfica y la depresión económica novohispanas durante el siglo xvii," *Historia Mexicana* 30 (1981).

33. Yautepec Parish Registers, GSU, microfilm, roll 655–833.

34. AGNHJ, leg. 312, exp. 10.

35. Miranda, "La población indígena," 187.

36. Gerhard, *Guide*, 97.

37. AGNHJ, vol. 49 (leg. 28), exp. 12.

38. Ward Barrett, in "Morelos and Its Sugar Industry in the Late Eighteenth Century," in *Provinces of Early Mexico: Variants of Spanish American Regional Evolution*, ed. Ida Altman and James Lockhart (Los Angeles, 1976), 157, gives additional figures for the numbers of tributaries in Cuernavaca, but the drastic fluctuations in his figures (for example, 2,500 for 1635; 5,438.5 for 1638; 2,013 for 1651; 4,767 for 1671; 2,110.5 for 1680; and 2,388 for 1686) suggest that the figures in the 4,000–5,000 range are for the entire alcaldía mayor of Cuernavaca, while those in the 2,000 range are only for Cuernavaca and its own sujetos, excluding other cabeceras in the alcalde mayor district.

39. Peter Gerhard, "Continuity and Change in Morelos, Mexico," *Geographical Review* 65 (1975), 347.

40. Gerhard, *Guide*, 97.

41. Pedro Carrasco, "La casa y hacienda de un señor tlahuica," *Estudios de Cultura Náhuatl* 10 (1972), 225; Carrasco, "The Joint Family in Ancient Mexico: The Case of Molotla," in *Essays on Mexican Kinship*, ed. Hugo G. Nuntini, Pedro Carrasco, and James M. Taggart, (Pittsburgh, 1976), 45.

42. Pedro Carrasco, "Tres libros de tributos del Museo Nacional de México y su importancia para los estudios demográficos," International Congress of Americanists, *Proceedings* 35 (1962); Carrasco, "La casa," 226; Carrasco, "Joint Family," p. 46.

43. GSU, microfilm, roll 655–833.

44. GSU, microfilm, roll 606–324.

45. AGNHJ, leg. 93, exp. 3, fols. 558–68.

46. AGNHJ, leg. 93, exp. 8, hoja suelta.

47. AGNHJ, leg. 312, exp. 6; see also AGNT, vol. 1501, exp. 6.

48. AGNT, vol. 1612, exp. 1; vol. 1958, exps. 1, 5.

49. AGNT, vol. 1779, exp. 4.

50. AGNT, vol. 1939, exp. 1; AGNCo, fols. 65–76.

51. AGNHJ, leg. 115, exp. 344.

52. AGNHJ, leg. 304, exp. 1.

53. AGNT, vol. 1779, exp. 4.

54. See, for example, Emmanuel LeRoy Ladurie, *Times of Feast, Times of Famine: A History of Climate since the Year 1000* (New York, 1971), 68–70; and citations given by Ward Barrett, "The Meat Supply of Colonial Cuernavaca," *Annals of the Association of American Geographers* 64 (1974), 537.

55. Elsa Malvido, "Factores de despoblación y reposición de la población indígena de Cholula (1641–1810)," *Historia Mexicana* 23 (1973), 68–73; Rosa Feijoo, "El tumulto de 1692," *Historia Mexicana* 14 (1965); Charles Gibson, *The Aztecs under Spanish Rule: A History of the Indians of the Valley of Mexico, 1519–1819* (Stanford, 1964), 450.

56. AGNHJ, vol. 49 (leg. 28), exp. 3.

57. Malvido, "Factores," 69.

58. Yautepec Parish Registers, GSU, microfilm, roll 655–850.

59. Claude Morin, *Santa Inés Zacatelco (1646–1812): Contribución a la demografía de México colonial* (Mexico City, 1973), 26.

60. Yautepec Parish Registers, GSU, microfilm, roll 655–850.

61. Yautepec Parish Registers, GSU, microfilm, rolls 655–834, 655–835.

62. Malvido, "Factores," 94–95; Claude Morin, *Michoacán en la Nueva España del siglo xviii: Crecimiento y desigualdad en una economía colonial* (Mexico City, 1979), 49; Morin, *Santa Inés Zacatelco*, 55–57.

63. Malvido, "Factores," 73–79; Morin, *Santa Inés Zacatelco*, 39–42; Thomas Calvo, "Demographie historique d'une paroisse Mexicaine: Acatzingo (1606–1810)," *Cahiers des Amériques Latines* 6 (1972), 14–16; Gibson, *Aztecs*, 450. Although most authors identify this epidemic as typhus, Malvido believes that it was an acute form of hepatitis.

64. AGNHJ, leg. 344, exp. 33.

65. Malvido, "Factores," 75.

66. Yautepec Parish Registers, GSU, microfilm, roll 655–910.

67. See, for example, David Brading, *Haciendas and Ranchos in the Mexican Bajío: León, 1700–1860* (Cambridge, 1978), 192.

68. Yautepec Parish Registers, GSU, microfilm, rolls 655–850, 655–851.

69. AGNHJ, leg. 344, exp. 33.

70. Morin, *Santa Inés Zacatelco*, 39–42.

71. Yautepec Parish Registers, GSU, microfilm, rolls 655–835, 655–836.

72. AGNT, vol. 1504, exp. 2, fols. 86v–87v.

Chapter 4

1. AGNHJ, leg. 294, exp. 95.

2. AGNHJ, leg. 96, exp. 1, fols. 235–36.

3. Ward Barrett, *The Sugar Hacienda of the Marqueses del Valle* (Minneapolis, 1970), 19.

4. AGNT, vol. 114, part 2, fol. 414.

5. AGNT, vol. 1761, fols. 89–92; Ward Barrett, "The Meat Supply of Colonial Cuernavaca," *Annals of the Association of American Geographers* 64 (1974), 536.

6. AGNT, vol. 139, exp. 1, fol. 38.

7. AGNT, vol. 1980, exp. 2; AGNBN, leg. 1215, exp. 3.

8. AGNT, vol. 114, part 1, fols. 92v–93.

9. AGNC, vol. 251, exp. 5.

10. AGNT, vol. 239, fols. 1–31.

11. AGNT, vol. 2868, exp. 4.

12. Jean-Pierre Berthe, "Xochimancas: Les travaux et les jours dans une *hacienda sucrière* de Nouvelle Espagne au xvii^c siècle," *Jahrbuch für Geschichte von Staat, Wirtschaft and Gesellschaft Lateinamerikas* 3 (1966), 92, 102–7; James D. Riley, "The Wealth of the Jesuits in Mexico, 1670–1767," *The Americas* 33 (1976).

13. AGNH, vol. 73, exp. 2; AGNBN, leg. 1215, exp. 1; Cheryl English Martin, "Crucible of Zapatismo: Hacienda *Hospital* in the Seventeenth Century," *The Americas* 38 (1981).

14. Eric Van Young, *Hacienda and Market in Eighteenth-Century Mexico: The Rural Economy of the Guadalajara Region, 1675–1820* (Berkeley and Los Angeles, 1981), 188.

15. AGNH, vol. 73, exp. 2; AGNBN, leg. 860, exp. 4; leg. 1010, exps. 4, 5; leg. 1116, exp. 4; leg. 1215.

16. AGNHJ, leg. 93, exps. 1, 2; Barrett, *Sugar Hacienda*, 111–12.

17. AGNT, vol. 1761.

18. AGNT, vol. 1501, exp. 6, fol. 34v.

19. AGNHJ, leg. 447, exp. 11; AGNT, vol. 1761, fol. 92.

20. AGNT, vol. 1742.

21. AGNHJ, leg. 447, exp. 11.

22. AGNT, vol. 343, exp. 3.

23. AGNT, vol. 1786, exp. 1.

24. AGNT, vol. 1780, exp. 6, fol. 11.

25. AGNT, vol. 343, exp. 3.

26. AGNBN, leg. 808, exp. 24.

27. AGNT, vol. 1761, fols. 229–229v; vol. 1943, fol. 236v; vol. 1970, exp. 7, fol. 31v; Barrett, *Sugar Hacienda*, 85.

28. AGNBN, leg. 131, exp. 10.

29. AGNT, vol. 2866, exp. 11.

30. AGNHJ, leg. 344, exp. 4; leg. 428, exp. 20; leg. 447, exp. 68.

31. AGNT, vol. 1969, exp. 1 cuaderno 3, fol. 62;, exp. 2, fol. 40.

32. Van Young, *Hacienda and Market*, 117; William B. Taylor, *Landlord and Peasant in Colonial Oaxaca* (Stanford, 1972), 141; Enrique Florescano, *Precios del maíz y crisis agrícolas en México (1708–1810)* (Mexico City, 1969), 183.

33. AGNT, vol. 1943 cuaderno 2, fol. 36v.

34. AGNT, vol. 522, exp. 5, fol. 39v.

35. AGNT, vol. 1566, fols. 151v–152.

36. AGNT, vol. 1935, exp. 1.

37. AGNT, vol. 1566, fols. 1–4.

38. AGNT, vol. 1564–69.

39. AGNT, vol. 1567, fol. 12v; vol. 1974, exp. 2.

40. AGNT, vol. 1935, exp. 1.

41. AGNHJ, leg. 304, exp. 1; leg. 447, exp. 12.
42. AGNHJ, leg. 115, exp. 373; leg. 304, exp. 1.
43. AGNHJ, leg. 447, exps. 6, 10, 92; "Cuaderno de las escrituras originales pertenecientes a la hacienda de Miacatlán," copy in CJD.
44. AGNHJ, leg. 128, exp. 5.
45. AGNT, vol. 1779, exp. 4.
46. AGNHJ, leg. 304, exp. 1.
47. AGNT, vol. 1779, exp. 4.
48. AGNHJ, leg. 447, exp. 29.
49. AGNHJ, leg. 93, exp. 22.
50. AGNT, vol. 1972, exp. 3; AGNHJ, leg. 90, exp. 4.
51. AGNHJ, leg. 447, exp. 6.
52. AGNHJ, vol. 48 (leg. 27), exps. 1, 2.
53. AGNHJ, leg. 304, exp. 1; leg. 344, exp. 1.
54. AGNCo, fol. 77v.
55. AGNT, vol. 1779, exp. 4.
56. AGNHJ, leg. 447, exp. 10.
57. AGNT, vol. 1779, exp. 4.
58. AGNHJ, leg. 344, exps. 29, 37; AGNT, vol. 1939, exp. 9; vol. 1941.
59. AGNHJ, vol. 73 (leg. 38), exp. 18.
60. AGNHJ, vol. 58 (leg. 31), exps. 1, 2; leg. 344, exp. 33.
61. AGNT, vol. 1972, exp. 4; AGNHJ, leg. 93, exp. 31; leg. 447, exps. 9, 87.
62. AGNT, vol. 1950, exp. 1.
63. AGNT, vol. 1742, fol. 395v; vol. 1940, exp. 2; AGNHJ, leg. 90, exp. 19.
64. AGNT, vol. 1951.
65. AGNT, vol. 1780, exp. 6.
66. AGNT, vol. 1566, exp. 1, fol. 104v.
67. AGNT, vol. 2868, exp. 4, fols. 344–357.
68. AGNT, vol. 2050, exp. 4.
69. AGNHJ, leg. 344, exp. 31; AGNT, vol. 1935, exp. 1, cuaderno 3, fol. 8.
70. AGNHJ, leg. 447, exp. 13.
71. AGNT, vol. 446, exp. 7.
72. AGNT, vol. 1948, exp. 3.
73. AGNT, vol. 1958, exp. 2.
74. AGNT, vol. 2752, fols. 265–272v.
75. Charles Gibson, *The Aztecs under Spanish Rule: A History of the Indians of the Valley of Mexico, 1519–1819* (Stanford, 1964), 456; Florescano, *Precios*, 115, 131.

76.   AGNHJ, leg. 321, exp. 12; Florescano, *Precios*, 203.
77.   AGNT, vol. 1566, exp. 1, fol. 104v; vol. 1567, exp. 5, fols. 72–165; vol. 1938, exp. 5; vol. 1939, exp. 2, fol. 8v; vol. 1964, exp. 1, cuaderno 3, fols. 52–59.
78.   AGNC, vol. 1827.
79.   David Brading, *Haciendas and Ranchos in the Mexican Bajío: León, 1700–1860* (Cambridge, 1978), 171–72.
80.   See, for example, AGNT, vol. 2157, exps. 5, 7, 8.
81.   AGNT, vol. 1541, exp. 2; AGNHJ, leg. 115, exp. 347.
82.   AGNT, vol. 2353, exp. 3.
83.   AGNHJ, vol. 78 (leg. 42), exps. 1–3.
84.   Villaseñor y Sánchez, *Teatro Americano: Descripción general de los reynos y provincias de la Nueva España, y sus jurisdicciones*, vol. 1 (Mexico City, 1746), 167–98.
85.   See, for example, AGNT, vol. 1962, exp. 1, fol. 152v.
86.   Womack, *Zapata*, 42–43.

Chapter 5

1.   For accounts of the economic growth in eighteenth-century Mexico, see Alexander von Humboldt, *Political Essay on the Kingdom of New Spain*, 4 vols. (New York, 1970); David Brading, *Miners and Merchants in Bourbon Mexico, 1763–1810* (Cambridge, 1971); Eric Van Young, *Hacienda and Market in Eighteenth-Century Mexico: The Rural Economy of the Guadalajara Region, 1675–1820* (Berkeley and Los Angeles, 1981); Doris Ladd, *The Mexican Nobility at Independence, 1780–1826* (Austin, 1976); John E. Kicza, "Business and Society in Late Colonial Mexico City" (Ph. D. diss., University of California, Los Angeles, 1979); Jaime E. Rodríguez O., "Down From Colonialism: Mexico's Nineteenth-Century Crisis" (Distinguished Faculty Lecture, University of California, 28 May 1980); Cheryl English Martin, "Haciendas and Villages in Late Colonial Morelos," *Hispanic American Historical Review* 62 (1982).
2.   Enrique Florescano, *Precios del maíz y crisis agrícolas en México (1708–1810)* (Mexico City, 1969); David Brading, *Haciendas and Ranchos in the Mexican Bajío: León, 1700–1860* (Cambridge, 1978), 174–204; Enrique Florescano, ed., *Fuentes para la historia de la crisis agrícola de 1785–1786*, 2 vols. (Mexico City, 1981).
3.   Gisela von Wobeser, "Las haciendas de Cuernavaca y Cuautla en la época colonial" (Paper presented at the conference on "La historia morelense en la investigación social," Cuernavaca, Morelos, September 1983).
4.   José Jesús Hernández Palomo, *El aguardiente de caña en México (1724–1810)* (Seville, 1974), 106–8, 114.

5. Ward Barrett, *The Sugar Hacienda of the Marqueses del Valle* (Minneapolis, 1970), 46–49.

6. Ward Barrett, "Morelos and Its Sugar Industry in the Late Eighteenth Century," in *Provinces of Early Mexico: Variants of Spanish American Regional Evolution*, ed. Ida Altman and James Lockhart (Los Angeles, 1976), 163–64.

7. AGNT, vol. 1974, exp. 2.

8. AGNT, vol. 1958, fol. 82.

9. AGNT, vol. 1567; vol. 1568; vol. 1974, exp. 2.

10. AGNT, vol. 1506, exp. 6.

11. AGNT, vol. 1396, pt. 1, exp. 4; vol. 1948, exp. 2; AGNHJ, leg. 373, exp. 15, fol. 103.

12. AGNT, vol. 1950, exp. 1 cuaderno 1; vol. 2420, exp. 1.

13. AGNT, vol. 1096, exp. 4; vol. 2157, exp. 8; vol. 2871, exp. 7; AGNHJ, leg. 327, exp. 1, fols. 58v, 67.

14. AGNT, vol. 1096, exp. 4, fol. 156.

15. Yautepec Parish Registers, GSU, microfilm, roll 655–851.

16. Yautepec Parish Registers, GSU, microfilm, roll 655–835, book 2, fols. 65, 81.

17. AGNT, vol. 2056, exp. 2.

18. See, for example, AGNHJ, leg. 327, exp. 2, fols. 65, 66v–68.

19. AGNT, vol. 1484, exp. 7; vol. 1938, exps. 6, 7; vol. 2048, exp. 1; vol. 2049, exp. 1; AGNA, vol. 12, fol. 11.

20. AGNT, vol. 1976, exp. 9; vol. 2159, exp. 1.

21. AGNHJ, leg. 81, exp. 1; leg. 327, exp. 3, fol. 204.

22. AGNT, vol. 1962, exp. 1, cuaderno 1.

23. AGNHJ, leg. 81, exp. 1; leg. 327, exp. 4, fol. 28v;, exp. 5, fol. 91v; AGNT, vol. 1371, exp. 1; vol. 253, exp. 1; vol. 2873, exp. 1.

24. Murdo J.MacLeod, "Forms and Types of Work, and the Acculturation of the Colonial Indian of Mesoamerica: Some Preliminary Observations," in *El trabajo y los trabajadores en la historia de México*, ed. Elsa Cecilia Frost, Michael C. Meyer, and Josefina Zoraida Vázquez (Mexico City and Tucson, 1979).

25. Florescano, *Precios*, 151, 174–76; Charles Gibson, *The Aztecs under Spanish Rule: A History of the Indians of the Valley of Mexico, 1519–1819* (Stanford, 1964), 316; Brading, *Haciendas and Ranchos*, 189.

26. AGIM, leg. 1418, microfilm in Bancroft Library, University of California, Berkeley, reel M-271, frame 35; reel M-272, frame 21.

27. Brading, *Haciendas and Ranchos*, p. 190; Elsa Malvido, "Factores de despoblación y reposición del la población de Cholula (1641–1810)," *Historia Mexicana* 23 (1973).

28. David Brading and Celia Wu, "Population Growth and Crisis: León, 1720–1860," *Journal of Latin American Studies* 5 (1973), 35.

29. Ibid, p. 17.

30. AGNC, vol. 1827; AGNA vol. 12, fols. 105ff; AGIM, leg. 1418, microfilm in Bancroft Library, University of California, Berkeley, reel M-271, frames 51–55; reel M-273, frames 17–18; José Antonio Alzate y Ramírez, *Consejos útiles para socorrer a la necesidad de comestibles en tiempo que escasesen los comestibles* (Mexico City, 1786); "Circular que acompaña representación y providencias de ciudadanos para esforzar las siembras de maíz, en las necesidades padecidas, y que de nuevo se recelan" (Mexico City, 13 December 1785), in *La crisis agrícola Novo-Hispana de 1784–1785*, ed. Luis Chávez Orozco (Mexico City, n. d.); *Gaceta de México*, 18 October 1785, 414.

31. AGIM, leg. 1418, microfilm in Bancroft Library, University of California, Berkeley, reel M-271, frame 51; reel M-273, frame 17.

32. AGNC, exp. 1, fols. 1–3; vol. 1827; *Gaceta de México*, 18 October 1785; 8 November 1785; 6 December 1785; 14 February 1786; 24 October 1786; Luis Chávez Orozco, *Alzate y la agronomía de la Nueva España* (Mexico City, n. d.), 1–2.

33. AGNT, vol. 1947, fol. 368v.

34. AGNT, vol. 2353, exp. 2.

35. AGNT, vol. 2049, exp. 1.

36. AGNT, vol. 1954, exp. 1.

37. AGNHJ, leg. 327, exp. 3, fols. 95, 97–97v, 103, 109v.

38. AGNT, vol. 927, exp. 3; vol. 1501, exp. 6; vol. 1538, exp. 4; vol. 1541, exp. 2; vol. 1937, exp. 1; vol. 1938, exp. 5; vol. 1948, exp. 2; vol. 1954, exp. 1; AGNHJ, leg. 81, exp. 2; leg. 373, exps. 14–18.

39. AGNT, vol. 1735, exp. 1.

40. AGNT, vol. 1938, exp. 6; vol. 1954, exp. 1; vol. 1976, exp. 8.

41. AGNT, vol. 1233, exp. 2.

42. AGNT, vol. 1653, exp. 9; vol. 1975, exp. 1.

43. AGNT, vol. 1504, exp. 2; vol. 1507, exp. 6; vol. 1596, exp. 8.

44. AGNT, vol. 2052, exp. 2.

45. AGNT, vol. 1504, exp. 2.

46. AGNCo, fol. 119.

47. AGNT, vol. 1612, exp. 1; vol. 1958, exps. 1, 5; AGNHJ, leg. 331, exp. 57.

48. AGNT, vol. 1096, exp. 4; vol. 2157, exp. 8; vol. 2871, exp. 7; AGNHJ, leg. 327, exp. 1, fols. 58v, 67; Yautepec Parish Registers. GSU, microfilm, roll 655–835, entry for 11 August 1746; roll 655–836, entries for 18 February 1754; 26 July 1755; 10 August 1758; 7 March 1764; AGNBN, leg. 573, exp. 3.

49. AGNCRS, vol. 74, exp. 9.

50. Manuel Mazari, "Un antiguo padrón itinerario del estado de Morelos," *Sociedad Científica "Antonio Alzate," Memorias* 48 (1927).

51. Kicza, "Business and Society," 26, 122–23.
52. John Tutino, "Creole Mexico: Spanish Elites, Haciendas, and Indian Towns, 1750–1810" (Ph. D. diss., University of Texas, 1976), 161.
53. AGNT, vol. 1980, exp. 1.
54. AGNT, vol. 1939, exp. 8.
55. AGNT, vol. 1981, exp. 3.
56. AGNHJ, leg. 327, exp. 2, fols. 66v–68, 91; exp. 3, fols. 21v, 24.
57. Mazari, "Un antiguo padrón."
58. AGNT, vol. 1972, exp. 4; AGNHJ, vol. 73 (leg. 38), exp. 15; leg. 93, exp. 31; leg. 447, exps. 9, 87.
59. See, for example, AGNT, vol. 1977, fol. 79v.
60. AGNHJ, leg. 406, exp. 2, cuadernos 84, 90.
61. AGNHJ, leg. 305, exp. 46, fols. 53v–54.
62. Florescano, *Precios*, 134; Gibson, *Aztecs*, 459.
63. AGNHJ, leg. 304, exp. 23.
64. AGNHJ, leg. 304, exp. 32.
65. Yautepec Parish Registers, GSU, microfilm, roll 655–851.

Chapter 6

1. Colin Palmer, *Slaves of the White God: Blacks in Colonial Mexico, 1570–1650* (Cambridge, Mass., 1976), 69–71, 80.
2. AGNHJ, leg. 312, exp. 10.
3. Murdo J. MacLeod, *Spanish Central America: A Socio-Economic History, 1520–1710* (Berkeley and Los Angeles, 1974), 226–27; Charles Gibson *The Aztecs under Spanish Rule: A History of the Indians of the Valley of Mexico, 1519–1819* (Stanford, 1964), 248.
4. Peter Gerhard, "Continuity and Change in Morelos, Mexico," *Geographical Review* 65 (1975), 347.
5. See lists in AGNHJ, leg. 312, exp. 10.
6. Gonzalo Aguirre Beltrán, *La población negra de México, 1519–1810: Estudio etnohistórico* (Mexico City, 1946), 39; Palmer, *Slaves of the White God*, 80.
7. Ward Barrett, *The Sugar Hacienda of the Marqueses del Valle* (Minneapolis, 1970), 78.
8. Jean-Pierre Berthe, "Xochimancas: Les travaux et les jours dans une *hacienda* sucrière de Nouvelle-Espagne au xviiᵉ siècle," *Jahrbuch für Geschichte von Staat, Wirtschaft und Gesellschaft Lateinamerikas* 3 (1966), 99.
9. GSU, microfilm, roll 659–065, entries for May 1684.
10. Herman Konrad has noted similar declines in the number of African-born slaves at the Jesuit hacienda Santa Lucía by the early eighteenth century.

Herman Konrad, *A Jesuit Hacienda in Colonial Mexico: Santa Lucía, 1576–1767* (Stanford, 1980), 252.

11. Barrett, *Sugar Hacienda*, 78; Palmer, *Slaves of the White God*, 48, 68.
12. Aguirre Beltrán, *La Población negra*, 162.
13. Barrett, *Sugar Hacienda*, 79.
14. AGNT, vol. 3428, exp. 1.
15. J. I. Israel, *Race, Class, and Politics in Colonial Mexico, 1610–1670* (London, 1975), 75–76.
16. Berthe, "Xochimancas," p. 93.
17. AGNBN, leg. 1215, exp. 3.
18. AGNT, vol. 1938, exp. 5.
19. AGNT, vol. 1974, exp. 2.
20. AGNT, vol. 2420, exp. 1.
21. GSU, microfilm, roll 641–723.
22. Oaxtepec Baptismal Registers, GSU, microfilm, roll 606–324, entries for October 1749; Oaxtepec Marriage Registers, GSU, microfilm, roll 606–329, entry for 5 June 1769.
23. AGNT, vol. 1974, exp. 2, fols. 27v–36.
24. Yautepec Parish Registers, GSU, microfilm, roll 655–836, entries for 28 September 1749; 15 March 1765.
25. See, for example, AGNT, vol. 2051, exp. 1.
26. Berthe, "Xochimancas," 101.
27. AGNT, vol. 240, fol. 526v; vol. 2676, exp. 7, fol. 37. In 1717, 7.5 fanegas of maize were planted for the exclusive purpose of feeding a slave force of about sixty-three adults and twenty-five children at Atlihuayan. Although maize yields are impossible to determine with precision, and 1717 was reportedly a relatively dry year, a yield of fifty to one (not an unreasonable estimate) would have provided 375 fanegas of maize. Subtracting 7.5 fanegas to be used for the next year's planting, we are left with 367.5 fanegas, or about 20,400 liters of maize, which would yield, in turn, a weekly allotment of 5.2 liters for each adult slave and 2.6 liters for every child. At the same hacienda in 1732, a harvest of 470 fanegas of maize was provided for eighty-five slaves, including both adults and children.
28. AGNT, vol. 1974, exp. 2, cuaderno 2.
29. AGNT, vol. 2880, exp. 1.
30. AGNHJ, leg. 344, exp. 29.
31. AGNT, vol. 1974, exp. 2, cuaderno 2; vol. 2880, exp. 2.
32. AGNHJ, leg. 344, exp. 29.
33. AGNT, vol. 1974, exp. 2, fol. 44v.
34. AGNT, vol. 239, fol. 262.
35. AGNT, vol. 1980, exp. 1, fols. 134v–136v.

36. AGNT, vol. 131, exp. 1, fol. 63; vol. 2880, exp. 2, fol. 52v.

37. AGNC, vol. 251, exp. 5, fol. 192v.

38. AGNT, vol. 2875, accounts for 1765.

39. AGNHJ, leg. 93, exp. 8, fol. 28.

40. AGNT, vol. 3428, exp. 1.

41. AGNHJ, leg. 93, exp. 35.

42. AGNT, vol. 1945, exp. 3, fol. 21v; AGNBN, leg. 573, exp. 3, fols. 125–127v.

43. AGNHJ, leg. 344, exp. 22.

44. AGNHJ, leg. 327, exp. 4, fol. 120v.

45. AGNT, vol. 1952, cuaderno 10, fol. 47.

46. See, for example, AGNHJ, leg. 344, exp. 29.

47. See Frank Tannenbaum, *Slave and Citizen: The Negro in the Americas* (New York, 1947).

48. Barrett, *Sugar Hacienda*, 77.

49. AGNT, vol. 2875, accounts for 1765.

50. AGNT, vol. 1938, exp. 7.

51. AGNT, vol. 1371, exp. 1, fol. 111v.

52. AGNT, vol. 1974, exp. 2, cuaderno 2; vol. 2880, exp. 2.

53. AGNHJ, leg. 344, exp. 29.

54. Claude Morin, *Michoacán en la Nueva España del siglo xviii: Crecimiento y desigualdad en una economía colonial* (Mexico City, 1979), 257.

55. AGNT, vol. 1761, fols. 229–229v; vol. 1943, fol. 236v; vol. 1970, exp. 7, fol. 31v; Barrett, *Sugar Hacienda*, 85.

56. AGNHJ, leg. 321, exp. 3; leg. 428, exp. 8; see alsoWard Barrett, "The Meat Supply of Colonial Cuernavaca," *Annals of the Association of American Geographers* 64 (1974), 530.

57. AGNT, vol. 1935, exp. 1.

58. AGNT, vol. 1974, exp. 2, cuaderno 3.

59. AGNT, vol. 1974, exp. 2.

60. Oaxtepec Parish Registers, GSU, microfilm, roll 606–325, entries for October 1749, May 1753.

61. Yautepec Parish Registers, GSU, microfilm, roll 655–911, entry for 11 October 1767.

62. AGNT, vol. 1959, exp. 1.

63. AGNT, vol. 1952, cuaderno 3. According to an inventory taken a few months before the fire, the hacienda's remaining slave force was composed entirely of children.

64. AGNT, vol. 2056, exp. 1, fol. 145.

65. AGNT, vol. 1945, exp. 3, fols. 1–4.

66. AGNHJ, leg. 305, exp. 40.

67. AGNHJ, leg. 305, exp. 19.

68. See, for example, AGNT, vol. 1945, exp. 2, fols. 2, 159; AGNHJ, leg. 327, exp. 5, fol. 4.

69. Barrett, *Sugar Hacienda*, 82; Morin, *Michoacán*, 257.

70. AGNT, vol. 927, fol. 71v.

71. AGNT, vol. 2880, exp. 2.

72. AGNT, vol. 2868, exp. 4, fol. 67.

73. AGNT, vol. 1935, exp. 7, fol. 83.

74. GSU, microfilm, roll 641–723.

75. AGNHJ, leg. 265, exp. 22.

76. AGNT, vol. 2875, accounts for 1765.

77. AGNC, vol. 1708, exp. 10, fol. 3.

78. AGNBN, leg. 593, exp. 42.

79. AGNT, vol. 1974, exp. 5, fols. 1, 26v.

80. AGNT, vol. 927, fol. 26; vol. 1974, exp. 5, fols. 28–28v; AGNC, vol. 251, exp. 5, fols. 193v–194v. Although in many parts of central Mexico the term "gañán" referred to a permanent resident worker, capitanes de gañanes in Morelos recruited temporary workers for the sugar estates. For a detailed discussion of gañanes, see James D. Riley, "Crown Law and Rural Labor in New Spain: The Status of Gañanes during the Eighteenth Century," *Hispanic American Historical Review* 64 (1984).

81. AGNT, vol. 1974, exp. 5.

82. AGNHJ, leg. 344, exp. 17.

83. AGNT, vol. 1545, exp. 1.

84. AGNT, vol. 1969, exp. 3, cuaderno 3, fol. 62.

85. Eric Van Young, *Hacienda and Market in Eighteenth-Century Mexico: The Rural Economy of the Guadalajara Region, 1675–1820* (Berkeley and Los Angeles, 1981), 249; David Brading, *Haciendas and Ranchos in the Mexican Bajío: León: 1700–1860* (Cambridge, 1978), 9, 76–77, 110; John Tutino, "Creole Mexico: Spanish Elites, Haciendas and Indian Towns, 1750–1810" (Ph. D. diss., University of Texas, 1976), 318; Gibson, *Aztecs*, 249–56.

86. Konrad, *A Jesuit Hacienda*, 232.

87. AGNT, vol. 1972, exp. 2, fol. 27v. See also Jan Bazant, "El trabajo y los trabajadores en la Hacienda de Atlacomulco," in *El trabajo y los trabajadores en la historia de México*, ed. Elsa Cecilia Frost, Michael C. Meyer, and Josefina Zoraida Vázquez (Mexico City and Tucson, 1979), 378–90.

88. AGNT, vol. 1940, cuaderno 3, fol. 64.

89. AGNT, vol. 1545, exp. 1.

90. AGNT, vol. 1096, exp. 4, fol. 34.

91. AGNT, vol. 2866, exp. 11.

92. Van Young, *Hacienda and Market*, 259.

93. AGNT, vol. 1980, exp. 2, fol. 142v.
94. See, for example, AGNBN, leg. 1215, exp. 3; AGNT, vol. 1958, exp. 3, fol. 2.
95. AGNT, vol. 1935, exp. 1, fol. 35; AGNT, vol. 1958, exp. 3.
96. AGNHJ, leg. 428, exp. 3.
97. AGNHJ, leg. 327, exp. 3, fol. 14v.
98. AGNT, vol. 1596, exp. 8, fols. 9–9v; vol. 1958, exp. 3, fols. 3–5; AGNHJ, leg. 344, exp. 29.
99. AGNHJ, leg. 428, exp. 20; AGNT. vol. 1945, exp. 1,fol. 10v.
100. AGNT, vol. 1974, exp. 2, cuaderno 2; vol. 2880, exp. 2.

Chapter 7

1. Ward Barrett, "Morelos and Its Sugar Industry in the Late Eighteenth Century," in *Provinces of Early Mexico: Variants of Spanish American Regional Evolution*, ed. Ida Altman and James Lockhart (Los Angeles, 1976), 171; Ward Barrett and Stuart B. Schwartz, "Comparación entre dos economías azucareras coloniales: Morelos, México y Bahia, Brasil," in *Haciendas, latifundios y plantaciones en America Latina*, ed. Enrique Florescano (Mexico City, 1975), 547.
2. See, for example, AGNHJ, leg. 128, exp. 5; leg. 312, exp. 10; AGNT, vol. 1475, exp. 1, cuaderno 4, fols. 102v–105v; vol. 1760, exp. 6.
3. AGNT, vol. 1773, exp. 1.
4. AGNHJ, leg. 356, exp. 8.
5. GSU, microfilm, roll 606–324, 606–325; 606–326.
6. Mazari, "Un antiguo padrón itinerario del estado de Morelos," Sociedad Científica "Antonio Alzate," *Memorias* 48 (1927); AGNHJ, leg. 356, exp. 8.
7. AGNHJ, leg. 312, exp. 13.
8. AGNHJ, vol. 49 (leg. 28), exps. 3, 12.
9. AGNHJ, leg. 304, exp. 36.
10. Mazari, "Un antiguo padrón; AGNHJ, leg. 358, exp. 30.
11. AGNHJ, leg. 135, exp. 6; vol. 49 (leg. 28), exp. 3; leg. 304, exp. 36.
12. Claude Morin, *Michoacán en la Nueva España del siglo xviii: Crecimiento y desigualdad en una economía colonial* (Mexico City, 1979), 59–60; Brading, *Haciendas and Ranchos in the Mexican Bajío: León, 1700–1860* (Cambridge, 1978), 49.
13. Elsa Malvido, "Factores de despoblación y reposición de la población indígena de Cholula (1641–1810)," *Historia Mexicana* 23 (1973), 62.
14. José Antonio Villaseñor y Sánchez, *Teatro americano: Descripción general de los reynos, y provincias de la Nueva España, y sus jurisdicciones*, vol. 1 (Mexico City, 1746), 171.

15. GSU, microfilm, roll 641–733; AGNT, vol. 1981, exp. 1.
16. AGNHJ, vol. 49 (leg. 28), exp. 3; leg. 304, exp. 36.
17. AGNT, vol. 1582, exp. 4; AGNHJ, leg. 305, exp. 2.
18. AGNHJ, leg. 327, exp. 5, fol. 130v.
19. AGNHJ, leg. 344, exp. 65; leg. 373, exps. 14–18; AGNT, vol. 1958, exp. 2.
20. AGNT, vol. 446, exp. 6.
21. AGNT, vol. 1504, exp. 2; vol. 1786, exp. 1.
22. AGNT, vol. 1964, exp. 4; AGNHJ, leg. 305, exp. 39, fol. 9.
23. GSU, microfilm, roll 655–836, entry for 5 February 1763; roll 655–837, entries for 22 August 1769; 19 April 1771; 10 November 1774; 22 May 1778; 23 April 1780; 3 December 1782; AGNHJ, leg. 406, exp. 2 cuaderno 90.
24. AGNP, vol. 8, fol. 26v.
25. AGNT, vol. 1487, exp. 4.
26. AGNT, vol. 1504, exp. 2.
27. John Tutino, "Creole Mexico: Spanish Elites, Haciendas, and Indian Towns, 1750–1810" (Ph. D. diss., University of Texas, 1976), 343–53.
28. Guillermo de la Peña, *A Legacy of Promises: Agriculture, Politics, and Ritual in the Morelos Highlands of Mexico* (Austin, 1981), passim.
29. AGNT, vol. 1612, exp. 1.
30. AGNT, vol. 1487, exp. 7.
31. AGNT, vol. 1981, exp. 1.
32. AGNBN, leg. 593, exp. 42; Jesús Sotelo Inclán, *Raíz y razón de Zapata: Anenecuilco* (Mexico City, 1970), passim.
33. AGNP, vol. 8.
34. AGNT, vol. 1487, exp. 7.
35. See, for example, AGNHJ, leg. 106, exps. 8, 9, 20, 21; leg. 327, exp. 3, fols. 40, 74, 191–92;, exp. 4, fols. 101–103, 210. For an interesting account of the factionalization of village politics in colonial Cuernavaca, see Robert S. Haskett, "Indian Cabildo Elections and Election Disputes in Cuernavaca, 1630–1766" (Paper presented at the Rocky Mountain Conference of Latin American Studies, Park City, Utah, April 1983).
36. See, for example, AGNHJ, leg. 106, exps. 1, 8.
37. William B. Taylor, *Landlord and Peasant in Colonial Oaxaca* (Stanford, 1972), 35–66.

Chapter 8

1. Major studies of the late eighteenth-century bureaucratic changes in Spain and in the colonies include Richard Herr, *The Eighteenth-Century Revolution in Spain* (Princeton, 1958); David Brading, *Miners and Merchants in Bour-*

bon Mexico, 1763–1810 (Cambridge, 1971); Christon I. Archer, *The Army in Bourbon Mexico, 1760–1810* (Albuquerque, 1977); N. M. Farriss, *Crown and Clergy in Colonial Mexico, 1759–1821: The Crisis of Ecclesiastical Privilege* (London, 1968); Brian R. Hamnett, *Politics and Trade in Southern Mexico, 1750–1821* (Cambridge, 1971); Mark Burkholder and D. S. Chandler, *From Impotence to Authority: The Spanish Crown and the American Audiencias* (Columbia, Mo., 1977); and Peggy K. Liss, *Atlantic Empires: The Network of Trade and Revolution, 1713–1826* (Baltimore, 1983).

2. AGNT, vol. 1501, exp. 6; vol. 1964, exp. 1; AGNHJ, leg. 332, exp. 19.

3. AGNHJ, vol. 73 (leg. 38), exp. 3.

4. AGNHJ, leg. 332, exp. 39; AGNCr, vol. 58, exp. 18, fol. 24.

5. AGNT, vol. 1975, exp. 4.

6. AGNCr, vol. 58, exp. 18; AGNT, vol. 1501, exp. 6, fol. 122; AGNHJ, leg. 305, exp. 3, fol. 12. For a description of Yautepec's existing jail, see AGNHi, vol. 578, fols. 60–62.

7. AGNT, vol. 1975, exp. 4.

8. AGNT, vol. 1975, exp. 4; AGNCRS, vol. 140, exp. 4; vol. 178, exp. 9.

9. AGNCRS, vol. 140, exp. 40, fol. 370. The baptismal registers of Yautepec indicate that Agüero was absent from the parish from 7 March 1796, just over a month after Cerro made his offer to build the new jail, until 1 January 1797. Agüero apparently regained control of the parish until May of the same year, during which time he won his ineffectual audiencia decree. From May 1797 until February 1802, Agüero signed no entries in the parish's registers. Although his signature appears occasionally after the latter date, as late as February 1805 he still had not been formally reinstated. GSU, micro-film, roll 655–838.

10. AGNBN, leg. 953, exp. 10; AGNT, vol. 2157, exp. 2.

11. AGNCRS, vol. 178, exp. 9; AGNBN, leg. 172, exp. 52; leg. 614, exp. 45.

12. AGNBN, leg. 953, exp. 10.

13. AGNT, vol. 1567, exp. 5, fol. 121v; vol. 1962, exp. 1, cuaderno 1, fols. 150–55; vol. 1972, exp. 1, fol. 70; vol. 1978, unnumbered expediente, last in volume; AGNBN, leg. 953, exp. 10; AGNHJ, leg. 327, exp. 3, fol. 204; leg. 332, exp. 50; AGNCr, vol. 58, exp. 18, fol. 3v; AGNCRS, vol. 178, exp. 9, fol. 295.

14. AGNHJ, leg. 332, exp. 50.

15. AGNT, vol. 1975, exp. 4; AGNCRS, vol. 84, exp. 7; vol. 140, exp. 4.

16. AGNBN, leg. 614, exp. 45.

17. Yautepec Parish Registers, GSU, microfilm, roll 655–911, entry for 23 February 1756; Peter Gerhard, *A Guide to the Historical Geography of New Spain* (Cambridge, 1972), 96; see also Cheryl English Martin, "Secularization and Clerical Finance in Eighteenth-Century Mexico: The Case of Morelos," paper presented to the Southern Historical Association, Memphis, Tenn., November 1982.

18. AGNCRS, vol. 140, exp. 4, fol. 99v.

19. Gerhard, *Guide*, 17; For a detailed discussion of the repartimiento and the effects of its abolition in Oaxaca, see Hamnett, *Politics and Trade*.

20. Gerhard, *Guide*, 93, 96; Bernardo García Martínez, *El Marquesado del Valle: Tres siglos de régimen señorial en Nueva España* (Mexico City, 1969), 129–30.

21. AGNHJ, leg. 332, exp. 39.

22. William B. Taylor, *Drinking, Homicide and Rebellion in Colonial Mexican Villages* (Stanford, 1979), 23, 141–42.

23. AGNT, vol. 1975, exp. 4.

24. AGNT, vol. 1396, part 1, exp. 4.

25. AGNHJ, leg. 305, exp. 28.

26. AGNHJ, leg. 304, exp. 3; leg. 305, exps. 28, 39.

27. AGNHJ, leg. 305, exp. 9, fol. 14; AGNT, vol. 1981, exp. 3.

28. AGNHJ, leg. 305, exp. 25.

29. AGNHJ, leg. 305, exps. 31, 39, 44.

30. Timothy E. Anna, *The Fall of the Royal Government in Mexico City* (Lincoln, 1978), 37–54; Timothy E. Anna, *Spain and the Loss of America* (Lincoln, 1983), xvii, 29–33.

31. AGNHJ, leg. 305, exps. 41, 44–46.

32. AGNHJ, leg. 305, exp. 31, fols. 21, 23. For additional details surrounding Porras' career prior to his aappointment as teniente in Yautepec, see Woodrow Borah, *Justice by Insurance: The General Indian Court of Colonial Mexico and the Legal Aides of the Half-Real* (Berkeley and Los Angeles, 1983), 160.

33. The Spanish Constitution of 1812 authorized the creation of ayuntamientos in some communities including Cuernavaca. Manuel de Porras, former teniente of Yautepec, held a position on Cuernavaca's council in 1814. AGNE, vol. 8, exp. 9, fol. 119. For a general discussion of the creation of these "constitutional ayuntamientos," see Borah, *Justice by Insurance*, 392, 297–98.

Conclusion

1. Hugh Hamill, *The Hidalgo Revolt: Prelude to Mexican Independence* (Gainesville, 1966).

2. Wilbert H. Timmons, *Morelos of Mexico: Priest, Soldier, Statesman* (El

Paso, 1963), passim; Wilbert H. Timmons, "José María Morelos: Agrarian Reformer?," *Hispanic American Historical Review* 45 (1965); Valentín López González, *La guerra de independencia en el estado de Morelos* (n. p., n. d.), 7–26.
3. AGNHi, vol. 108, exp. 28.
4. Peter Gerhard, "Continuity and Change in Morelos, Mexico," *Geographical Review* 65 (1975), 349.
5. AGNCr, vol. 48, exp. 11.
6. AGNT, vol. 1981, exp. 3.
7. AGNT, vol. 1376, exp. 4.
8. John Tutino, "Hacienda Social Relations in Mexico: The Chalco Region in the Era of Independence," *Hispanic American Historical Review* 55 (1975), 528.
9. María Teresa Huerta, "La familia Yermo, 1750–1850" (Paper presented at the Sixth Conference of Mexican and United States Historians, Chicago, September 1981).
10. Domenico E. Sindico, "Santa Ana Tenango: A Morelos Sugar Hacienda" (Ph. D. diss., University of Minnesota, 1980).
11. AGNBN, leg. 369, exp. 60; Manuel Mazari, "Un antiguo padrón itinerario del estado de Morelos," Sociedad Científica "Antonio Alzate," *Memorias* 48 (1927).
12. AGNBN, leg. 369, exp. 60.
13. John Womack, *Zapata and the Mexican Revolution* (New York, 1969), 6.
14. For discussions of Porfirian Morelos, see Womack, *Zapata*, 37–66; Arturo Warman, *"We Come to Object": The Peasants of Morelos and the National State* (Baltimore, 1981), 42–90; Roberto Melville, *Crecimiento y rebelión: El desarrollo económico de las haciendas azucareras en Morelos (1880–1910)* (Mexico City, 1979).
15. Peter Gerhard, "La evolución del pueblo rural mexicano: 1519–1975," *Historia Mexicana* 24 (1975), 576.
16. Jan Bazant, *A Concise History of Mexico: From Hidalgo to Cárdenas, 1805–1940* (Cambridge, 1977), 30–94; Jean Meyer, *Problemas campesinos y revueltas agrarias (1821–1910)* (Mexico City, 1973), 28, 116–17.
17. Womack, *Zapata*, 43.
18. See, for example, AGNT, vol. 1504, exp. 2, fol. 194.
19. Otumba, in the Valley of Mexico, for example, exhibited many of the same political characteristics as Yautepec in the late colonial era. See John Tutino, "Provincial Spaniards, Indian Towns, and Haciendas: Interrelated Agrarian Sectors in the Valleys of Mexico and Toluca, 1750–1810," in *Provinces of Early Mexico: Variants of the Spanish American Regional Experience*, ed. Ida Altman and James Lockhart (Los Angeles, 1976).
20. AGNT, vol. 1475, exp. 1, cuaderno 4, fol. 231v.

21. For a discussion of the relationship between acculturation and the production of indigo, cochineal, and sugarcane, see MacLeod, "Forms and Types of Work, and the Acculturation of the Colonial Indian of Mesoamerica: Some Preliminary Observartions," in *El trabajo y los trabajadores en la historia de México*, ed. Elsa Cecilia Frost, Michael C. Meyer, and Josefina Zoraida Vázquez (Mexico City and Tucson, 1979).

Glossary

Alcabala. Sales tax

Alcalde mayor. Spanish official in charge of a district

Alcaldía mayor. District of an alcalde mayor's jurisdiction

Audiencia. Supreme tribunal of New Spain, consisting of a president and four associate justices (oidores)

Avío. Capital for investment or current operation of an enterprise

Barrio. Section of a town; ward

Bozal. African-born slave

Caballería. Unit of agricultural land, equal to 105.8 acres

Cabecera. Head town

Cabildo. Municipal council

Cacica. Feminine form of cacique

Cacicazgo. Estate or office of a cacique

Cacique. Indian lord or chief

Capellanía. A chaplaincy or chantry fund, yielding 5 percent annual interest

Casco. Compound or permanent buildings of a hacienda

Castizo. Person of one-fourth Indian, and three-fourths Spanish, ancestry

Censo. Mortgage or loan

Censo perpetuo. Emphiteutic grant; a kind of perpetual rent

Cofradía. Sodality, lay brotherhood responsible for designated religious observances or objects

Compadrazgo. Ritual kinship; relationship between the parents and godparents of a child

Compadre. Person to whom one is related by virtue of compadrazgo
Composición. Confirmation and legalization of land title
Concurso de acreedores. Judicial procedure, allocating one's assets among one's creditors
Congregación. Congregation or concentration of scattered settlements into one community
Cura. Parish priest
Depositario. Appointed receiver of goods embargoed in judicial proceedings
Encomienda. Grant of Indian tributaries
Encomendero. Possessor of an encomienda
Español. Person claiming pure Spanish ancestry
Fanega. Unit of dry measure; about 1.5 bushels, or 55.5 liters
Fanega de sembradura. Area planted with one fanega of seed; for maize, about 8.8 acres
Frijol. American bean
Fundo legal. Townsite to which every community was entitled; 600 varas square in the late colonial period
Gachupín. Spaniard born in Spain, resident in Mexico
Gañán. Hacienda laborer
Gente de razón. Non-Indians
Gobernador. Governor; native ruler of an Indian community
Hacendado. Proprietor of a hacienda
Hacienda. A large rural estate
Huerta. Orchard or garden
Ingenio. Water-powered sugar mill
Labrador. Farmer
Lobo. Person of mixed Indian and African ancestry
Maestro de azúcar. Sugar master; chief technician in the manufacture of sugar
Marqués del Valle. Title granted to Fernando Cortés and his descendants
Marquesado del Valle. Estate of the Marqués del Valle
Matlazáhuatl. Epidemic disease of which Indians were the chief victims; probably a form of typhus or typhoid fever
Mayordomo. Majordomo; custodian
Merced. Grant, usually of land
Mestizo. Person of mixed white and Indian ancestry
Mulatto. Person of mixed white and African ancestry; in colonial Mexico, used also to designate a person of mixed Indian and African ancestry
Ojo. A spring
Oidor. Judge of the audiencia of Mexico
Padrón. Census
Pardo. Person of dark complexion; implies substantial proportion of African ancestry

Peso. Monetary unit; eight reales

Pegujalero. Tenant of a small parcel of agricultural land

Principal. Member of the Indian upper class

Pueblo. Town or village, usually a small or medium-sized Indian community

Ranchero. Owner or tenant of a rancho

Rancho. A small landed property; a subordinate section of a hacienda

Real. Monetary unit, one-eighth of a peso

Regidor. Councilman; member of a cabildo

Repartimiento. Labor draft or public distribution, often forced, of merchandise by a district magistrate

Sitio de ganado mayor. Land granted (in theory) for grazing cattle and horses, equal to 4,398 acres or 1,756 hectares

Sitio de ganado menor. Land granted (in theory) for grazing sheep and goats, equal to 1,928 acres or 780 hectares

Solar. House site

Sujeto. Subject town

Teniente. Lieutenant, especially of an alcalde mayor

Terrazguero. Tenant of a small plot of agricultural land

Tienda. Store

Tierra caliente. Hot, tropical lowlands

Tierra fria. Cold lands, at higher elevations

Tierra templada. Temperate lands

Trapiche. Animal-powered sugar mill

Vara. Unit of measure, roughly thirty-three inches

Vecino. Citizen or householder

Bibliography

Aguirre Beltrán, Gonzalo. *La población negra de México, 1519–1810: Estudio etnohistórico*. Mexico City: Ediciones Fuente Cultural, 1946.

Altman, Ida, and James Lockhart, eds. *Provinces of Early Mexico: Variants of Spanish American Regional Evolution*. Los Angeles: Latin American Center, University of California, 1976.

Alzate y Ramírez, José Antonio. *Consejos útiles para socorrer a la necesidad de comestibles en tiempo que escasesen los comestibles*. Mexico City: Felipe de Zúñiga y Ontiveros, 1786.

———. *Tabla rural en que se manifiestan las épocas mas oportunas de cada mes para el cultivo de las hortalizas, legumbres, flores y frutos*. Mexico City: Imprenta del Aguila, 1830.

Anna, Timothy E. *The Fall of the Royal Government in Mexico City*. Lincoln: University of Nebraska Press, 1978.

———. *Spain and the Loss of America*. Lincoln: University of Nebraska Press, 1983.

Apuntamientos sobre la necesidad de promover el cultivo de azúcar y otros frutos. Mexico City: José María Ramos Palomera, 1822.

Archer, Christon I. *The Army in Bourbon Mexico, 1760–1810*. Albuquerque: University of New Mexico Press, 1977.

Atlas Nacional del medio físico. Mexico City: Secretaría de Programación y Presupuesto, 1981.

241

Bakewell, Peter J. *Silver Mining and Society in Colonial Mexico: Zacatecas, 1546–1700*. Cambridge: Cambridge University Press, 1971.

Barrett, Ward. "The Meat Supply of Colonial Cuernavaca." *Annals of the Association of American Geographers* 64 (1974): 525–40.

———. "Morelos and Its Sugar Industry in the Late Eighteenth Century." In *Provinces of Early Mexico: Variants of Spanish American Regional Evolution*, edited by Ida Altman and James Lockhart. Los Angeles: Latin American Center, University of California, 1976.

———. *The Sugar Hacienda of the Marqueses del Valle*. Minneapolis: University of Minnesota Press, 1970.

Barrett, Ward, and Stuart B. Schwartz, "Comparación entre dos economías azucareras coloniales: Morelos, México y Bahia, Brasil." In *Haciendas, latifundios y plantaciones en America Latina*, edited by Enrique Florescano. Mexico City: Siglo Veintiuno, 1975.

Bazant, Jan. *A Concise History of Mexico: From Hidalgo to Cárdenas, 1805–1940*. Cambridge: Cambridge University Press, 1977.

———. "El trabajo y los trabajadores en la Hacienda de Atlacomulco." In *El trabajo y los trabajadores en la historia de México*, edited by Elsa Cecilia Frost, Michael C. Meyer, and Josefina Zoraida Vázquez. Mexico City and Tucson: El Colegio de México and University of Arizona Press, 1979.

Berthe, Jean-Pierre. "Xochimancas: Les travaux et les jours dans une *hacienda* sucrière de Nouvelle-Espagne au xviie siècle." *Jahrbuch für Geschichte von Staat, Wirtschaft und Gesellschaft Lateinamerikas* 3 (1966): 88–117.

Borah, Woodrow. *Justice by Insurance: The General Indian Court of Colonial Mexico and the Legal Aides of the Half-Real*. Berkeley and Los Angeles: University of California Press, 1983.

———. *New Spain's Century of Depression*. Berkeley and Los Angeles: University of California Press, 1951.

Brading, David. "La estructura de la producción agrícola en el Bajío de 1700 a 1850." *Historia Mexicana* 23 (1973): 197–237.

———. *Haciendas and Ranchos in the Mexican Bajío: León, 1700–1860*. Cambridge: Cambridge University Press, 1978.

———. *Miners and Merchants in Bourbon Mexico, 1763–1810*. Cambridge: Cambridge University Press, 1971.

Brading, David, and Celia Wu. "Population Growth and Crisis: León, 1720–1860." *Journal of Latin American Studies* 5 (1973): 1–36.

Burkholder, Mark, and D. S. Chandler. *From Impotence to Authority: The Spanish Crown and the American Audiencias*. Columbia: University of Missouri Press, 1977.

Calderón de la Barca, Frances. *Life in Mexico*. New York: Dutton, 1973.

Carta de Mexico: Topográfica, 1:250,000. Mexico City: Secretaría de Programación y Presupuesto, 1982.

Calvo, Thomas. "Demographie historique d'une paroisse Mexicaine: Acatzingo (1606–1810)." *Cahiers des Amériques Latines* 6 (1972): 7–41.

Carrasco, Pedro. "La casa y hacienda de un señor tlahuica." *Estudios de Cultura Náhuatl* 10 (1972): 225–44.

———. "The Joint Family in Ancient Mexico: The Case of Molotla." In *Essays on Mexican Kinship*, edited by Hugo G. Nutini, Pedro Carrasco, and James M. Taggart. Pittsburgh: University of Pittsburgh Press, 1976.

———. "Tres libros de tributos del Museo Nacional de México y su importancia para los estudios demográficos." International Congress of Americanists, *Proceedings* 35 (1962): 373–78.

Chávez Orozco, Luis, ed. *Alzate y la agronomía de la Nueva España*. Mexico City, Banco Nacional de Crédito Agrícola y Ganadero, n. d.

———, ed. *La crisis agrícola Novo-Hispana de 1784–1785*. Mexico City: Banco Nacional de Crédito Agrícola y Ganadero, n. d.

Chevalier, Francois. *La formation des grands domaines au Mexique, terre et société aux xvi⁻–xvii⁺ siècles*. Paris: Université de Paris, Institut d'Ethnologic, 1952. English version: *Land and Society in Colonial Mexico: The Great Hacienda*. Edited by Lesley Byrd Simpson; translated by Alvin Eustis. Berkeley and Los Angeles: University of California Press, 1966.

Chiaramonte, José Carlos. "En torno a la recuperación demográfica y la depresión económica novohispanas durante el siglo xvii." *Historia Mexicana* 30 (1981): 561–604.

Cline, Howard. "Civil Congregations of the Indians in New Spain." *Hispanic American Historical Review* 29 (1949): 349–69.

———. "Viceroyalty to Republics, 1786–1952: Historical Notes on the Evolution of Middle American Political Units." In *Handbook of Middle American Indians*, edited by Robert Wauchope. Vol. 12, part 1, 138–65. Austin: University of Texas Press, 1972.

Cook, Sherburne F., and Woodrow Borah. *The Aboriginal Population of Central Mexico on the Eve of the Spanish Conquest*. Berkeley and Los Angeles: University of California Press, 1963.

———. *Essays in Population History*. 3 vols. Berkeley and Los Angeles: University of California Press, 1971–79.

———. *The Indian Population of Central Mexico, 1531–1610*. Berkeley and Los Angeles: University of California Press, 1960.

———. *The Indian Population of Central Mexico in 1548*. Berkeley and Los Angeles: University of California Press, 1960.

Deerr, Noel. *The History of Sugar*. 2 vols. London: Chapman and Hall, 1949.

de la Peña, Guillermo. *A Legacy of Promises: Agriculture, Politics, and Ritual in the Morelos Highlands of Mexico*. Austin: University of Texas Press, 1981.

Denevan, William M., ed. *The Native Population of the Americas in 1492*. Madison: University of Wisconsin Press, 1976.

Díaz del Castillo, Bernal. *The Conquest of New Spain.* Translated by J. M. Cohen. Baltimore: Penguin Books, 1963.

Dubernard, Juan. *Santa Ana Amanalco (Cuernavaca, Morelos).* Cuernavaca: n. p., 1975.

Farriss, N. M. *Crown and Clergy in Colonial Mexico, 1759–1821: The Crisis of Ecclesiastical Privilege.* London: Oxford University Press, 1968.

————. "Nucleation versus Dispersal: The Dynamics of Population Movement in Colonial Yucatán." *Hispanic American Historical Review* 58 (1978): 187–216.

Feijoo, Rosa. "El tumulto de 1692." *Historia Mexicana* 14 (1965): 656–79.

Florescano, Enrique, ed. *Fuentes para la historia de la crisis agrícola de 1785–1786.* 2 vols. Mexico City: Archivo General de la Nación, 1981.

————. *Precios del maíz y crisis agrícolas en México (1708–1810).* Mexico City: El Colegio de México, 1969.

García Martínez, Bernardo. *El Marquesado del Valle: Tres siglos de régimen señorial en Nueva España.* Mexico City: El Colegio de México, 1969.

Gerhard, Peter. "Continuity and Change in Morelos, Mexico." *Geographical Review* 65 (1975): 335–52.

————. "La evolución del pueblo rural mexicano: 1519–1975." *Historia Mexicana* 24 (1975): 566–78.

————. *A Guide to the Historical Geography of New Spain.* Cambridge: Cambridge University Press, 1972.

Gibson, Charles. *The Aztecs under Spanish Rule: A History of the Indians of the Valley of Mexico, 1519–1810.* Stanford: Stanford University Press, 1964.

Greenleaf, Richard E. "Viceregal Power and the Obrajes of the Cortés Estate, 1595–1708." *Hispanic American Historical Review* 48 (1968) 365–79.

Hamill, Hugh. *The Hidalgo Revolt: Prelude to Mexican Independence.* Gainesville: University of Florida Press, 1966.

Hamnett, Brian R. *Politics and Trade in Southern Mexico, 1750–1821.* Cambridge: Cambridge University Press, 1971.

Haskett, Robert S. "Indian Cabildo Elections and Election Disputes in Cuernavaca, 1630–1766." Paper presented at the Rocky Mountain Conference of Latin American Studies, Park City, Utah, April 1983.

Henige, David. "On the Contact Population of Hispaniola: History as Higher Mathematics." *Hispanic American Historical Review* 58 (1978): 217–37.

————. "Reply." *Hispanic American Historical Review* 58 (1978): 709–12.

Hernández Palomo, José Jesús. *El aguardiente de caña en México (1724–1810).* Seville: Escuela de Estudios Hispano-Americanos, 1974.

Herr, Richard. *The Eighteenth-Century Revolution in Spain.* Princeton: Princeton University Press, 1958.

Huerta, María Teresa. "La familia Yermo, 1750–1850." Paper presented at the Sixth Conference of Mexican and United States Historians, Chicago, September 1981.

Humboldt, Alexander von. *Political Essay on the Kingdom of New Spain*. 4 vols. New York: AMS Press, 1970.

Israel, J. I. "Mexico and the 'General Crisis' of the Seventeenth Century." *Past and Present* 63 (1974): 33–57.

———. *Race, Class and Politics in Colonial Mexico, 1610–1670*. London: Oxford University Press, 1975.

Kicza, John. "Business and Society in Late Colonial Mexico City." Ph.D. dissertation, University of California, Los Angeles, 1979.

———. "The Great Families of Mexico: Elite Maintenance and Business Practice in Late Colonial Mexico City." *Hispanic American Historical Review* 62 (1982): 429–57.

Konrad, Herman. *A Jesuit Hacienda in Colonial Mexico: Santa Lucía, 1576–1767*. Stanford: Stanford University Press, 1980.

Ladd, Doris M. *The Mexican Nobility at Independence, 1780–1826*. Austin, University of Texas Press, 1976.

LeRoy Ladurie, Emmanuel. *Times of Feast, Times of Famine: A History of Climate since the Year 1000*. New York: Doubleday, 1971.

Liss, Peggy K. *Atlantic Empires: The Network of Trade and Revolution, 1713–1826*. Baltimore: Johns Hopkins University Press, 1983.

López González, Valentín. *La guerra de independencia en el estado de Morelos*. N. p., n. d.

MacLeod, Murdo J. "Forms and Types of Work, and the Acculturation of the Colonial Indian of Mesoamerica: Some Preliminary Observations." In *El trabajo y los trabajadores en la historia de Mexico*, edited by Elsa Cecilia Frost, Michael C. Meyer, and Josefina Zoraida Vázquez. Mexico City and Tucson: El Colegio de México and University of Arizona Press, 1979.

———. *Spanish Central America: A Socio-Economic History, 1520–1710*. Berkeley and Los Angeles: University of California Press, 1973.

McNeill, William H. *Plagues and Peoples*. New York: Anchor-Doubleday, 1976.

Malvido, Elsa. "Factores de depoblación y de reposición de la población indígena de Cholula (1641–1810)." *Historia Mexicana* 23 (1973), 52–110.

Martin, Cheryl English. "Crucible of Zapatismo: Hacienda *Hospital* in the Seventeenth Century." *The Americas* 38 (1981): 31–43.

———. "Haciendas and Villages in Late Colonial Morelos." *Hispanic American Historical Review* 62 (1982): 407–27.

———. "The San Hipólito Hospitals of Colonial Mexico, 1566–1702." Ph.D. dissertation, Tulane University, 1976.

———. "Secularization and Clerical Finance in Eighteenth-Century Mexico:

The Case of Morelos." Paper presented at the Southern Historical Association, Memphis, Tenn., November 1982.

Mazari, Manuel. "Un antiguo padrón itinerario del estado de Morelos." Sociedad Científica "Antonio Alzate," *Memorias* 48 (1927): 149–70.

Melville, Roberto. *Crecimiento y rebelión: El desarrollo económico de las haciendas azucareras en Morelos (1880–1910)* Mexico City: Editorial Nueva Imagen, 1979.

Meyer, Jean. *Problemas campesinos y revueltas agrarias (1821–1910)*. Mexico City: SepSetentas, 1973.

Miranda, José. "La población indígena de México en el siglo xvii." *Historia Mexicana* 12 (1962): 182–89.

Moreno Toscano, Alejandra. "Tres problemas en la geografía del maíz, 1600–1624." *Historia Mexicana* 14 (1965): 631–55.

Morin, Claude. *Michoacán en la Nueva España del siglo xviii: Crecimiento y desigualdad en una economía colonial.* Mexico City: Fondo de Cultura Económica, 1979.

――――. *Santa Inés Zacatelco (1646–1812): Contribución a la demografía del México colonial.* Mexico City: Instituto Nacional de Antropología e Historia, 1973.

Normales climatológicas, período 1941–1970. Mexico City: Dirección General de Geografía y Meteorología, 1976.

Palmer, Colin. *Slaves of the White God: Blacks in Mexico, 1570–1650.* Cambridge, Mass.: Harvard University Press, 1976.

Ponce, Alonso. *Relación breve y verdadera de algunas cosas de las muchas que sucedieron al Padre Fray Alonso Ponce en las provincias de la Nueva España.* 2 vols. Madrid: Viuda de Calero, 1878.

Riley, G. Michael. *Fernando Cortés and the Marquesado in Morelos, 1522–1547.* Albuquerque: University of New Mexico Press, 1973.

Riley, James D. "Crown Law and Rural Labor in New Spain: The Status of Gañanes during the Eighteenth Century." *Hispanic American Historical Review* 64 (1984): 259–85.

――――. "The Management of the Estates of the Jesuit Colegio Máximo de San Pedro y San Pablo of Mexico City During the Eighteenth Century." Ph.D. dissertation, Tulane University, 1972.

――――. "The Wealth of the Jesuits in Mexico, 1670–1767." *The Americas* 33 (1976): 226–66.

Rodríguez O., Jaime E. "Down from Colonialism: Mexico's Nineteenth Century Crisis." Distinguished Faculty Lecture, University of California, 28 May 1980.

Rosenblat, Angel. *La población de América en 1492: Viejos y nuevos cálculos.* Mexico City: El Colegio de México, 1967.

Rounds, Christopher R. "From Hacienda to Ejido: Land Reform and Economic Development in Yautepec, Morelos, 1920–1970." Ph.D. dissertation, State University of New York, Stony Brook, 1977.

Ruíz de Velasco, Felipe. *Historia y evoluciones del cultivo de la caña y de la industria azucarera en México hasta el año de 1910*. Mexico City: Editorial Cultura, 1937.

Sanders, William T. "The Population of the Central Mexican Symbiotic Region, the Basin of Mexico, and the Teotihuacán Valley in the Sixteenth Century." In *The Native Population of the Americas in 1492*, edited by William M. Denevan. Madison: University of Wisconsin Press, 1976.

Sandoval, Fernando B. *La industria del azúcar en Nueva España*. Mexico City: Instituto de Historia, 1951.

Simpson, Lesley Byrd. *The Encomienda in New Spain: The Beginning of Spanish Mexico*. Berkeley and Los Angeles: University of California Press, 1950.

Sindico, Domenico E. "Modernization in Nineteenth-Century Sugar Haciendas: The Case of Morelos (From Formal to Real Subsumption of Labor to Capital." *Latin American Perspectives* 7 (1980): 83–99.

———. "Santa Ana Tenango: A Morelos Sugar Hacienda." Ph.D. dissertation, University of Minnesota, 1980.

Sotelo Inclán, Jesús. *Raíz y razón de Zapata: Anenecuilco*. Mexico City: Editorial CFE, 1970.

Tannenbaum, Frank. *The Mexican Agrarian Revolution*. New York: Macmillan, 1929.

———. *Slave and Citizen: The Negro in the Americas*. New York: Knopf, 1947.

Taylor, William B. *Drinking, Homicide and Rebellion in Colonial Mexican Villages*. Stanford: Stanford University Press, 1979.

———. "Landed Society in New Spain: A View from the South." *Hispanic American Historical Review* 54 (1974): 387–413.

———. *Landlord and Peasant in Colonial Oaxaca*. Stanford: Stanford University Press, 1972.

TePaske, John, and Herbert S. Klein. "The Seventeenth-Century Crisis in New Spain: Myth or Reality?" *Past and Present* 70 (1981): 116–35.

Timmons, Wilbert H. "José María Morelos: Agrarian Reformer?" *Hispanic American Historical Review* 45 (1965): 183–95.

———. *Morelos of Mexico: Priest, Soldier, Statesman*. El Paso: Texas Western Press, 1963.

Tutino, John. "Creole Mexico: Spanish Elites, Haciendas, and Indian Towns, 1750–1810." Ph.D. dissertation, University of Texas, 1976.

———. "Hacienda Social Relations in Mexico: The Chalco Region in the Era of Independence." *Hispanic American Historical Review* 55 (1975): 496–528.

———. "Provincial Spaniards, Indian Towns, and Haciendas: Interrelated Agrarian Sectors in the Valleys of Mexico City and Toluca, 1750–1810."

In *Provinces of Early Mexico: Variants of Spanish American Regional Evolution*, edited by Ida Altman and James Lockhart. Los Angeles: Latin American Center, University of California, 1976.

Van Young, Eric. *Hacienda and Market in Eighteenth-Century Mexico: The Rural Economy of the Guadalajara Region, 1675–1820*. Berkeley and Los Angeles: University of California Press, 1981.

————. "Tuxtla in the Sixteenth Century: A Study in Decline." Unpublished manuscript, 1971.

————. "Urban Market and Hinterland: Guadalajara and Its Region in the Eighteenth Century." *Hispanic American Historical Review* 59 (1979): 593–635.

Vecinos de Tetelcingo. *Historia del poblado de Tetelcingo, antes Xochimilcatzingo y Zumpango*. Cuernavaca: Emilio J. Bejarano, 1981.

Venegas Ramírez, Carmen. *Régimen hospitalario para indios en la Nueva España*. Mexico City: Instituto Nacional de Antropolgía e Historia, 1973.

Villaseñor y Sánchez, José Antonio. *Teatro americano: Descripción general de los reynos, y provincias de la Nueva España, y sus jurisdicciones*. 2 vols. Mexico City: Viuda de Joseph Bernardo de Negal, 1746–1748.

Von Wobeser, Gisela. *San Carlos Borromeo: Endeudamiento de una hacienda colonial (1608–1729)*. Mexico City: Universidad Nacional Autónoma de Mexico, 1980.

————. "Las haciendas de Cuernavaca y Cuautla en la época colonial." Paper presented at the conference on "La historia morelense en la investigación social," Cuernavaca, Morelos, September 1983.

Warman, Arturo. *"We Come to Object": The Peasants of Morelos and the National State*. Translated by Stephen K. Ault. Baltimore: Johns Hopkins University Press, 1981.

West, Robert C., and John Augelli. *Middle America: Its Lands and Peoples*. Englewood Cliffs, N.J.: Prentice-Hall, 1966.

White, C. Langdon, and George T. Renner. *Human Geography: An Ecological Study of Society*. New York: Appleton-Century-Crofts, 1948.

Womack, John. *Zapata and the Mexican Revolution*. New York: Knopf, 1969.

Zambardino, R. A. "Critique of David Henige's 'On the Contact Population of Hispaniola: History as Higher Mathematics.' " *Hispanic American Historical Review* 58 (1978): 700–708.

Zavala, Silvio. *La encomienda indiana*. Madrid: Centro de Estudios Históricos, 1935.

Zavala, Silvio, and María Castelo, eds. *Fuentes para la historia del trabajo en Nueva España*. 8 vols. Mexico City: Fondo de Cultura Económica, 1939–1945.

Index